COLLINS
COBUIL

VERBS:
PATTERNS & PRACTICE

SELF-STUDY EDITION
WITH ANSWERS

THE UNIVERSITY
OF BIRMINGHAM

COLLINS
COBUILD

HarperCollins*Publishers*

HarperCollins Publishers
77-85 Fulham Palace Road
London W6 8JB

COBUILD is a trademark of William Collins Sons & Co Ltd

First published 1997

2 4 6 8 10 9 7 5 3 1

ISBN 0 00 375092 2

Design and typesetting by
eMC Design, Bromham, Bedfordshire

Corpus Acknowledgements

We would like to acknowledge the assistance of the many hundreds of
individuals and companies who have kindly given permission for
copyright material to be used in The Bank of English. The written
sources include many national and regional newspapers in Britain and
overseas; magazine and periodical publishers; and book publishers in
Britain, the United States, and Australia. Extensive spoken data has
been provided by radio and television broadcasting companies; research
workers at many universities and other institutions; and numerous
individual contributors. We are grateful to them all.

Printed and bound in Great Britain by
Scotprint Ltd, Musselburgh

Note

Entered words that we have reason to believe constitute trademarks have been
designated as such. However, neither the presence or the absence of such designation
should be regarded as affecting the legal status of any trademark.

http://www.cobuild.collins.co.uk

The COBUILD Series

Founding Editor-in-Chief   John Sinclair
Publishing Director   Gwyneth Fox

Editorial Team

Senior Editors

Gill Francis
Elizabeth Manning
Susan Hunston

Editorial Consultant   Eugene Gatt Winter
Computer Officer   Tim Lane
Illustrations   Ela Bullon

We would like to thank Elaine Watton and Deborah Orpin for their help with the Practice pages, and Philippe Humblé and John Todd for their detailed comments on the text.

Contents

Introduction

Verb patterns

This book presents the major patterns of English verbs, and relates these patterns to meaning.

A verb pattern is, in most cases, a verb and the words that come after it. These words might be a noun group, an adjective group, a prepositional phrase, an adverb group, or a clause. In some cases, the Subject is restricted – for example it is always *it*, or always plural – and so can be considered part of the verb pattern.

We have devised a simple way of referring to patterns whereby the elements in each pattern are set out in the order in which they occur. For example:

V n	means 'verb followed by a noun group'
V n that	means 'verb followed by a noun group and a that-clause'
V *for* n	means 'verb followed by *for* and a noun group'
V n *for* n	means 'verb followed by a noun group, *for* and another noun group'

A list of the elements and their abbreviations is given at the end of this Introduction.

A pattern of a verb includes only those words that are significant for that particular verb, not those that are just part of general clause structure. For example, most verbs in English can be followed by adverb groups or prepositional phrases indicating manner, time, or place. When information about manner, time, or place is not essential, the adverb group or prepositional phrase is not considered to be part of the pattern.

The Units

In this book, we present information on each verb pattern on the left-hand pages, with practice material on the right-hand pages. Sometimes a pattern is described in two or three successive Units. Sometimes a Unit deals with two or three major patterns, in which case each section is numbered.

Left-hand pages: Patterns

Each Unit begins with a simple description of each pattern. For each major pattern, there is a table with a shaded area showing the pattern and simplified examples of verbs used with this pattern. There is also a table illustrating the passive pattern, if it occurs frequently.

Meaning groups

The verbs with a particular pattern have been divided into groups according to their basic meaning. For example, in the Unit on **V n *into* -ing** (Unit 62), there is a group of verbs which indicate that someone makes someone do something by using force or pressure. This group includes the verbs *force*, *frighten*, *nag*, *pressure*, *push*, *scare*, and *terrify*. This division into meaning groups means that this book can be used as a grammatically-based thesaurus.

Examples

Each meaning group has examples to show the verbs being used with the pattern in question. These examples are actual examples of current English, taken from the Bank of English. The verb pattern is highlighted in bold, and the verb group itself is underlined.

This example illustrates the pattern **V adj** with the verb *feel*:

> I **was <u>feeling</u>** a bit lonely.

Note that the verb group includes any auxiliaries (forms of *be*, *do*, and *have*), modals (for example *may* or *will*), and phrasal modals (for example *used to* or *have to*).

The negative word *not*, or its contracted form *n't*, is also included in the verb group:

> Chandler **<u>did not notice</u>** him enter.

A group of examples may contain active and passive examples, and examples of phrasal verbs. The passive examples are labelled.

Lists

The lists contain the verbs which most frequently or typically have the pattern in question. Phrasal verbs are included, as well as ordinary verbs.

If a verb is usually or always used with a negative such as *not* or a modal such as *can* or *would*, that word is given in brackets before the verb. Verbs preceded by *can* in the lists can also be preceded by *could*.

If a verb is always passive when used with the pattern, its passive form (for example *be seen*) is given in the list. If a verb is usually used in continuous tenses, that form (for example *be dying*) is given.

Sometimes a verb may appear in more than one list in a Unit, because it has more than one meaning when used with the pattern concerned.

Phrasal verbs

Where necessary, we give brief information on the position of the different parts of phrasal verbs in a pattern. We refer to the adverb or preposition in a phrasal verb as the **particle**. Where we say that the particle comes either after the noun group or after the verb, it should be noted that it does not come after the noun group if that noun group is a personal pronoun. For example, you should say *They pulled it down*, not *They pulled down it*. If we give no special information on phrasal verbs, the particle always comes immediately after the verb.

Different forms of the pattern

One of the difficulties in recognising patterns comes about because patterns can take different forms, for example in questions or in relative clauses. At the end of the information on a pattern, we give some of the different forms a pattern can take.

For example, the verbs *do, buy, make, train* and *choose* are used with the pattern **V n for n** (see Units 51 and 52), as in these made-up examples:

(a) *I can do something for you.*

(b) *I will buy something for my mother.*

(c) *Her mother had made a dress for her.*

(d) *We've been trained for this job.* (passive)

(e) *I chose Roger, Lawrence and John for the interviews.*

But the order of elements in this pattern may be different. In a question or clause beginning with *what*, the *what* replaces the first noun group and comes at the beginning of the clause:

(a) *What can I do for you?*

(b) *I was trying to work out what to buy for my mother.*

If the verb comes in a relative clause, the relative pronoun may replace one of the noun groups and come at the beginning of the clause:

(c) *She was wearing a dress that her mother had made for her.*

(d) *This is a real opportunity to go and do the job that we've been trained for.*

The relative pronoun can be omitted: *She was wearing a dress her mother had made for her.*

If the first noun group is very long, it may be moved to the end of the clause:

(e) *I chose for these interviews Roger de Grey, Lawrence Gowing, and John Piper.*

Productive uses

If a pattern is particularly productive – that is, many verbs with a particular basic meaning can be used with the pattern – we mention it in a special note.

Right-hand pages: Practice

The right-hand pages contain practice material relating to the patterns on the left-hand pages. This material is based on real examples taken from the Bank of English. Where necessary, the first question has been done for you to provide a model. In the Self-Study edition, an Answer Key is given at the back of the book.

There are many different types of exercise in this book, so you should read the instructions carefully. Here are some comments on the most common types of exercise.

Introduction

'Find the pattern' exercises

In these exercises, you are asked to put a dotted line under the verb used with the pattern being practised, and then to underline the other parts of the pattern. For instance, in Unit 42 you will see this example:

Top executives around the country have rated Atlanta as the nation's best city for business.

and you are asked to pick out the pattern **V n *as* n**. The verb with this pattern is *rate*, and the parts of the pattern are:

V	have rated
n	Atlanta
as	as
n	the nation's best city for business

Using underlining to show the pattern, the example looks like this:

Top executives around the country have rated Atlanta as the nation's best city for business.

Often, the example shows a different form of the pattern, and this is more difficult to identify (see 'Different forms of the pattern' above). In the following example, the verb which occurs in the pattern **V n *as* n** is *address*, but it is in a relative clause.

When he reached the back porch, he met an officer, whom he addressed as captain.

The parts of the pattern are:

V	addressed
n	whom
as	as
n	captain

Using underlining to show the pattern, the example looks like this:

When he reached the back porch, he met an officer, whom he addressed as captain.

Where we ask you to put a dotted line under the verb used with a pattern, we mean you to mark the whole verb group, including any auxiliaries or modals.

'Filling in gaps' exercises

Some of the exercises in this book ask you to fill in the gap in each of a number of sentences by choosing the correct word from a list. These exercises both practise the pattern and develop your knowledge of what words go together. Usually, some of the questions in these exercises are easier than others, so do the ones that you know first, then fill in the others. Unless you are told otherwise, each of the words in the list will be used in only one example. If you are filling in a verb, you should use an appropriate tense or form of the verb.

'Rewriting' exercises

In these exercises you are asked to rewrite an example so that it uses a given verb and the pattern you are practising. The examples also help you to understand what the verb and its pattern mean. For example, in Unit 47, you will see this example:

He took hold of my hair and pushed me roughly up the trailer steps.

You are asked to rewrite this sentence using the verb *grab* in the pattern **V n *by* n**. So instead of *took hold of my hair* you write *grabbed me by the hair*. The complete answer is:

He grabbed me by the hair and pushed me roughly up the trailer steps.

'Matching sentences' exercises

In the 'matching sentences' exercises you don't have to write anything. You simply draw a line to match the first part of the sentence with the second part. As with the 'filling in gaps' exercises, you are developing your knowledge of which verbs and nouns go together. Do the easy ones first, then puzzle out the others.

Extra Practice

On pages 202-205 there is some extra practice material, in which each exercise tests your knowledge of more than one pattern.

Verb Index

To find out which patterns a particular verb has, look it up in the **Verb Index** (p 206) and turn to the Unit(s) where it is listed, along with other verbs with the same pattern and meaning.

Glossary

There is a Glossary of grammatical terms on page x.

More detailed information about verbs can be found in Collins Cobuild Grammar Patterns 1: Verbs. This book was the winner of the **Duke of Edinburgh English-Speaking Union Award 1996.**

Words and abbreviations used in the patterns

/	or
adj	an adjective group
adv	an adverb group
amount	a word or phrase indicating an amount
as if	a clause beginning with *as if*
as though	a clause beginning with *as though*
inf	the bare infinitive form of a verb
-ed	a clause beginning with the past participle of a verb
-ing	a clause beginning with the '-ing' form of a verb
it	'introductory' or 'general' *it*
like	a clause beginning with *like*
n	a noun group
pl-n	a plural noun group
prep	a prepositional phrase
pron-refl	a reflexive pronoun
quote	a quoted clause in direct speech
that	a that-clause
to-inf	a clause beginning with the to-infinitive form of a verb
V	a verb group
way	*way* preceded by a possessive determiner
wh	a finite clause beginning with a wh-word
when/if	a finite clause beginning with *when* or *if*
wh-to-inf	a non-finite clause beginning with a wh-word and a to-infinitive form
with	more than one order of elements is possible

Glossary of grammatical terms

active voice If a verb is in the active voice, the Subject of the clause indicates the person or thing doing the action or responsible for it, e.g. *Anne* **has given** *me a tiny black kitten.* Compare **passive voice**.

adjective group An adjective group may consist of just one adjective, e.g. *I was* **glad**. Or the adjective may have words before it, such as an adverb, e.g. *I was* **very happy**, or words after it, such as a non-finite clause or a prepositional phrase, e.g. *I was* **pleased to see her**... *That was* **kind of you.** An adjective group is used to describe someone or something, or to give information about them.

adverb group An adverb group usually consists of just one adverb, e.g. *He swung* **round** *to see who was there... She is doing* **well** *at school*, but the adverb may also have another adverb before it, e.g. *Young skin burns* **very easily.** Adverb groups which are part of verb patterns are usually concerned with place or manner.

amount An amount is a word or phrase indicating an amount of something, for example *a lot, nothing, three percent, four hundred pounds, more, much*, e.g. *Her style of cooking owes* **much** *to her mother-in-law.*

auxiliary An auxiliary is one of the verbs *be, have*, and *do*, when they are used with a main verb to form tenses, passives, negatives, interrogatives, imperatives, etc.

bare infinitive A bare infinitive is the infinitive without *to*, e.g. *Thomas did not dare* **approach** *the great man... She heard the girl* **laugh**.

bare infinitive The base form is the most basic form of the verb, e.g. *go, run* and *walk*.

co-ordinated Two parts of a group or clause which are co-ordinated are joined together with a **co-ordinator** such as *and, or*, or *than*, e.g. *In his 68 years,* **he and Diana** *quarrelled only once.*

'-ed' clause An '-ed' clause is a non-finite clause beginning with the '-ed' form of a verb, e.g. *Rose had all her shops* **decorated in pink**.

'-ed' form The '-ed' form of a verb is its past participle form. This usually ends in '-ed' but it sometimes ends in '-en'. There are also several irregular verbs which have special forms, for example, the past participle of *put* is *put*. The '-ed' form is used, for example, in all passive patterns, e.g. *The cliffs were* **formed** *when the sea level was higher.*

ergative verb An ergative verb has two patterns, most commonly V and V n. The V pattern indicates that something happens to the Subject, or that the Subject does something, e.g. *The car* **stopped**. The V n pattern indicates that someone or something causes something to happen, e.g. *The driver* **stopped** *the car.* The Subject in the V pattern is the Object in the V n pattern. See Units 90-93.

finite clause In a finite clause, the verb group includes an indication of tense or modality, e.g. *A man was swimming fast to the canoe.* Compare **non-finite clause**.

general it General *it* is used in some patterns and phrases to refer vaguely to a general situation, e.g. **It's** *raining... Cut* **it** *out.* See Unit 99.

imperative When a clause is in the imperative, the base form of the verb is used and the clause usually has no Subject. The imperative is typically used to tell someone what to do, e.g. **Stand** *with your feet about a foot apart.*

'-ing' clause An '-ing' clause is a non-finite clause beginning with the '-ing' form of a verb, e.g. *His wife did not like him* **drinking so much**... *You should consider* **supplementing your diet with vitamins and minerals.**

'-ing' form The '-ing' form of a verb is the form that ends with '-ing'. It is used, for example, to form continuous tenses, e.g. *I've been* **thinking** *about it*, or to make an action nominal, e.g. **Swimming** *is good exercise.*

introductory it Introductory *it* functions as a 'dummy' Subject or Object in a sentence, without contributing to its meaning. It points forward to another clause in the sentence, e.g. **It** *is not clear who will get the money... He made* **it** *clear that he would not negotiate.* See Units 94-98.

modal verb There are eleven modal verbs in English: *can, could, dare, may, might, must, need, shall, should, will,* and *would*. They are used to add meaning to a main verb, for example to indicate how certain or possible something is, or whether a course of action is recommended or allowed. See also **phrasal modal**.

non-finite clause In a non-finite clause, the verb group does not include an indication of tense or modality, e.g. *I can just see him* **swimming in clear blue water**. Compare **finite clause**.

noun group A noun group may consist of just one noun, e.g. **Children** *roamed the streets.* Or the noun may have words before it, such as a determiner, adjective, or other modifier, e.g. *He and* **the children** *drove down to the beach... She was raising* **two little children**; or words after it, such as a prepositional phrase or a relative clause, e.g. **Children under twelve** *are half-price...* **Children who eat with their parents** *can choose from an adult menu.* A noun group may also consist of a pronoun, e.g. **They** *were enjoying* **themselves**... **He** *didn't say* **anything**. It may be an amount, e.g. *Jack owes his mother* **a lot**.

Object An Object is a part of an active clause that refers to the person or thing that is involved in an action but does not perform the action, e.g. *I was eating* **my dinner**... *They painted* **the outside of the house**. An Object is typically a noun group, but it may also be a non-finite clause, e.g. *I'd like* **to see you**. When an Object is a clause it indicates a situation or action. An Object typically comes after the verb, but in questions it may be a wh-word and occur at the beginning of the clause, e.g. **What** *do you want?.* See also **introductory it**.

ordinal An ordinal is a word such as *first, last*, or *tenth*. It is used to indicate where something comes in a sequence.

particle 'Particle' is the term used to refer to adverbs or prepositions such as *in, on, up*, or *down* when they combine with verbs to form phrasal verbs, e.g. *He was trying to break* **up** *the fight... They burned the school* **down**... *I'll look* **after** *it for you.*

passive voice If a verb is in the passive voice, the Subject of the clause is affected by the action and is not responsible for it, e.g. *He* **was given** *a bone marrow transplant.*

personal pronoun The personal pronouns are *I, me, you, he, him, she, her, it, we, us, they*, and *them*. They are used to refer to people or things whose identity is clear.

phrasal modal A phrasal modal is a phrase which forms a single verb group with another verb and which affects the meaning of that verb in the same way that a modal verb does, e.g. *I **have to** go... **You're bound to** like him.*

phrasal verb A phrasal verb consists of a verb and one or more particles. Its meaning is different from that of the verb and the particle(s) taken separately. Phrasal verbs have patterns that are similar to those of ordinary verbs, except for the presence of the particle(s). Some examples of phrasal verbs are *back down, die out, look after,* and *put up with.*

plural noun group With some verbs, the noun group which comes before the verb or after the verb has to be plural. A plural noun group may consist of one noun group which indicates two or more people or things, e.g. *Combine **all the ingredients** in a pan.* Or it may consist of two or more co-ordinated noun groups, linked by *and*, e.g. ***Molly and Simon** were always arguing.*

prepositional phrase A prepositional phrase typically consists of a preposition and a noun group, e.g. *He dived **into the river***, but it may also consist of a preposition and an adjective group, e.g. *She is described **as critically ill***; an '-ing' clause, e.g. *They will work **towards removing the underlying causes** of famine;* or a wh-clause, e.g. *They are preparing to vote **on whether to begin a full investigation**.* A prepositional phrase indicates the circumstances of an action or event, for example, its time or place, its frequency, its degree, or the manner in which it occurs. Prepositional phrases which are part of verb patterns are either concerned with place or manner, e.g. *Place the mixture **in a saucepan***, or they indicate a person or thing that is directly involved in the action or state indicated by the verb, e.g. *A practical program of reform must be based **on firm principles**.*

quote A quote gives the words that someone has said, written, or thought. There are usually quotation marks round a quote, e.g. *'I don't want you to leave,'* he said.

reciprocal pronoun There are two reciprocal pronouns, *each other* and *one another*. They indicate that what one person or thing does to another, the other does to them, e.g. *They looked at **one another**... They hated **each other**.*

reciprocal verb A reciprocal verb indicates a process which two or more people, groups, or things are involved in mutually, for example, they do the same thing to each other or they take part jointly in the same action or event. Reciprocal verbs are used in patterns with a plural Subject, where the Subject indicates both people, groups, or things, e.g. *We **argued** about politics... The two leaders **met** in New York yesterday.* They are also used in patterns where the Subject indicates one person, group, or thing, in which case the other participant is mentioned in another part of the pattern, e.g. *I **argued** with Dick about the rules... I **met** him in Switzerland.*

reflexive pronoun The reflexive pronouns are *myself, yourself, himself, herself, itself, ourselves, yourselves,* and *themselves*, e.g. *The government will continue to dedicate **itself** to peace.*

relative clause A relative clause is a subordinate clause which gives more information about someone or something mentioned in the main clause. Relative clauses are often introduced with a relative pronoun, e.g. *who, that* or *which*.

Subject In an active clause, the Subject is the part of the clause that refers to the person or thing that does the action indicated by the verb, or that is in the state

indicated by the verb, e.g. ***The children** have eaten all the biscuits... **The brain** consists of billions of nerve cells.* In a passive clause, the Subject typically indicates the person or thing that is affected by an action, e.g. ***The house** has been restored.* It may be something that is in the state indicated by the verb, e.g. ***Her mother** was known to be a rich woman... **This factory** is comprised of just three rooms.* The Subject is typically a noun group, but it may also be a wh-word, e.g. ***What** is happening here?;* a clause beginning with *what* or *all*, e.g. ***What I need** is some accurate information;* a non-finite clause, e.g. ***Thinking about it** makes me feel unhappy;* or, infrequently, a that-clause. The Subject typically begins the clause, and comes before the verb, but in questions it may come after an auxiliary verb such as *do* or *have*, e.g. *Do **you** think he will make a good president?*

subjunctive The subjunctive form of a verb is in most cases the base form, used in certain clauses in place of the present or past tense, e.g. *I suggested that he **call** me Pinky.*

that-clause A that-clause is a finite clause that follows a verb group or a noun group and often, though not always, begins with *that*, e.g. *She thought **that he was heading west**... Gertrude told him **he would soon be a father**.*

to-infinitive A to-infinitive is the base form of a verb preceded by *to*, e.g. *The number of victims continues **to rise**.* A passive to-infinitive form consists of *to be*, and the '-ed' form of a verb, e.g. *He refused **to be silenced**.*

to-infinitive clause A to-infinitive clause is a clause beginning with the to-infinitive form of a verb, e.g. *She persuaded him **to leave the office**... The President agreed **to be interviewed** the next day.*

verb group A verb group may consist of just one verb, e.g. *I **went** to Wales last year;* or it may also contain one or more auxiliaries, e.g. *I **have been thinking** about your offer;* a modal, e.g. *Colleges **should provide** needed information;* a phrasal modal, e.g. *I **have to leave** immediately;* or the negative form *not*, e.g. *Grace **did not answer** the question directly.* A verb group tells you, for example, what someone or something does or what happens to them.

wh-clause A wh-clause is a finite clause that begins with a wh-word, e.g. *I wondered **why the children weren't home yet**... I asked her **whether I should inform the police**.* A wh-clause indicates that something is uncertain or unknown. Wh-clauses usually follow verb groups or noun groups, although they occasionally occur as the Subject of a clause. In this book, we sometimes use the term 'wh-clause' as a general term covering both the finite clause and the non-finite wh-to-inf clause. See **wh-to-inf clause**.

when/if clause The term 'when/if clause' is used in Units 96-98 to indicate a finite clause beginning with *when* or *if* which is not a wh-clause because it does not indicate that something is uncertain or unknown. It refers to a situation that occurs, or may occur, e.g. *I used to like it **when you came round for coffee and a game of cards**.*

wh-to-inf clause A wh-to-inf clause is a non-finite clause that begins with a wh-word and a to-infinitive, e.g. *I still have not decided **what to spend the money on**.* Wh-to-inf clauses refer to something that is uncertain or unknown.

wh-word The wh-words are *what, who, whom, when, where, why, which, whose, whether, how,* and *if*.

Verbs used on their own

The simplest verb pattern of all is where the verb can be used on its own, without anything following it. For example, in *She laughed*, there is nothing following the verb *laugh*. This pattern is **V**.

	Verb group
The meeting	had ended.
The amount of desert in the world	is increasing.

This is one of the most frequent patterns in English. In this book we can list only a small number of the verbs which have this pattern. Here are some of the meaning groups they belong to:

■ **verbs indicating that someone or something moves or stays where they are**

approach	fall	leave	set off	turn
arrive	fly	move	sit down	wait
climb	get up	open	stand up	walk
come	go	pass	stay	
dance	go out	remain	stop	
emerge	jump	return	swim	
enter	land	run	travel	

*Menti shook hands with her and **left**.*

*She **turned** and stared at him.*

*At this moment the screen door **opened** and John McGinnis **emerged**.*

*The car **stopped**.*

■ **verbs indicating that something happens or exists**

continue	go on	last	result
exist	happen	occur	

*The accident **occurred** when a pilot crossed a runway during foggy conditions.*

*The relationship **didn't last**.*

*Hundreds of their villages no longer **exist**.*

■ **verbs concerned with beginning and ending**

begin	finish	start
end	open	stop

*The talks **began** on Monday.*

*We**'ll** never **finish** in time.*

*The rain **had stopped**.*

■ **verbs concerned with changing**

change	expand	grow	increase
decline	fall	grow up	rise
develop	go up	improve	

*Things **have changed** in the fashion world.*

*Inflation **is rising**.*

*Reading standards **have improved**.*

■ **verbs concerned with being successful, failing, or managing to do something in difficult circumstances**

cope	lose	pass	survive	work out
fail	manage	pay off	win	
lead	miss	succeed	work	

*I've made a big effort to improve my discipline and, to a large extent, I think I**'ve succeeded**.*

*Many are finding it difficult to **cope** because of unpaid wages and lost savings.*

*Other swimmers got him ashore, but attempts to revive him **failed**.*

*Didn't I tell you things **would work out**?*

■ **verbs indicating that someone makes a sound or puts on an expression, or that someone's body does something involuntarily**

cough	frown	shiver	sneeze
cry	laugh	sleep	wake up
faint	pass out	smile	

*She **smiled** weakly.*

*We both **laughed**.*

*Then they both drank so much that they **passed out** in their hotel.*

■ **verbs concerned with talking or thinking**

agree	argue	explain	reply	talk
answer	care	lie	speak	think

*'This is your last chance', her father said. Erin **didn't reply**.*

*He never **spoke** unless he was spoken to.*

*She pauses and **thinks** for a moment.*

■ **other common verbs**

break	draw	hurt	run out	teach
carry on	dress	(not) matter	settle down	wash
cook	drink	paint	show off	work
count	drive	pay	sing	write
die	eat	read	smoke	

*From an early age he loved to **draw** and **paint**.*

*Suppose we meet somewhere for a drink? I**'ll pay**.*

*She'd be late for work, but it **didn't matter**.*

*I went to Dent's to get some more books 'cos I**'ve run out**.*

*I **work** hard.*

A Fill in the gaps in the sentences below using the verbs in this list. Use each verb once.

arrive   begin   continue   die   explain   go up   happen   jump   laugh   pay off   smoke

1 'What's ....?' she asked.
2 There was no way to escape from the building except to ....
3 The train .... on time this morning.
4 When she said that nothing seemed to be working right, I asked her to ....
5 Two boys were sitting close together, whispering and ....
6 I'm afraid, though, the price has .... a little bit.
7 I was happy that all of the hard work I had done in practice had finally ....
8 When he .... in 1985, few people noticed.
9 Most people are now aware of the risks to their health if they ....
10 The radio said the fighting .... on Sunday and was .... in the
    region around the capital.

B In the list of verbs beginning with *approach*, find:

1 five verbs which indicate that someone leaves a place

   ....

2 four verbs which indicate that someone or something does not move or no longer moves

   ....

3 three verbs which indicate that someone or something moves through the air

   ....

4 one verb which indicates that someone moves through water ....

C From the list of verbs beginning with *cough*, select the right verb to put into the following
dictionary definitions.

1 When you ...., tears come from your eyes, usually because you are unhappy or
   hurt.
2 When you ...., you suddenly and involuntarily take in your breath and then blow
   it down your nose noisily.
3 If you .... or ...., you lose consciousness for a short time,
   especially because of hunger, pain, heat, or shock.
4 When you ...., your body shakes slightly because you are cold or frightened.
5 When you ...., you force air out of your throat with a sudden, harsh noise.
6 When you ...., you become conscious again after being asleep.
7 When someone ...., their eyebrows become drawn together, because they are
   annoyed, worried, or puzzled, or because they are concentrating.
8 When you ...., the corners of your mouth curve upwards and you sometimes show
   your teeth. People .... when they are pleased or amused or when they are being
   friendly.

Verbs used with a noun group: 1

Some verbs are followed by a noun group. For example, in *She was eating a biscuit*, the verb *eat* is followed by the noun group *a biscuit*. This pattern is **V n**.

Active pattern

	Verb group	noun group
He	hit	me.
I	made	a shallow box.

Passive pattern

	Verb group
The system	has been improved.
The posters on the fence	were removed.

(With most of the phrasal verbs listed in these units, the particle comes either after the noun group or after the verb. With a few, the particle always comes after the verb. If there are two particles, as in *look forward to*, the particles come after the verb.)

This is the most frequent pattern in English. In this book we can list only a small number of the verbs which have this pattern. Here are some of the meaning groups they belong to:

■ **verbs concerned with harming, breaking, destroying, or attacking someone or something**

attack	burn	fight	injure	shoot down
beat	burn down	hang	kill	take apart
beat up	cut	harm	pull down	
blow up	cut down	hit	run over	
break	destroy	hurt	shoot	

She **broke her leg**, and can't get to work.

One civilian and one soldier **were killed**. (passive)

A four-storey hotel in Hull **has been destroyed** by fire. (passive)

■ **verbs concerned with mending things**

do up	maintain	repair
fix	mend	restore

I hope Rudolph **can fix your car**.

■ **verbs concerned with making or producing something**

bring about	complete	design	found	produce
build	cook	finish	make	
cause	create	form	prepare	

They**'re building a prison** a few miles from town.

I **have completed my greatest work of art**.

It is doubtful if such a response **would produce the required results**.

The bridge **was designed** by Brunel. (passive)

■ **verbs concerned with changing or affecting something**

affect	cut	improve	limit	reduce
change	extend	increase	raise	

I am proud that we helped **change the world**.

We **have to reduce our costs** now.

■ **verbs concerned with moving or holding something**

add	close	hang up	pick	remove
arrange	cut off	hide	pick up	shake
bear	deliver	hold	press	shut
break off	draw	lift	pull	take
bring	drop	move	push	turn
carry	give back	open	put away	
catch	hand over	pass round	raise	

Add the garlic, onion and carrots.

I**'ll bring some more plates and cutlery**.

Opening her bag again, Nancy **handed over another envelope**.

Michelle remembers the first time she **held the new baby**.

■ **verbs concerned with operating machinery or vehicles**

blow	operate	ring	start	work
drive	play	set	start up	
fire	play back	set off	stop	
fly	ride	sound	use	

Charles came and **operated the security lock**.

The second time we **played the record**, it sounded twice as fast.

Well, you **can't ride your bicycle** today, and that's final.

Eileen smiled, and **started up the engine** without speaking.

Practice

A Fill in the gaps in the sentences below using the verbs in this list. Use each verb once.

fire   operate   play back   ring   set   set off   use

1 I had to .... the bell for the nurse to come.
2 Never .... a mobile phone in a restaurant.
3 I haven't .... the gun in over five years.
4 He .... the tape ...., listening intently.
5 Another gang of criminals .... the burglar alarm in a store across the road.
6 He needs money to pay the technicians who .... his equipment.
7 I forgot to .... my alarm clock and I overslept.

B In the pieces of text below, put a dotted line under the verbs used with a noun group in the pattern **V n**. Then underline the noun groups. The verbs may not appear in the lists in this Unit.

1 Trim and peel the carrots. Cut them crosswise into 2-inch lengths. Coarsely chop the red bell pepper, discarding the seeds. Peel and chop the garlic. In an electric blender combine the red bell pepper, garlic, lime juice, sugar, and salt. Taste the dressing; you may wish to add a little more salt.
2 We poison our hearts and lungs, we give ourselves bronchitis, we alter the enzymes in our blood and make our children hyperactive. And we give ourselves cancer. We do these things by burning coal, making and driving motorcars, by growing crops and spraying them against infection, and then spraying them again to keep the weeds down.

C Each of the sentences below shows a verb from this Unit used in a relative clause. Say what the verb is, and whether it is active or passive.

1 Those who were injured are recovering slowly. .... *injure, passive* ....
2 The woman, who was carrying a shoulder bag, left because the guesthouse was full.
   ....
3 Most people know someone who's been affected and I'm no exception.
   ....
4 This is a model of a bridge which is being built in Japan right now.
   ....
5 Troops also searched houses in the port area, which the rebels have attacked twice in the past week.
   ....
6 The catastrophe which destroyed the dinosaurs happened sixty-five million years ago.
   ....
7 The Park once surrounded Marbury Hall, which was pulled down in 1968.
   ....
8 A new rail timetable, which will reduce services, will be introduced from September.
   ....
9 The University of Deusto, which was founded in 1886, owed its existence to a number of leading industrialists. ....
10 He said she should admit her economic failures and announce policies to deal with the problems her mistakes had created. ....

Verbs used with a noun group: 2

Here are some more groups of verbs which are followed by a noun group:

■ **verbs concerned with thinking, feeling, perceiving, and discovering**

accept	expect	like	see
(cannot) bear	face up to	look forward to	(cannot) stand
believe	fear	look up	study
blame	feel	look up to	support
check	find out	love	think over
compare	forget	miss	understand
consider	hate	notice	want
determine	hear	plan	watch
discover	ignore	prefer	welcome
enjoy	investigate	read	
establish	know	recall	
examine	learn	remember	

I **would** certainly **consider** any offer very carefully.

I'm very much **looking forward to** the challenge of editing a weekly newspaper.

If you'**d like** a copy of those recipes, we can easily let you have one.

Tommy **didn't notice** him.

I **was watching** television with the cat on my lap.

With *compare*, the noun group following the verb is always a **plural noun group**.

Compare the two lists.

■ **verbs concerned with speaking and writing**

announce	describe	predict	repeat	talk over
answer	discuss	promise	report	teach
ask	explain	propose	reveal	tell
ask after	express	put forward	say	threaten
confirm	go into	quote	speak	urge
declare	mention	raise	suggest	write
deny	point out	recommend	talk	write down

I **didn't say** anything.

Let's **talk business**.

I can't believe that Paul **wrote** that letter.

Now Britain **has put forward** an alternative proposal.

With *ask after* and *go into*, the particle always comes after the verb.

They refused to **go into** details.

With the following verbs, the noun group following the verb always or sometimes indicates the person who is spoken to:

address	ask	tell	thank	warn
answer	teach	tell off	threaten	write

The girls **thanked** him and left.

Did you **tell** anyone?

■ **verbs used when indicating what something includes, shows, or is connected with**

concern	demonstrate	include	mean	show
contain	determine	indicate	prove	
cover	feature	involve	represent	

Fifteen percent of detective work **concerns divorces**.

The law **covers religions in general**.

The price **includes air travel from London, rail travel, and coach transfers**.

The row **shows the different approaches of the two governments**.

■ **delexical verbs**. The verb and noun group together indicate that someone performs an action, rather than that someone affects something.

carry out	fight	hold	perform	take
commit	fire	keep	play	
deliver	give	make	score	
do	have	pay	sit	

Melody **gave a nervous laugh**.

Tanya **had a hot bath**, hoping it would relax her.

We **might be able to do some work** this afternoon.

Last month he **held a big party** to mark his 60th birthday.

I need to **make a phone call**.

He **fired a shot** to wake the others.

Only six students **sat the exam**.

■ **verbs concerned with starting, stopping, or continuing an activity**

begin	continue	finish	prevent	stop
break up	end	keep up	start	

How have your opinions of people changed since you **started** this project?

Diplomatic efforts to **prevent a civil war** have so far been unsuccessful.

It is questionable whether the agreement **will stop the killing**.

I want to **continue my career** in Spain or Italy.

A From the list of verbs beginning with *accept*, select the right verb to put into the following dictionary definitions.

1 If you .... something, you believe that it will happen.

2 If you .... something, you feel a desire or a need for it.

3 If you .... someone or something, you are frightened because you think they will harm you.

4 If you .... a fact, a piece of information, or an answer, you have it correctly in your mind.

5 If you .... people or events from the past, you still have an idea of them in your mind.

6 If you .... someone or .... what they are saying, you know what they mean.

7 If you .... someone, especially someone older than you, you respect and admire them.

8 If you .... someone who is no longer with you or who has died, you feel sad and wish that they were still with you.

B Rewrite these sentences using one of the verbs and noun groups in these lists. Use each verb once.

commit   do   fight   give   have   make   take
a long campaign   a decision   lectures   murder   a sip   a sleep   some thinking

1 I am not going to decide now. *I am not going to make a decision now.*

2 She sipped her drink. ....

3 I generally sleep for a while in the afternoon. ....

4 They have long campaigned for full compensation. ....

5 I was asked to lecture on political economics in the mathematics department.

   ....

6 I don't think your father killed anyone. ....

7 I've been thinking about the plan, and there's a question I forgot to ask you.

   ....

C In each of the sentences below, one of the verbs from this list is missing. Mark where it goes and say what it is. Use each verb once.

begin   contain   demonstrate   finish   predict   prove   quote   threaten

1 He kept coming round and / me. ....*threatening*........

2 Meryl was able to finish college and a successful career. ....

3 I had no experience running anything, but I did a good knowledge of the industry. ....

4 Since the era of the Babylonians it's been possible to an eclipse years in advance. ....

5 Sugary desserts such as pie, cookies and cake often more carbohydrates than do chocolate-flavored foods. ....

6 They won't have much trouble finding the evidence to his guilt. ....

7 He did another ten thousand words in America and the book in November. ....

8 I shall one example that I happen to know from first-hand experience. ....

Verbs used with a noun group: 3

Here are some more groups of verbs which are followed by a noun group:

■ **verbs concerned with having, getting, losing, or selling things**

accept	find	have	own	steal
buy	get	keep	receive	take
choose	give away	lose	sell	

*I decided I **would** never **own** a TV.*

*The thieves **kept** my credit card, which the bank immediately stopped.*

*When I left the army I came back home and **bought** a house.*

*We **gave away** some of our old furniture and started to search for new pieces.*

■ **verbs concerned with amounts of money**

ask	cost	get	make	pay
charge	earn	live on	offer	

*Things are expensive: a jar of black caviar **costs** 1,700 roubles.*

*Psychiatrists tend to **charge** more than other types of mental health counselors.*

*The job now **pays** £135,000 a year.*

■ **verbs indicating the position, extent, or course of something or someone**

approach	face	keep to	occupy
cover	fill	lead	pass
cross	follow	leave	reach
enter	join	meet	surround

*The resort is situated where the Atlantic Ocean **meets** the Gulf of Mexico.*

*Beyond the pub, the road **passes** a farmyard and becomes a grass track.*

*Martin **crossed** the road and headed into the trees.*

Follow me.

■ **verbs concerned with moving or travelling.** The noun group following the verb indicates the distance travelled.

go	march	swim	walk
jump	run	travel	

*Joseph **walked** over four miles in 90 degree heat.*

*She **had to travel** more than five miles by bus every day.*

Productive use: Most verbs which involve moving or travelling can be used with this pattern.

■ **other common verbs**

avoid	drink	look after	require	test
beat	eat	need	run	touch
call	grow	paint	save	visit
combine	help	protect	sort out	wait
control	interest	provide	surprise	wear
draw	last	record	take	win

*England **can** now **beat** any team in the world.*

*I'**ll call** you tonight.*

*People **need** homes, not just houses.*

*She **runs** a restaurant in San Francisco now.*

*Four lives **were saved** because of Chloe. (passive)*

With *combine*, the noun group following the verb is always a **plural noun group**.

***Combine** the yoghurt, honey and cinnamon.*

Last, take, and *wait* are followed by a noun group referring to a period of time.

*The trial **lasted** five weeks.*

With *look after*, the particle always comes after the verb.

*Who'**ll look after** the baby?*

Different forms of the pattern

*What **did** you **say**?*

*I asked **what** he **had bought**.*

*I just want to spend a little time with **the girl** I **love**.*

***Such changes** can be hard to **accept**.*

***The wine** is then ready for **drinking**.*

*It was **a rotten trick** to **play**.*

***This** I **knew** already.*

***What** we **need** is democracy.*

Some verbs are sometimes used in a pattern with *than*.

*Don't order more than you **need**.*

A Put the different parts of these sentences in the right order.

1 he / with a knife / and / money and jewellery / stole / them / threatened

....

2 all their money / decided / they / they / away / should give

....

3 as a result of / people / might lose / market reform / four million / their jobs

....

4 chose / with / the best view / the bedroom / Simon ....

5 and / crisps / the group / drank / ate / white wine ....

B In the piece of text below, put a dotted line under the verbs used with a noun group in the pattern **V n**. Then underline the noun groups. The verbs may not appear in the lists in this Unit.

The track passes a small lodge. On meeting a main road turn left up the approach to Abbey Lodge, which guards a fine avenue of trees. Cross the bridge and bear right to an iron gate. Walk along the weir and over the lock gates. To reach Henley turn right and follow the river for 2 miles.

C In the sentences below, there is a dotted line under a verb used with a noun group. Underline the noun group, which may occur before the verb.

1 What are you trying to say?
2 Who did this?
3 What I want is more money.
4 He was the best golfer I've ever seen.
5 That's a horrible thing to say.
6 I found the radar extremely easy to use.
7 I asked her what that meant.
8 This she agreed to do.
9 The fish here are not suitable for eating.
10 The present system does not give us the information that we require.

D Fill in the questions, starting with the words provided.

1 'I saw something.' 'What *did you see?'* ....
2 'I've forgotten something.' 'What ....
3 'Let's play a game.' 'What ....
4 'We need something else.' 'What ....
5 'Yes, I heard something about that.' 'What ....
6 'Let's go out and buy something.' 'What ....
7 'I was watching television.' 'What programme ....
8 'I would prefer someone else.' 'Who ....

Verbs used with a noun group: 4

In the case of some verbs with the pattern **V n**, the noun group after the verb describes the Subject. Most of these verbs do not have passives.

	Verb group	noun group
My husband	is	a doctor.
It	seemed	an ordinary place.

These verbs belong to the following meaning groups:

■ **verbs indicating that a person or thing is something, or is made up of something**

be	constitute	make up	represent
compose	form	prove	stay
comprise	make	remain	

*That story **is a good example** of Crane's greatness as a writer.*

*Do you think he**'d make a good president**?*

*Two and two **make four**.*

*How many players **comprise a team** in netball?*

*The agreement **represents an important victory** for the union.*

The verbs *compose*, *comprise*, and *make up* have a passive pattern in which the verb group is followed by a prepositional phrase beginning with *of*.

*This machine **is composed** of three parts.*

*The Chinese character for 'wise leader' **is made up** of three symbols.*

■ **verbs indicating that a person or thing becomes something**

become	form	make	turn

*She eventually gave up her job and **became a full-time singer**.*

*After about 10-15 minutes, the police quietly began **forming a line across the road**.*

In the case of *turn*, the noun group is always singular but without a determiner.

*Both **turned informer** and were the main prosecution witnesses in the trial of the other men.*

■ **verbs indicating that a person or thing seems to be something**

appear	feel	look	seem	sound

*He **seems a reasonable man**.*

*That **sounds a good idea**.*

Feel indicates how someone seems to themselves.

*For the first year after the divorce I **felt a real failure**.*

■ **verbs indicating that someone behaves like a kind of person they are not**

act	play

The noun group after the verb always begins with *the*.

*The more the parents **act the boss**, the less control they seem to have and the more miserable they are.*

■ **verbs used when indicating the size or weight of something or someone**

average	cover	measure	weigh
be	extend	stand	

*Twenty years ago, supermarkets **averaged 20,000 square feet**.*

*He **weighs 8st 7lb**.*

Be and *stand* are always followed by a noun group and an adjective group, adverb group, or prepositional phrase when used to indicate size, and *measure* and *extend* usually are.

*The fence **was two and a half metres high**.*

*The river **was only fifty yards across** and we were over in a minute.*

*The brooch **measures 2 inches in length**, and the clip-on earrings **are 1 inch in diameter**.*

Different forms of the pattern

*Who **are you**?*

*What **is your favourite book**?*

*I did not know what the problem **was**.*

*What it **is** is a civil war.*

Some verbs are sometimes used in a pattern with *than*.

*I feel I am a better player than I **was** in 1985.*

A The sentences below indicate someone's opinion of a person or thing. Fill in the gaps using the nouns in this list. Use each noun once.

arrangement   boy   business   experience   girl   people   place   thing

1 He's a charming ....

2 She seems a bright, happy .... who will fit in well here.

3 That looks a nice ....

4 That sounds a sensible ....

5 That sounds a ridiculous .... to say, but it's exactly how it felt.

6 They were decent ....

7 Growing up is a painful ....

8 A holiday in the Himalayas is an unforgettable ....

B For each pair of sentences, say whether the noun group after the verb describes the Subject or not.

1 a) She weighed 175 pounds. ...*yes*........
   b) He weighed the gun in his hands. ...*no*........

2 a) They make some good music. ....
   b) They would have made very good teachers. ....

3 a) He felt a stranger in this country. ....
   b) He felt a strange mix of emotions. ....

4 a) He represents a group of five artists, none of them yet over 30. ....
   b) The $4.7 billion deal represents a major victory for McDonnell Douglas. ....

5 a) The individual cells that make up the brain are well understood. ....
   b) Parliament can make up the rules as it goes along. ....

6 a) Riot police formed a human barrier between the two sides. ....
   b) He had formed a poor opinion of his forthcoming rival, Jimmy Carter. ....

C Express these measurements in sentences. There may be more than one way of doing it.

1 a hole – width: 12 feet; depth: 2 feet.
   The hole was 12 feet wide and 2 feet deep.

2 a bridge – length: 130 metres; height: 30 metres.
   ....

3 an insect – length: 2 inches; diameter: 1 inch.
   ....

4 an oil slick – length: 10 miles; width: 2 miles.
   ....

5 a man – height: 5 feet 8 inches; weight: 11 stone.
   ....

UNIT 6

Verbs used with or without a noun group

Many verbs can be used on their own (the pattern **V**) or can be followed by a noun group (the pattern **V n**).

Some verbs that have these two patterns are **ergative verbs**, for example *break*, as in *A window broke*, *They broke the window*. These verbs are dealt with in Units 90-92.

The other verbs with these two patterns can be divided into two groups:

Group 1

When the verb is used on its own, something else involved in the action must have been previously mentioned or indicated. For example, you do not say *I'll check* unless it is clear what you will check.

accept	cut down	hear	pay	sell
answer	defend	help	play	start
approach	do without	help out	promise	stop by
ask	drink	investigate	publish	strike
attack	enter	know	pull	survive
attend	explain	lead	push	take over
call	fight	leave	remember	visit
call back	find out	lose	repeat	watch
check	finish	(not) mind	resign	win
choose	fire	miss	ring	
claim	fit	notice	ring back	
clear up	follow	order	rule	
count	give up	pass	see	

Here are some pairs of examples, one with the pattern **V** and one with the pattern **V n**.

*To our great relief, she **accepted**.*
*He offered to help me, and I **accepted** the offer.*

*But what if Jay **found out**?*
***Have** you **found out** something?*

***Have** you **finished**?*
*There were further cheers when the old man **had finished** his speech.*

*He took his pistol and **fired**.*
*Pagan **fired** his gun again.*

*He talked softly so that nobody **could hear**.*
*I thought I **heard** a noise.*

*Tony grabbed the wire and **pulled**.*
*Reggie put a gun to his head and **pulled** the trigger.*

*You helped him once before, **do** you **remember**?*
*I **remember** the day he was born.*

*She'**ll ring back** later.*
*I'**ll ring** you **back** in the morning.*

*The chauffeur **survived** and identified Garcia.*
*Several people **survived** the crash.*

Group 2

The verb can be used freely on its own because the general type of thing involved is obvious from the meaning of the verb. For example, you can say *She was singing*, and it is obvious that she was singing a song of some kind. More detail about the thing involved can be given with the pattern **V n**, as in *She was singing a song about me*.

act	draw	marry	run	study
adopt	drive	move	save	suffer
answer back	eat	negotiate	shoot	teach
change	fly	paint	sing	travel
charge	go without	perform	sing	wait
cook	kill	please	speak	write
deliver	learn	read	steal	

Here are some pairs of examples.

*She taught me how to **cook**.*
***Cook** the carrots, onions, celery and diced bacon until golden.*

*Cocaine **can kill**.*
*A series of explosions **have killed** three soldiers and wounded at least three others.*

*He never **married**.*
*He **married** a local woman.*

*I was thrilled when we **scored**.*
*Carey **scored** five runs.*

*He **has taught** at Princeton, Harvard and Yale.*
*She **taught** English Literature.*

With many of these verbs, the noun group in the **V n** pattern sometimes does not add any meaning. For example, *Uruguay had just scored a goal* means the same as *Uruguay had just scored*. Here are some further examples:

*She went upstairs to **change**.*
*When he came out he'**d changed** his clothes.*

*Unable to have children of their own, Penny and Rodney decided to **adopt**.*
*Eventually we decided to **adopt** a child instead.*

12

A Fill in the gaps in the pairs of sentences below using the verbs in this list. Say which sentence shows the pattern **V** and which shows the pattern **V n** or its passive.

attack   attend   enter   follow   help   notice   pay   push

1 a) Your hotel bill's been ....*paid.*............ .....*V n (passive)*..........
   b) You must let me ....*pay.*............ ....*V*...............

2 a) Sutcliffe knocked on the door and ....
   b) Quickly Nancy .... the shop. ....

3 a) Then I .... her eyes. ....
   b) The cake was trampled under their feet, but they didn't ....

4 a) The message merely reported that the French had .... at dawn. ....
   b) The victim was .... at about midnight on Thursday last week. ....

5 a) I can .... you. ....
   b) I just wanted to ....

6 a) The public was invited to ....
   b) About eight-hundred delegates .... the conference. ....

7 a) Don't look now, but I think we're being ....
   b) She went up the stairs, and Jake ....

8 a) He .... harder, and then fell on his face as the door was opened suddenly.
   ....
   b) She .... the buttons, but they didn't light up. ....

B In each case, say whether sentence b) means the same as sentence a).

1 a) He has never bothered to learn to drive.
   b) He has never bothered to learn to drive a car. .....*yes*.....

2 a) I love learning.
   b) I love learning English. ....

3 a) The sport has given me the opportunity to travel.
   b) The sport has given me the opportunity to travel the world. ....

4 a) You can easily take it with you when you move.
   b) You can easily take it with you when you move house. ....

5 a) She was reading.
   b) She was reading a magazine. ....

6 a) They cheated. They stole. And they lied.
   b) They cheated. They stole cars. And they lied. ....

7 a) Trying too hard to please can be harmful.
   b) Trying too hard to please others can be harmful. ....

8 a) He scored twice in their comfortable 3-nil win over Norway.
   b) He scored two goals in their comfortable 3-nil win over Norway. ....

Verbs used with a reflexive pronoun

Some verbs are followed by a reflexive pronoun. For example, in *She enjoyed herself*, the verb *enjoy* is followed by the reflexive pronoun *herself*. This pattern is **V pron-refl.**

	Verb group	reflexive pronoun
History	Behave repeats	yourself! itself.

(With phrasal verbs, the particle comes after the reflexive pronoun.)

Verbs with this pattern belong to the following meaning groups:

■ **verbs concerned with injuring yourself accidentally, or killing yourself**

burn	drown	hurt	kill
cut	hang	injure	starve

*If you **burn yourself** in the kitchen, put your hand into the freezer and put ice on the burn.*

*She wanted to die and tried to **drown herself** in the river.*

*Police say he **hanged himself**, but there are suspicions that he may have been killed.*

■ **verbs concerned with doing something with a lot of effort or enthusiasm, or taking something seriously**

apply	commit	stir
assert	exert	wear out

*Potential buyers had been reluctant to **commit themselves**.*

*He never seemed to hurry or **exert** himself.*

■ **verbs concerned with controlling your feelings or behaviour**

behave	compose	limit	pull together
collect	control	organize	

*She tried to **control herself**, but there were tears in her eyes.*

***Pull yourself together**. Go wash your face. Freshen up.*

■ **verbs concerned with talking, often about yourself**

explain	express	introduce	repeat

*Godard sat down and prepared to **explain himself**.*

*Johnson pretended not to be able to hear anything Shaw said, so Shaw **had to repeat** himself in a louder voice.*

■ **verbs indicating that someone moves their body or changes position**

cross	raise	shake	support
draw up	seat	stretch out	

*The old woman glared at him, **drew herself up** and stormed into the building.*

*'Nothing is wrong now,' laughed Bess as she **stretched herself out** lazily.*

*She knelt, **crossed herself** and prayed.*

■ **verbs concerned with enjoying yourself or treating yourself well**

enjoy	help	spoil
fulfil	indulge	suit

*I **do enjoy myself**, I love sports, travelling and socializing.*

*This is the time to **indulge yourself**. Go on, treat yourself to a new dress.*

*He has already arranged his life to **suit himself**.*

■ **verbs concerned with hiding or keeping away from other people**

hide	isolate	lock away	shut away	shut off

*His first instinct was to **hide himself**.*

*I always **lock myself away** to write.*

■ **verbs concerned with being or becoming successful**

better	distinguish	excel	prove

*Sheppard **excelled herself**, breaking her own 50m time and setting a new British record.*

*He never felt pressured to **prove himself** in a fight.*

■ **other common verbs**

be	dress	present	reproach
disgrace	kid	repeat	work out

*'What do I have to do?' I asked. Tony laughed. 'Just **be yourself**. Nothing more.'*

*An opportunity soon **presented itself**, which he eagerly seized.*

*Just how this situation **will work itself out** remains to be seen.*

A Fill in the gaps in these sentences with a reflexive pronoun.

1 Losing her balance, she had landed on her back and hurt .... badly.
2 All the children in the class have to behave ....
3 How often do I have to repeat .... ?
4 It's your body and your life, so don't be frightened to assert ....
5 Let me introduce ....
6 If we isolate ...., we die.
7 The problem is not going to work .... out.
8 You must pull .... together.
9 He cut .... shaving.
10 Don't work so hard. You'll wear .... out.
11 She was allowed to leave the court for a few minutes to compose ....
12 He'd been terrified of making a wrong step and disgracing ....

B Rewrite these sentences using the verb given in brackets with the pattern **V pron-refl**.

1 He committed suicide. (kill)
He killed himself. ....

2 You must get your personal life in order. (organize)
....

3 He refused to give any explanation. (explain)
....

4 Have a good time! (enjoy)
....

5 He was finding it difficult to describe how he felt. (express)
....

6 It is only with friends that most people feel they can relax and behave naturally. (be)
....

7 She took an unnecessarily long time to bath and put her clothes on. (dress)
....

8 He worked really hard and got into Magdalene, his father's college. (apply)
....

9 They appear to be rewriting the rules to fit in with what they want. (suit)
....

10 He was poor at maths and English but did very well in French. (distinguish)
....

Verbs used with two noun groups: 1

Some verbs are followed by two noun groups. For example, in *I bought him lunch*, the verb *buy* is followed by the noun groups *him* and *lunch*. This pattern is **V n n**. The first noun group always indicates a person, and the second noun group indicates the thing that is involved in the action.

Active pattern

	Verb group	noun group	noun group
Her boyfriend	gave	her	a diamond ring.
I	wrote	him	a letter.

Passive pattern

	Verb group	noun group
Natalia	was offered	a job in New York.
We	were brought	the lunch menu.

(With phrasal verbs, the particle comes either after the first noun group or after the second noun group.)

Verbs with this pattern belong to the following meaning groups:

■ **verbs concerned with giving, selling, or offering someone something, or refusing to do so**

accord	deny	hand back	pay	serve
advance	feed	lease	pay back	slip
allow	give	leave	permit	throw
assign	give back	lend	promise	tip
award	grant	offer	refuse	toss
deal	hand	pass	sell	

*That year for Christmas my parents **gave** me a microscope kit.*

*She **gave** me **back** my ring.*

*The club's representative had arranged to **sell** him a ticket for the match.*

*Throughout history, females **have been denied** many roles in society.* (passive)

■ **verbs concerned with doing something for someone, usually something which is beneficial to them**

assure	cook	fix	order	sing
bear	cut	get	play	
book	do	guarantee	pour	
bring	fetch	make	prescribe	
buy	find	mix	secure	

*She asked me to **bring** her some tea.*

*They offered to **cook** us a Swiss lunch the following day.*

*They **can book** you a room by phone and tell you how to get there.*

■ **verbs concerned with communicating**

ask	give	post	shoot	write
bid	kiss	quote	teach	
cast	mail	read	tell	
fax	make	send	throw	

*She asked me to **read** her a story.*

*I **sent** you a postcard from Nevada.*

*He's a good man and I**'ve taught** him everything I know.*

*Let me **give** you some advice.*

*Paul and Penny came to **bid** us good-bye.*

Cast, shoot, and *throw* indicate that someone looks or smiles at someone else.

*She **shot** Brian a quick look.*

■ **verbs concerned with causing someone to gain, lose, or suffer something**

cause	cost	earn	save	spare
charge	do	lose	set back	win

*He**'s caused** us all sorts of problems this season.*

*The man's identity is not being revealed to **spare** him further embarrassment.*

*It was a fight that **cost** him his life.*

*A basic meal **will set** you **back** about eight to ten pounds.*

■ **other common verbs**

envy	let off	put off	show	wish
forgive	owe	set	take	

*She **envied** them their freedom.*

*Putting too much on the plate **may put** your child **off** his food.*

*It didn't turn out to be a difficult job, though it **took** me two hours.*

In the case of *owe*, the second noun group is often an amount.

*Now more and more I see I **owe** her everything.*

Different forms of the pattern

*What **did** she **give** you?*

*Robina did not know what Martha **told** the police.*

*He refused to accept the six dollars she **offered** him.*

*I can't think of anything to **tell** him.*

*'Thirty-five pounds it **cost** me,' she said.*

A In the sentences below, put a dotted line under the verb used with the pattern described in this Unit. Then underline each of the other parts of the pattern.

1 I'll show <u>you</u> <u>a photograph</u>.
2 On the way out of town, he stopped by the florist and bought her a bouquet of white flowers.
3 Children between 1 and 5 are charged a small flat daily rate.
4 Dr Brock was extremely helpful and promised me a written report in a week's time.
5 Dad handed me a big box wrapped in gold foil and tied with a red ribbon.
6 The message you send your adolescent about drug and alcohol use is important.
7 I would do a 12-hour shift, come home and spring-clean the flat and then cook my flatmates a wonderful meal.
8 That will set you back a few pounds.
9 Elizabeth Dekker was refused employment as a teacher at a training centre on the grounds that she was three months pregnant.
10 What were you offered, George?

B Match up the two halves of each sentence.

1 My homework took me ...   a ... every success.
2 I envy him ...   b ... money.
3 He owes me ...   c ... hours.
4 We wish them ...   d ... a lovely birthday card.
5 He poured her ...   e ... his cheerful good nature.
6 He sent me ...   f ... a glass of soda.

C Rewrite these sentences using the verb given in brackets with the pattern **V n n**.

1 Ginny said goodbye to her with a kiss at Victoria station. (kiss)
Ginny kissed her goodbye at Victoria station. ....

2 Tod looked at them angrily. (throw)
....

3 He smiled at me gratefully. (shoot)
....

4 There had been barely time for Rose to say good-bye to Philip. (bid)
....

5 From time to time a passer-by would glance suspiciously at him. (cast)
....

6 I thought you might be able to advise me. (give)
....

Verbs used with two noun groups: 2

In addition to those described in Unit 8, there are other verbs which are followed by two noun groups. For example, in *I considered him a friend*, the verb *consider* is followed by the noun groups *him* and *a friend*. The second noun group – *a friend* – describes the first noun group – *him*.

Verbs of this kind are very frequently used in the passive.

Active pattern

	Verb group	noun group	noun group
They	named	their daughter	Mary.
He	proclaimed	it	a masterpiece.

Passive pattern

	Verb group	noun group
He	will be nominated	prime minister.
The hotel	is rated	one of the best in town.

These verbs belong to the following meaning groups:

■ **verbs concerned with naming or labelling someone or something in a particular way**

acclaim	christen	dub	name	rename
brand	code-name	hail	nickname	tag
call	declare	label	pronounce	term

*My children **called him Uncle Frankie** and were always delighted to see him.*

*If she makes a mess of this marriage she**'ll be labelled a complete and utter failure** for the rest of her life.* (passive)

*I **was branded** a liar and a show-off.* (passive)

■ **verbs concerned with nominating or choosing someone for a particular position**

anoint	declare	name	proclaim	vote
appoint	elect	nominate	pronounce	
crown	make	ordain	rule	

*In 1987, the BBC **appointed** him their Deputy Editor of News and Current Affairs.*

*If you **elect me president**, you will be better off four years from now than you are today.*

*He **was named** full professor in 1941 and chaired the university's economics department for 10 years.* (passive)

■ **verbs concerned with having a particular idea regarding someone or something**

account	consider	deem	feel	prove
adjudge	count	fancy	find	rate

*The government **considers** him a threat.*

*I**'ve** always **found** him a pleasant man.*

*We have 10 industries in the constituency that **are rated** a pollution risk.* (passive)

In the case of *fancy* and *feel*, the noun group following the verb is always a reflexive pronoun.

*His son **fancied** himself a poet and a man of letters.*

■ **other common verbs**

be born	bring up	hold	make	prove

*In Mexico, his writing **has made** him a well-known public figure.*

*Two furious motorists **held a man prisoner in his own car** when they found him drunk on a motorway.*

*I **was brought up** a strict Catholic.* (passive)

In the case of *prove*, the noun group following the verb is always a reflexive pronoun.

*He **proved** himself a remarkably effective prime minister.*

Different forms of the pattern

*What **are** you **going to call it**?*

*In 1722 he accompanied a missionary from Canton back to France, **which** he **found** an altogether bewildering place.*

*The Lodge, they **call** it.*

*They are displeased with **what** they **consider** a lack of concern for patients' needs.*

Some verbs are sometimes used in a pattern with *as*.

*Bob III, as he **is called**, shares his father's pride in the business.*

A In the sentences below, put a dotted line under the verb used with the pattern described in this Unit. Then underline each of the other parts of the pattern.

1 He felt himself a fraud.

2 In 594 he proclaimed Buddhism the official state religion.

3 September 9 has been declared a day of action for press freedom.

4 We haven't got what you might term a school policy on assessment.

5 He consistently underestimated the Englishman, whom he considered an idiot.

6 It's not surprising, then, that fans throughout the United States have now voted him Entertainer of the Decade.

7 It was among the oldest of the Academy's buildings and was nicknamed 'Perilous Hall', with good reason.

8 I had been driving at about 35mph, which I considered a safe speed for the narrow, wet and winding road.

B Rewrite these sentences using the verb given in brackets with the pattern **V n n** or its passive.

1 They gave her the name of 'The Angel'. (call)
   They called her 'The Angel'.

2 He was referred to as 'The King of Wessex'. (dub)

3 He was made into a priest. (ordain)

4 US officials are saying that the mission was a military success. (hail)

5 Always sun-tanned, he believed he was an athlete. (fancy)

6 Some people discover that relaxation is a useful way of calming down. (find)

7 He claimed he had been given the reputation of a liar and a hypocrite. (brand)

8 General Powell could be chosen as the country's first black President. (elect)

C *Find* and *make* have the pattern **V n n** with more than one meaning. For each sentence, say whether or not the second noun group after the verb describes the first one.

1 You find him a stupid man, I think. ....*yes*.....

2 We have to find him a job. ....

3 Joanna found her an inspiration to work with. ....

4 The next morning she made them a real farmhand's breakfast. ....

5 His business had made him a very wealthy man. ....

6 She had made us an offer too good to refuse. ....

Verbs used with an adjective group: 1

Some verbs are followed by an adjective group. For example, in *I was hungry*, the verb *be* is followed by the adjective *hungry*. This pattern is **V adj**.

	Verb group	adjective group
He	was feeling	unwell.
She	looked	happy.
The door	slammed	shut.

Verbs with this pattern belong to the following meaning groups:

■ **verbs indicating that someone or something has a particular quality or is in a particular state**

be	go	lie	prove	stand
feel	keep	pass	remain	stay

She **was not young**, but she **was beautiful**.

I **was feeling** a bit lonely.

The law **has proved** difficult to implement.

The verbs *go* and *pass* are followed by negative adjectives such as *unnoticed* and *undetected*.

Adler wasn't going to let such behaviour **go unnoticed**.

Be is sometimes followed by an '-ed' clause indicating the state someone or something is in.

An old, yellowing card **was fixed** to the gate.

■ **verbs indicating that someone or something starts to have a particular quality or be in a particular state**

become	come over	finish up	grow	wind up
come	end up	get	turn	
come out	fall	go	turn out	

If your boss is opposed to your idea, your task **becomes more difficult**.

Does your father ever **get cross**?

He **came over** all dizzy, he said, when he stood up.

Swanson's face **turned white** as he realized what was about to happen.

Become and *get* are sometimes followed by an '-ed' clause indicating the state someone or something ends up in.

The whales often **become trapped** in fishing nets.

A thorny branch **had** just **got tangled** in my hair.

■ **verbs indicating that someone or something seems to have a particular quality or be in a particular state**

appear	look	smell	taste
feel	seem	sound	

The Government **seems unable to take control of the situation**.

Bottled fruit not only **tastes delicious** but it also **looks terrific** displayed in the kitchen.

Appear, feel, look, and *seem* are sometimes followed by an '-ed' clause indicating the state someone or something seems to be in. *Feel* indicates how someone seems to themselves.

The enemy **seemed stunned by the suddenness of the attack**.

He **felt betrayed**.

■ **verbs indicating that something such as a door moves, or makes a sound as it moves**

bang	burst	slide	spring
blow	slam	snap	swing

As Adam and Zelikov entered, the heavy steel doors **banged shut** behind them.

The door **slid open** to admit Blake.

■ **verbs indicating that a person manages to get free, or that an object comes away from or out of something**

break	roll	spring	work
pull	shake	struggle	

The more I struggled to **break free**, the more I became entangled.

The cable **had worked loose**.

■ **verbs indicating that something gives out or reflects light**

flash	gleam	glisten	shine

The metal box **gleamed silver** in the sun.

Behind us the white cliffs of Dover **shone bright** in the morning sun.

Different forms of the pattern

I see now **how stupid** I **was**.

Terrible he **was**.

He's **smarter** than I **am**.

Note that questions are often asked using *what...like* or *how*:

What did it **look like**?

How do you **feel**?

A Fill in the gaps in the sentences below using the verbs in this list. Use each verb once.

fall   feel   get   look   pass   seem

1 He keeps buying me things and trying to make me .... guilty.
2 I found it hard to .... fit this season.
3 It now .... certain that the country's next President will be a woman.
4 She was .... strikingly attractive, as usual.
5 A health alert has been issued after 29 people .... ill after eating cucumber.
6 Without that, my mistake would have .... unnoticed.

B Fill in the gaps in the sentences below using the adjectives in this list. Use each one once.

bright   free   loose   open   shut   silver

1 The stream glistened .... in the sunlight.
2 Gordon tried to grab him by the arm, but the boy pulled ....
3 The heavy door swung .... and the lock snapped into place.
4 His eyes still shone .... in the wrinkled face.
5 Noting that the ropes around the bags on my sled had worked ...., I retied them carefully.
6 In the same moment, the outer door burst .... and several police constables stormed in.

C Put the different parts of these questions in the right order.

1 your brother / what / does / look / like ....
2 the party / how / was ....
3 it / what / did / feel / like ....
4 I / how / do / look ....
5 the food / what / was / like ....

D Complete the second sentence in each pair.

1 Life was dull.
  He complained about how ..*dull life was.*..............
2 Middle America is flat and empty.
  I had forgotten how ....
3 She looked fresh and pretty.
  I thought how ....
4 His family are important to him.
  He told them how ....
5 She seemed modest.
  I was struck by how ....
6 This must have sounded suspicious.
  I was uncomfortably aware how ....

Verbs used with an adjective group: 2

Here are some more groups of verbs which are followed by an adjective group:

■ **verbs concerned with actions or processes**

arrive	die	emerge	grow up	return

*My father **died young**.*

*I want him to **grow up** happy and healthy*.

*None of them **returned** alive*.

The verbs listed above are the ones most frequently used with this meaning. However, it is often the adjective, rather than the verb, which makes this pattern possible. There are a lot of adjectives which are used with a much wider variety of verbs referring to actions and processes. Most of these adjectives have a negative meaning, especially those formed with 'un'. Here is a list of adjectives which are often used after an action verb.

barefoot	unafraid	unescorted	unnoticed
blindfold	unaided	unharmed	unprotected
breathless	unannounced	unheard	unpunished
drunk	unarmed	unhurt	unread
empty-handed	unasked	unimpaired	unrecognized
free	unassisted	uninjured	unseen
naked	unattended	uninterrupted	untouched
straight-faced	undetected	uninvited	

*A teenager named John Rush **came uninvited** to one of Stef's parties.*

*The man's car was hit by rifle fire but he **escaped unhurt**.*

*They all **walked barefoot** across the damp sand to the water's edge.*

■ **verbs indicating the position or posture of someone or something, or indicating that something stays in the same state**

hang	lie	sit	stand

The following adjectives are frequently used with *hang*:

loose	low	motionless	open

*Straight ahead of me the thunderclouds **hung low** over the highway.*

*Her head was on her knees, long dark hair **hanging loose**.*

The following adjectives are frequently used with *lie*:

awake	empty	idle	open	unconscious
dead	flat	motionless	quiet	undiscovered
deep	helpless	naked	silent	undisturbed

*He went in and found Stevens **lying dead** on the floor in the library.*

*The cave's entrance **lies deep beneath the sea**.*

The following adjectives are frequently used with *sit*:

empty	idle	naked	silent
erect	low	quiet	straight
high	motionless	rigid	

*The man **sat silent and motionless**.*

*8,000 unsold flats **are sitting** empty.*

The following adjectives are frequently used with *stand*:

empty	high	naked	ready	straight
erect	idle	open	rigid	tall
free	motionless	proud	silent	unused

*The corn **stood higher than the car**.*

*Very little work has been done and the flats still **stand empty**.*

■ There are a lot of other verbs which are followed by an adjective, but in many cases only one or two adjectives are used. Examples are *marry young, plead guilty/innocent, wear thin, sit up straight* and *fall down dead*.

*Her grandmother **married young** and divorced soon afterwards.*

*She was advised to **plead guilty** and accept a fine.*

A Rewrite the sentences below using the adjectives in this list. Use each adjective once.

barefoot   blindfold   empty-handed   unaided   uninterrupted   unseen

1 He was unable to walk without help. ....*He was unable to walk unaided.*....................
2 The troops were marching without shoes to maintain silence.

....

3 His opponent was playing with a blindfold on. ....
4 I was hoping to work without anyone interrupting me.

....

5 There was barely time for the two boys to escape without anyone seeing them.

....

6 Her home was broken into by robbers, who miraculously left without taking anything.

....

B Fill in the gaps in the sentences below using the adjectives in this list. Use each one once.

alive   unheard   uninjured   uninvited   unpunished

1 His house was demolished but he escaped ....
2 Celebrities are welcome to show up ....
3 Women who say they feel unsafe are going ....
4 I don't think the man who killed that little girl should go ....
5 We didn't know whether they would return ....

C In each of the sentences below, one of the verbs from this list is missing. Mark where it goes and say what it is.

hang   lie   sit   stand

1 His mouth / open, his eyes grew wide, the blood drained from his face. ....*hung*..........
2 Grace lifted the child into a corner of a deep chair. 'You have to quiet while Mommy makes a little music.' ....
3 When the newly-weds emerged from the church, a gleaming horse-drawn carriage ready to transport them to their reception. ....
4 Fiona fell to the ground and motionless for a few seconds. ....
5 Her fair hair loose on her shoulders. ....

D Fill in the gaps in these sentences with the correct adjectives.

1 There was a terrible flash of lightning and he fell down ....
2 Crook's expression made it clear that his patience was wearing ....
3 The actor vehemently denies the charges and will plead .... when the case opens on February 15 next year.
4 Sit up .... when you are having your hair cut to ensure an even line.
5 Lunn had married .... and had a boy and a girl aged four and six.

Verbs used with an adjective group: 3

Some verbs are followed by a noun group and an adjective group. For example, in *I like my tea sweet*, the verb *like* is followed by the noun group *my tea* and the adjective *sweet*. This pattern is **V n adj**.

Active pattern

	Verb group	noun group	adjective group
They	considered	these meetings	important.
He	wished	both of them	dead.

Passive pattern

	Verb group	adjective group
The party	was declared	illegal.
He	was proved	wrong.

Verbs with this pattern belong to the following meaning groups:

■ **verbs concerned with declaring or proving someone or something to have a particular quality**

brand	confess	find	pronounce	rule
call	declare	label	prove	
certify	diagnose	pass	report	

The journal 'Nature' **called** this book dangerous.

Keating sampled the wine and **pronounced** it drinkable.

I **was** placed in a mental institution and **diagnosed** *schizophrenic*. (passive)

At the last moment he **was passed** fit to compete. (passive)

In the case of *confess*, the noun group following the verb is always a reflexive pronoun. *Prove* often has this pattern as well.

I **confess** myself very hurt by this neglect.

He **proved** himself worthy of the task in front of him.

■ **verbs indicating that someone has a particular opinion about someone or something**

account	count	hold	rate
believe	deem	judge	think
consider	find	presume	

I **cannot believe** him capable of feeling for another human person.

At 48 he **is considered** too young to be prime minister. (passive)

The pair **are thought** likely to divorce later this year. (passive)

Some of these verbs are used only with a very restricted range of adjectives; for example *hold* is used only with *accountable*, *liable*, and *responsible*.

They **were held** responsible for the harm they caused. (passive)

■ **verbs indicating that someone likes, wants, or needs someone or something to have a particular quality or to be in a particular state**

like	need	prefer	want	wish

The Dutch spread jam on bread for breakfast, so they **like** it smooth.

I **want** everything perfect.

Note that these verbs cannot be used in the passive with this pattern.

A In the sentences below, put a dotted line under the verb used with an adjective group. Then underline each of the other parts of the pattern. (For different forms of the pattern, see Unit 13.)

1 Readers, it seems, prefer their authors female.
2 Surveys suggest that people like their councils small and local.
3 It was six months before Joanna was diagnosed pregnant.
4 Courts should be given the power to declare invalid contracts written in complex or obscure language.
5 Mr. Schorr showed that the news media consider financial gains more important than ethics.
6 According to his mother he was a sober character, but I found him capable of profound emotion.
7 All the crew members of the oil tanker are reported safe, but a huge oil slick is reported to be spreading around the two vessels.
8 He presented himself at the library at a little after ten-thirty – an hour he judged appropriate for cornering an American scholar.
9 The lighting crew avoided directing very bright lights at him, which he found uncomfortable.
10 Whatever your reasons for pursuing a language course, you will soon find yourself able to speak and write with much greater confidence and clarity.

B Rewrite these sentences using the verb given in brackets and the pattern **V n adj** or its passive.

1 You're lucky it's still necessary to me that you remain alive. (need)
You're lucky I still need you alive.

2 She admits that she is unable to give a definite view of the situation. (confess)

3 Her doctor said she was unfit to travel. (rule)

4 We think that we are lucky to have such a skilled worker around. (count)

5 According to Patterson's wife, he was intelligent and well educated. (think)

6 The owner cannot be regarded as responsible for injury or damage. (hold)

7 Everyone knows the railway line should be built, but no one is in favour of having it close to their own village. (want)

8 The jury decided that he was guilty. (find)

9 In this instance a fine was considered to be appropriate. (deem)

10 Sammy was not a nice man. Many people hoped he would die. (wish)

Verbs used with an adjective group: 4

Here are some more groups of verbs which are followed by a noun group and an adjective group:

■ verbs used to indicate that something is opened or shut

blow	force	pull	slide
close	kick	push	tear
ease	open	shut	

They **had to force** the door **open** to get in.

He went inside his cell and **pulled** the door **shut** behind him.

Close your eyes **tight**.

He rose, **opened** the window **wide**, and let in a blast of freezing air.

■ verbs used with adjectives indicating the physical state of a person or thing after an action has been completed

draw	set	squash	sweep
leave	shake	squeeze	wipe
pull	shoot	stuff	

She took off her cap and threw it in Leigh's direction, **shaking** her hair **loose**.

A head-on collision between a bus and another passenger vehicle **has left** eighteen people **dead** and two more **injured**.

Whole neighbourhoods **have been squashed** flat by shelling. (passive)

■ verbs concerned with holding or keeping someone or something in a particular position or state

have	hold	keep	leave

I had problems **holding** the camera **steady**.

His snores **kept me awake** all night.

■ verbs used with adjectives indicating someone's mental or psychological state after an action has been completed

beat	knock	send
drive	scare	strike

I won't take this new job, it **scares me silly**.

It turns out he was in a fight and **was knocked unconscious**. (passive)

■ verbs concerned with changing the colour of something

colour	paint	spray	turn

We **painted the walls white**.

Cut a rectangle from the card and **colour it green**.

■ verbs concerned with catching or finding someone or something in a particular state

capture	catch	find

He is a different man if ever you **catch** him **relaxed**.

One inmate **had been found** dead after a fire in his cell. (passive)

■ verbs indicating ways in which people or animals get killed

boil	burn	bury	skin	swallow

The adjective used with these verbs is *alive*.

For many centuries the Christian Church **burned** heretics **alive**.

We feel terror at the thought of **being buried** alive. (passive)

Some of these verbs are sometimes used metaphorically.

They are fiercely competitive. If they **can skin us alive** in business, they will.

■ other common verbs

be born	imagine	render
get	make	serve

Bake them for 8 to 10 minutes and **serve them hot from the oven**.

The government considered **making** such experiments **illegal**.

All men, whites and blacks, **are born** free and equal. (passive)

Different forms of the pattern

What **do** people **consider** important?

Army commanders have been given full powers to carry out **any operation** they **consider** necessary to restore law and order.

The Court of Appeal yesterday **declared** illegal prison rules allowing the authorities to censor prisoners' letters.

Black leather jeans are easy to **keep** clean.

A Put the different parts of these sentences into the right order.

1 removed / in order to / his glasses / them / dry / wipe / he

....

2 after / John / kicked / the door / him / shut

....

3 the unlocked door / he / a wall cupboard / of / eased / open

....

4 well / with / a few pistachio nuts / chilled / the pudding / serve

....

5 maybe / think / unlucky / I / I / was born

....

B Fill in the gaps in the sentences below using the adjectives in this list. Use each one once.

alight   alive   brown   exhausted   loose   mad   shut   steady   unconscious   white

1 Large quantities of iron may turn the water ....
2 Eye-witnesses said that cars were set ...., shop windows were broken and people passing by were beaten up.
3 They knew that the darkness could drive a man ....
4 The man picked up the tool and left. Gibson kicked the door .... after him.
5 German houses were usually painted ...., with blue roofs.
6 Bill recalls, 'I had problems holding the camera .... while shaking from loss of energy in the heat.'
7 I'd rather be buried .... than stuck in a lift with you.
8 They beat him .... with their pistols.
9 It is tragic when a rock shaken .... by an earthquake causes the death of a child.
10 It seemed to take him forever to get out of the river, and the effort left him ....

C Fill in the gaps in the sentences below using the verbs in this list. Use each verb once.

be born   capture   force   keep   make   send   squash   tear

1 The man escaped from the back of the house, while his captors slept, after .... a window open with a spoon.
2 No one .... happy. Everyone has to make his own happiness.
3 Shock can .... people sad or angry.
4 They .... animals alive to sell to animal dealers, who sold them to zoos.
5 They've installed an irrigation scheme to .... the trees alive.
6 I stood outside with my suitcases and .... open the letter.
7 She made clay models and .... them flat again.
8 I can't help but feel that an obsessive search for our inner selves – far from saving the world – could .... us all mad.

UNIT 14 Verbs used with an '-ing' clause: 1

Some verbs are followed by an '-ing' clause. For example, in *She started walking away*, the verb *start* is followed by the '-ing' clause *walking away*. This pattern is **V -ing**.

	Verb group	-ing clause
He You She	kept risk hated	saying he was sorry. losing everything. being called Dora.

Verbs with this pattern belong to the following meaning groups:

■ **verbs concerned with starting, stopping, continuing, or doing an action**

begin	come	give up	keep	resume
burst out	continue	go	keep on	start
carry on	finish	go around	leave off	stop
cease	get	go on	quit	take to

*I hope you're not going to **start** crying.*

***Stop** treating me like a schoolgirl.*

*I **gave up** swimming in the sea years ago.*

*Rather than correct her, I **kept** trying to change the subject.*

■ **verbs indicating that someone does not do something**

avoid	(not) bother	escape	omit	resist

*I thought, I **won't bother** washing my hair – I'll wash it tomorrow.*

*He left word that he had rung, but carefully **omitted** leaving his own number.*

*He moved silently in the darkness to **avoid** awakening his wife and two sons.*

■ **verbs concerned with doing something which may not be successful or may be dangerous**

chance	risk	try

*I **tried** ringing his home, but they told me he wasn't there.*

*He did not want to **risk** going back to his apartment.*

*Since race cars aren't insured, you **risk** losing everything if you hit something solid.*

Note that these two examples of *risk* are different. In the first the '-ing' clause refers to an action which might have unpleasant consequences, and in the second the '-ing' clause refers to something that might happen as a result of an action.

■ **verbs indicating that someone takes part in an activity, often shopping or a leisure activity**

come	go

*The next afternoon Amy **went** riding with Gerald.*

■ **verbs indicating that someone likes or dislikes something**

adore	dislike	like	resent
appreciate	(cannot) endure	love	(cannot) stand
(cannot) bear	enjoy	mind	(not) tolerate
detest	hate	prefer	

*I **don't** really **like** having people round.*

*Many people **prefer** living alone, even if it means loneliness.*

*I **don't appreciate** being treated like a suspect.*

*I hate the sight of guns and **dislike** touching them.*

*Many other people today said they **could not tolerate** doing nothing.*

■ **verbs concerned with attitudes towards the future, for example looking forward to something or being afraid of something**

dread	(cannot) face	fancy	fear	look forward to

*She **was looking forward to** taking a two-week holiday at the beach.*

*She was hungry, but she **couldn't face** eating.*

■ **verbs concerned with plans or ideas about the future**

anticipate	count on	imagine	plan on
consider	debate	intend	reckon on
contemplate	figure on	look into	see about

*I haven't been in any trouble and I **don't intend** getting into any.*

*In this case, you **should consider** seeking professional help.*

*He **debated** taking his car, but decided to go on foot.*

A Rewrite these sentences using the verb given in brackets in combination with the underlined verb.

1 We <u>wrote</u> our witty letters again as if nothing was wrong. (begin)
We began writing our witty letters again as if nothing was wrong.

2 I <u>lived</u> with my mum right up until we moved into this house. (carry on)

....

3 The team <u>has not analysed</u> that data yet. (finish) ....

4 I <u>asked</u> people how they felt about America. (go around)

....

5 I couldn't sleep and <u>thought</u> of the wonderful dancing I'd seen. (keep)

....

6 Dunne looked up at the ceiling and then <u>stared</u> at the fire. (resume)

....

7 He <u>walked</u> long distances in an attempt to physically exhaust himself. (take to)

....

B Rewrite these sentences using the verb given in brackets.

1 People did not talk about the problem. (avoid) *People avoided talking about the problem.*

2 When I was young, people didn't lock their doors. (not bother)

....

3 The dustmen made so much noise that I did not try to sleep. (give up)

....

4 'Don't read those books,' he said. 'They put ideas into your head.' (quit)

....

5 Hughes didn't use a wheelchair for almost two years. (resist)

....

6 His old comrades don't write to him any more. (stop) ....

C Rewrite these sentences using the verb given in brackets with the pattern **V -ing**.

1 45 per cent of British people might possibly vote Green in a general election. (consider)
45 per cent of British people would consider voting Green in a general election.

2 They are hoping that they will get money from the government. (count on)

....

3 I had been self-employed for so long that I couldn't think what it would be like to work for someone
else. (imagine)

....

4 He thought he'd continue work on his writing. (intend) ....

5 You should expect to pay around £25,000 for a one-bedroomed flat. (reckon on)

....

6 I shall go and consult my lawyer. Then I must make arrangements to sell the house. (see about)

....

29

Here are some more groups of verbs which are followed by an '-ing' clause:

■ verbs concerned with attitudes and ideas about the past, for example remembering or forgetting something, or regretting something

forget	miss	recall	regret	remember

She **can't remember committing the murder**, although all the evidence points to her guilt.

I'll never **forget going to Sunday school as a kid.**

Whatever the future holds, I **will** never **regret meeting him**.

■ verbs concerned with speaking or writing

acknowledge	advocate	describe	mention	report
admit	debate	forbid	propose	suggest
advise	deny	justify	recommend	urge

He **denied causing death by reckless driving.**

The judges **recommended giving more modest prizes.**

I **suggest following a simple rule:** never ask anyone anything about his or her life that you are not prepared to reveal about your own.

■ verbs concerned with a logical relation between two actions, events, or states

allow	justify	permit	save
involve	mean	prevent	

His route to school **involves crossing three main roads.**

Nothing **could** ever **justify destroying such a life.**

My brother had suggested that I take the bus because it **would save having to find a place to park in Manhattan.**

■ verbs indicating that someone postpones an action

delay	postpone	put off

Many young couples **have postponed having families** because of the recession.

■ verbs concerned with needing or deserving action or treatment of some kind

deserve	need	require	want

I asked if there were any more problems that **needed sorting out.**

Miles is in good health and doesn't cry unless he **wants feeding or changing.**

■ verbs concerned with beginning, ending, or spending time in a particular way

die	finish up	start off
end up	hang around	wind up

The soldiers reasoned that they'd prefer to **die fighting rather than waiting.**

Their boat **finished up pointing the wrong way.**

■ other common verbs

discourage	get away with	(cannot) help
encourage	go towards	play at
endure	go without	practise

Parents **should encourage learning** but not push children beyond their current abilities.

The profits **will go towards fighting pollution and the destruction of rainforests.**

They say that when you're playing chess you **can go without eating.**

I **couldn't help feeling ashamed.**

Practise giving your speech in front of a mirror.

A Rewrite each of the following pairs of sentences as one sentence.

1 I used to be homeless. I'll never forget that.
   I'll never forget being homeless.

2 He made the telephone calls. He admitted it.

3 I feel resentful. I can't help it.

4 She didn't want to tell Ida. She put it off until the last minute.

5 He cheated. He believed he might be able to get away with it.

6 They charge £22.50 for a fishing licence. I don't know how they can justify this.

7 People cannot campaign in the final two days before voting. The law forbids it.

B For each of the sentences below, say whether the underlined phrase indicates a past action or a possible future action.

1 The boys were expelled after admitting smoking cannabis. ....*past*..............
2 For best results, Virginia advises using olive oil rather than vegetable oil. ....
3 Witnesses described hearing a loud bang. ....
4 The committee recommended increasing the tax on fuels. ....
5 I don't regret telling her my suspicions. ....
6 I can remember sitting on the floor and eating an egg sandwich. ....
7 Several passengers reported seeing smoke coming from the engine. ....
8 They suggest opening up unused land around the airport. ....

C Match up the two halves of each sentence.

1 Many women delay ...   a ... removing the surface layer of the bone.
2 These criminals deserve ...   b ... doing harm.
3 To improve your skills, practise ...   c ... cycling on major roads.
4 He appears gentle but ends up ...   d ... throwing and catching balls.
5 The official policy is not to encourage ...   e ... having children until later in life.
6 This technique involves ...   f ... locking up.

Verbs used with a to-infinitive: 1

Some verbs are followed by a to-infinitive clause. For example, in *He expects to fly to Paris soon*, the verb *expect* is followed by the to-infinitive clause *to fly to Paris soon*. This pattern is **V to-inf**.

	Verb group	to-infinitive clause
The arrangements	appeared	to be satisfactory.
The President	agreed	to be interviewed.

Verbs with this pattern belong to the following meaning groups:

■ **verbs concerned with starting, stopping, or continuing an action, or doing something next**

begin	come	get	grow	start
cease	continue	go on	proceed	

Edgar **began to laugh** again.

He treated us okay but I never **got to like him**.

Linda **continued to lose weight**.

Phil **went on to enjoy more success at cricket than he had at football**.

■ **verbs concerned with what something is or appears to be**

appear	pretend	prove	seem	turn out

The diagnosis **turned out to be her worst nightmare**.

He'd only **pretended to be sleeping**. He'd really been watching her all the time.

■ **verbs indicating that someone tries to achieve something**

attempt	fight	strive	try
battle	labour	struggle	

That's what he's doing, though he **tries to ignore it**.

A lot of people **struggled to understand why they were doing this**.

■ **verbs emphasizing that something is successfully done, especially something that is difficult or is easily forgotten**

get	manage	remember	serve

With some difficulty he **managed to stretch out an arm and get hold of the chocolate**.

Remember to tell us if you change your address.

What he learned **served** to improve the managerial skills needed in his present employment.

■ **verbs indicating that someone does not, need not, or cannot do something**

(cannot) begin	decline	forget	omit	(not) trouble
(not) bother	fail	neglect	refuse	

The peace talks collapsed when the rebels **failed to turn up**.

Jane went back to bed and fell promptly asleep, **forgetting to turn off the light**.

I **cannot begin to describe the things I miss**.

■ **verbs concerned with the manner or attitude of the person doing an action**

care	dare	hesitate	regret

I **regret to tell you that very many American lives have been lost**.

Each time the phone rings I **hesitate to answer**.

The roads are safer now, and people **dare to emerge from their homes at night**.

■ **verbs concerned with talking or thinking about a future action, or preparing for something that will happen in the future**

agree	determine	intend	pledge	set out
arrange	elect	mean	prepare	swear
choose	fix	offer	promise	threaten
contract	go out	opt	propose	undertake
decide	guarantee	plan	resolve	vote

Chloe **had promised to take her shopping as soon as she arrived**.

At one stage in the political crisis, the prime minister himself **threatened to resign**.

I **had planned to stay longer**, but something came up.

You **can choose to repay your loan over 60 months**.

A These sentences are about actions that are done or not done. Rewrite them using the verb given in brackets with the pattern **V to-inf**.

1 I didn't tell Ellen about this development. (neglect)
I neglected to tell Ellen about this development.

2 Keep the list in a safe place. (remember) ....

3 He escaped during the night. (manage) ....

4 I hadn't brought a towel. (forget) ....

5 The man was nervous and would not give his name. (refuse)
....

6 The number of people who vote in these elections is small. (bother)
....

7 And did you meet Warhol? (get) ....

8 Mr. King, the contractor, has not answered our numerous phone calls. (decline)
....

9 This is the first time in nine years that the Lakers have not reached the finals. (fail)
....

B These sentences show the pattern **V that** (see Units 24 and 25). Rewrite them using the pattern **V to-inf**.

1 Lorraine just pretended she didn't hear. *Lorraine just pretended not to hear.*

2 He decided he would ask Claire to marry him. ....

3 I promised I would have a word with Nick when he returned.
....

4 We have agreed that we have to follow up this incident.
....

5 She swore she wouldn't tell anyone. ....

6 He had already resolved that he would agree to nothing at this first meeting.
....

7 He kept threatening that he'd push the button on this remote control bomb device.
....

C Fill in the gaps in the sentences below using the verbs in this list. Use each verb once.

begin   cease   intend   seem   struggle

1 This was the first death in Trish's life and she had to .... to control her tears.

2 I .... to find that the subject of opera was becoming interesting.

3 It's funny how I never .... to get a thing accomplished on my day off.

4 We .... to invest 238 billion roubles over the next fifteen years.

5 Well, you never .... to learn in this life is what I always say.

33

Verbs used with a to-infinitive: 2

Here are some more groups of verbs which are followed by a to-infinitive clause:

- **verbs concerned with asking to do something or asking for something to be done**

apply	beg	campaign	plead
ask	bid	demand	pray

*The police **asked** to use Keith's video as evidence.*

*He **demanded** to be flown to Sweden, but the pilot landed instead at Helsinki.*

- **verbs concerned with wanting or expecting to do something**

aim	fear	long	reckon	want
be dying	hope	(would) love	seek	wish
expect	(would) like	queue up	(cannot) wait	

*He **wanted** to forget.*

*We **expect** to see her back on the screen in the autumn.*

*He'd had his eyes on the telephone all during breakfast and he **couldn't wait** to get out of his chair and get at it.*

- **verbs concerned with liking or disliking something**

(cannot) bear	like	prefer
hate	love	(cannot) stand

*She **likes** to entertain, shop and go to the theatre.*

*Douglas **preferred** to do his own driving.*

- **verbs concerned with going somewhere in order to do something**

come	flock	go	hurry	rush

*Franklin **hurried** to catch the last train back to Washington.*

*Audiences **flocked** to see the Beatles in their screen appearances.*

- **other common verbs**

(can) afford	happen	need	remain	train
claim	help	negotiate	stop	wait
compete	learn	pay	survive	
deserve	live	qualify	tend	

*I want my books to be as cheap as possible so that more people **can afford** to buy them.*

*He **claims** to have had no inside knowledge.*

*Women **deserve** to be treated as professionals.*

*She never **learned** to read or write.*

*If you take Joey's advice, I'm convinced you**'ll live** to regret it.*

*Britain's 27 million motorists **may have to pay** to drive on motorways within five years.*

*Low-heeled comfortable shoes are best, too, as feet **tend to** swell if you sit still for too long.*

*Women **can** also **train** to become fast jet pilots.*

*The entire household **waited** to greet them.*

In the case of *remain*, the verb is always followed by a passive to-infinitive.

*A lot of questions **remain** to be answered.*

Productive use: A to-infinitive clause after a verb often has the meaning 'in order to do something'. An example is *He smiled to hide his fear*, which means that hiding his fear was the purpose of his smiling.

Different forms of the pattern

*Don't **take me**, if you **don't want to**.*

Some verbs are sometimes used in a pattern with *as* or *than*.

*He did as his sister **asked**.*

*Kelly stayed at the disco much later than she**'d planned**.*

UNIT 17 Practice

A Fill in the gaps in these sentences using the to-infinitive form or the '-ing' form of the verb given in brackets. (See also Units 14 to 16.)

1 He longed .... her voice. (hear)
2 The woman admitted .... the bombing. (carry out)
3 We couldn't afford .... another actor. (hire)
4 She asked .... home. (be taken)
5 Lisa suggested .... a bonfire. (make)
6 He couldn't practise .... much, except when he hunted. (shoot)
7 I tend .... a bit of a perfectionist. (be)
8 He decided .... the matter to the women. (leave)
9 I would recommend .... your doctor. (consult)
10 Always give a toddler who is learning .... something to hold on to. (walk)
11 At least six states have passed laws that discourage .... by car. (commute)
12 The number of people applying .... physics and chemistry at British universities fell last year. (study)

B Fill in or complete the replies, using the verb given in brackets.

1 'Do you intend to keep playing until then?' (hope) ....*Yes, I hope to.*...........
2 'Would you like to have coffee?' (would love) ....
3 'Put a T-shirt on.' (don't want) 'No, ...
4 'So you're learning Italian?' (try) ....
5 'Are you leaving tomorrow?' (plan) ....
6 'Are you finding plenty of work?' (would like)
  'Well, not as much as ....
7 'You could have phoned me.' (mean)
  .... but I didn't get the chance.'
8 'Does he in fact have most of the power at the moment?' (appear)
  'Well, this is always hard to say, but ....

C Put the different parts of these sentences into the right order.

1 all / the most popular / they / in the school / to be / long / girl
  ....
2 in the competition / would love / more women / they / to see
  ....
3 for / expect / in hospital / I / about / to be / five days
  ....
4 everything / dropped / to help / and / rushed / everyone
  ....
5 to be / with young children / most mothers / at home / would prefer
  ....

35

Verbs used with an '-ing' clause or a to-infinitive

Some verbs may be followed either by an '-ing' clause or by a to-infinitive clause.

A With some verbs, the meaning is almost the same.

■ verbs concerned with beginning, ending, or continuing an action
■ verbs concerned with someone's feelings or attitudes
■ verbs concerned with not doing something

(cannot) bear	cease	intend	omit
begin	continue	like	prefer
(not) bother	hate	love	start

They **began going out together** and some ten months later decided to marry.
As time passed and he grew colder, he also **began to grow tired**.

I **can't bear being shouted at**.
I **cannot bear to watch the film from beginning to end** because of the bad memories it brings back.

Some people have said they **will not** even **bother going back to their destroyed homes**.
He ran out, **not bothering to close the door**.

Note that you use a to-infinitive clause after *would like* or *would love* meaning 'want'. You cannot use an '-ing' clause.

She **would like to be more financially independent**.

B With some verbs, the two meanings are different.

1 After *come* and *go*, you use an '-ing' clause to indicate that someone moves or does something in a particular way.

Bob **came running from the room next door**.
They **go looking for trouble** just for something to do.

You use a to-infinitive clause to indicate that someone goes somewhere in order to do something.

I actually **came to apologize**.
I **went to see him** last week.

After *go*, you can also use an '-ing' clause to indicate that someone goes shopping or takes part in a leisure activity.

My kids **go swimming in the sea**.

After *come*, you can also use a to-infinitive clause to indicate that someone gradually begins to do something, or does something eventually.

Phil **came to understand that it is impossible to control another person**.

2 If you *go on* doing something, you continue to do it. If you *go on* to do something, you do it after you have finished doing something else.

He disregards what others say, quietly planning to **go on doing things his own way**.
After the calf muscles, **go on to exercise the knees, then the upper leg**.

3 After *remember*, *forget*, and *regret*, you use an '-ing' clause if you are referring to an event which actually happened.

I **remember visiting them just before his sixtieth birthday**.
I'll never **forget living next to her**.
I think they **regret selling it to us** now.

After *remember* and *forget*, you use a to-infinitive clause when talking about something that you had planned or are planning to do, or that you should do.

Remember to lock the door.
Too often we **forget to laugh**, taking ourselves and life too seriously.

After *regret*, in formal English, you use a to-infinitive clause with verbs like *say* and *inform* to indicate that you are sorry for what you are saying.

I **regret to inform you he died as a consequence of his injuries**.

4 After *need* and *deserve*, you use a to-infinitive clause if the Subject of the verb is also the Subject of the to-infinitive clause.

I **need to talk to you**.
The gunmen **deserve to be locked up**.

You can use an '-ing' clause instead of a passive to-infinitive clause.

The plants **need watering**.
Local residents agree that the wildlife **deserves protecting**.

5 If someone or something *helps* to do something, they assist in an action. If you *cannot help* doing something, you cannot prevent yourself from doing it.

Careful exercise or gentle massage **can help to relax the muscles**.
I **couldn't help overhearing the argument**.

6 If you *try* to do something, you make an effort to do it. If you *try* doing something, you do it as an experiment, for example to see if you like it or if it solves a problem.

Defence lawyers **tried to have the case dismissed**.
Try drinking your tea or coffee without sugar.

A These sentences show the pattern **V -ing**. Rewrite them using the pattern **V to-inf**.

1 James started talking about the quiz show.

....

2 The sport continued growing through the Seventies.

....

3 She said that she wouldn't bother coming to the meeting.

....

4 I tried to remember what I like eating.

....

5 I can't bear not seeing him.

....

B These sentences show the pattern **V to-inf**. Rewrite them using the pattern **V -ing**.

1 The team will begin to build the observatory later this year.

....

2 The firm ceased to operate three weeks ago.

....

3 He'd omitted to tell the police about the missing cash.

....

4 First of all, he loves to make movies, he loves the process.

....

5 You prefer to be taught by somebody who has actually done the job rather than somebody who's studied the job.

....

C Fill in the gaps in these sentences using the '-ing' form or the to-infinitive form of the verb given in brackets.

1 He came .... me on Monday. (see)
2 I went .... down the stairs and bruised my thigh. (tumble)
3 She enjoyed talking to her neighbour, and they often went .... together. (shop)
4 Did you remember .... your voting form? (post)
5 I'll never forget .... Barcelona to win the Cup-Winner's Cup. (beat)
6 I regret .... that I am unfamiliar with her work. (say)
7 The rule needs .... at. It should be changed. (look)
8 They were a better team than us and deserved .... (win)
9 Again and again I tried ...., but no sound came. (speak)
10 I couldn't help .... sorry for him. (feel)

Verbs used with an '-ing' clause: 3

Some verbs are followed by a noun group and an '-ing' clause. For example, in *They caught him stealing money*, the verb *catch* is followed by the noun group *him* and the '-ing' clause *stealing money*. This pattern is **V n -ing**.

	Verb group	noun group	-ing clause
I	don't like	them	pointing at me.
She	noticed	a man	sitting alone on the grass.

Verbs with this pattern belong to the following meaning groups:

- **verbs indicating that someone thinks about an event, or has a particular feeling about an event or situation**

anticipate	forget	(not) mind	(cannot) stand
appreciate	hate	put up with	tolerate
(cannot) bear	(will not) have	recall	(not) want
contemplate	imagine	remember	
fear	like	(can) see	

*Nobody **can** ever **recall** him firing anybody.*

*Her husband **doesn't like** her talking to us.*

*I hope you **don't mind** me calling in like this, without an appointment.*

- **verbs concerned with a logical relation between two processes or things**

entail	involve	justify	mean

*A move there **would involve** him taking a cut in salary.*

*We get another customer for our hospital, and this **justifies** us spending money on new equipment.*

- **verbs concerned with stopping someone doing something, or preventing something happening**

avoid	prevent	resist	save	stop

*They hope to reach an agreement to **avoid** the case ending up in court.*

*I think she really would have liked to **stop** us seeing each other.*

- **verbs concerned with perceiving, finding, or showing someone doing something**

catch	find	notice	see	watch
feel	hear	observe	show	

*As she left, she **could feel** his eyes following her.*

Most of these verbs are sometimes used in the passive.

*Men **had been observed** entering and leaving the house with large bags, the police were told.* (passive)

The Subject usually indicates a human being, but *see* and *show* sometimes have inanimate Subjects.

*The picture **showed** Joey jumping into the air, his arms and legs spread wide.*

In the case of *catch*, *feel*, and *find*, the noun group is often a reflexive pronoun.

*I **caught** myself wondering why we ever imagine children will bring us happiness.*

*She **felt** herself beginning to cry.*

- **verbs concerned with causing someone or something to do something or remain in a particular state**

bring	keep	send
have	leave	set

*Edna Lawrence survived a gas blast which **brought** her home crashing down on top of her.*

*The film **had** the audience cheering and crying.*

All these verbs except *have* are sometimes used in the passive.

*Mathis **was sent** flying onto his back.*

- **verbs concerned with passing time in a particular way, or starting or ending a period of time in a particular way**

begin	finish	pass	take
busy	kill	spend	waste
end	occupy	start	

***Don't waste** time talking.*

*Liberal Democrats **started** this day making their objections to the Republican plan clear.*

In the case of *busy* and *occupy*, the noun group is always a reflexive pronoun.

*He **busied** himself rinsing the washcloth, soaping it again.*

- *Risk* also has this pattern.

*Glover **could not risk** four men standing up in court and telling the judge he had ordered them to kill someone.*

Different forms of the pattern

He was the first man I'd seen wearing blue jeans.

A In the sentences below, put a dotted line under the verb used with an '-ing' clause. Then underline each of the other parts of the pattern.

1 She wouldn't tolerate any of us going into the armed services.
2 When I was in my twenties, she put up with me drifting in and out of her life.
3 Despite Robin's importance he was kept waiting a long time.
4 I was amazed that I could watch Nicholas being delivered without feeling funny.
5 She wrote in her diary of two small boys she had seen begging in the street.
6 All the unaccompanied children had been taken away, except for the boys whom she had heard being rejected.

B Rewrite these sentences using the verb given in brackets with a noun group and an '-ing' clause.

1 They saw that a police car was following them. (notice)
   They noticed a police car following them.
2 He pulled in three or four huge lungfuls of smoke that made him cough. (set)
   ....
3 At the start of his career he played in dance bands. (begin)
   ....
4 Every day I keep myself busy by doing chores about the house. (occupy)
   ....
5 When she came back with the vase, he was staring at the picture of himself. (find)
   ....
6 During the process of digestion, the animal uses energy. (involve)
   ....

C Rewrite each of the following pairs of sentences as one sentence.

1 He was about to go into hospital. I couldn't bear that.
   I couldn't bear him going into hospital.
2 He said, 'You don't have to say anything, just be here.' I'll never forget that.
   I'll never forget ....
3 The room is hot. You have to put up with that.
   You have to put up with ....
4 Don't chase around the streets. That's a waste of time.
   Don't waste ....
5 Her father might see them together. Erin didn't want to risk that.
   Erin didn't want to risk ....
6 He could not see whether he had done any damage. The rifle's smoke prevented him.
   The rifle's smoke prevented ....

Verbs used with a to-infinitive: 3

Some verbs are followed by a noun group and a to-infinitive clause. For example, in *She persuaded him to leave*, the verb *persuade* is followed by the noun group *him* and the to-infinitive clause *to leave*. This pattern is **V n to-inf**.

Active pattern

	Verb group	noun group	to-infinitive clause
They	would prefer	the truth	to remain untold.
She	nagged	me	to cut my hair.

Passive pattern

	Verb group	to-infinitive clause
He	was begged	to stay on.
We	will be forced	to make some difficult decisions.

(With phrasal verbs, the particle comes either after the noun group or after the verb.)

Verbs with this pattern belong to the following meaning groups:

■ **verbs concerned with what someone wants to happen**

(would) hate	(would) love	prefer	wish
(would) like	need	want	

Treating others as you **would like** *them to treat you is easier said than done.*

*I'**d love** her to go into politics or on the stage.*

I **need** *you to do something for me.*

Note that these verbs cannot be used in the passive with this pattern.

■ **verbs concerned with making requests, or giving advice or orders**

advise	counsel	forbid	pressure	tell
ask	dare	invite	push	urge
beg	defy	nag	recommend	warn
challenge	direct	order	remind	
command	encourage	press	request	

She looked at him, waiting for him to **ask** *her to come with him.*

He **advised** *me to go home and rest.*

I **told** *him to get out and stay out.*

Last night, he **urged** *them to give up their fight.*

■ **verbs concerned with making or causing someone to do something**

(cannot) bring	force	lead	pay	tempt
cause	get	be made	persuade	
condemn	induce	motivate	prompt	
convince	influence	move	sentence	
drive	inspire	oblige	spur	

The force of her push **caused** *me to crack my head against someone else's.*

It was September 1982 when his love for books **drove** *him to open his own shop.*

Kim's guilt **led** *her to overeat.*

Their fairytale marriage **prompted** *Jane to write a book on romantic living.*

Make occurs in this pattern only in the passive: the corresponding active pattern is **V n inf** (see Unit 22).

*I did nothing wrong, yet I'**m being made** to suffer like this.*

In the case of *bring*, the noun group is always a reflexive pronoun.

Even now she **couldn't bring** *herself to tell John the whole truth.*

■ **verbs concerned with allowing, enabling, or helping someone to do something**

allow	entitle	help	qualify
assist	equip	permit	teach
enable	free	prepare	train

My dad **helped** *me to buy it.*

He **taught** *us all to swim when we were quite young.*

We obediently awaited the signal **permitting** *us to enter.*

The basic course **does not qualify** *you to practise as a therapist, but it does give you an adequate foundation.*

A Rewrite these sentences using the verb given in brackets with the pattern **V n to-inf**.

1 It would be awful if he lost his job. (would hate) *I would hate him to lose his job.*

2 It would be nice if you could see the house. (would like)

....

3 They would rather that the talks were held in a neutral country. (would prefer)

....

4 His wife wishes he would give up his job. (would love)

....

5 Why can't they leave me alone? (want) ....

B Put these quotes into reported speech using the verb given in brackets and the words provided.

1 'You should go to bed immediately.' (tell)
The doctor ....*told*............ me ....*to go to bed immediately.*...........

2 'Please don't go!' (beg)
I .... her ....

3 'Tell me everything you can about the product.' (ask)
I .... him ....

4 'Don't leave the room.' (forbid)
He .... me ....

5 'You ought to take responsibility for yourself.' (urge)
I .... Jennifer ....

6 'I wouldn't talk to the press, if I were you.' (advise)
His lawyer .... him ....

7 'The public should be on the look-out for other bombs.' (warn)
Police .... the public ....

C Fill in the gaps in these sentences using the '-ing' form or the to-infinitive form of the verb given in brackets. (See also Unit 15.)

1 It was Pam who finally persuaded him .... to Britain. (return)
2 They said they were allowed .... everything they wanted to see. (see)
3 Environmentalists advise .... a damp cloth over the mouth and nose for protection. (wear)
4 All bicyclists are encouraged .... helmets. (wear)
5 Donna taught herself .... the piano. (play)
6 Guns enable men .... at a distance. (kill)
7 The rules forbid .... in the building. (cook)
8 I recommend .... water or mild soap and water, depending on how dirty the surface is. (use)

Verbs used with a to-infinitive: 4

Here are some more groups of verbs which are followed by a noun group and a to-infinitive clause:

■ **verbs concerned with appointing or choosing someone to do something, or with allocating or assigning something to a particular use**

appoint	choose	detail	nominate	use
assign	commission	employ	recruit	

Belgium **chose** *her to represent the country again the following year and she became a star there.*

It is never too late to **use** *new information to improve the situation.*

He **was nominated** *to be the director of a computer company.* (passive)

■ **verbs concerned with thinking, saying, or showing something**

acknowledge	declare	know	be reputed	think
allege	discover	make out	be rumoured	understand
assume	feel	prove	be said	
believe	find	reckon	be seen	
consider	judge	report	show	

They **have declared** *the north to be an independent republic.*

60 per cent of 900 firms surveyed **judge** *their business to be bad.*

About eighty people **are believed** *to have died in the attack.* (passive)

Islands **are seen** *to offer solitude, relaxation and a safe retreat.* (passive)

She left the course by ambulance and **was thought** *to have suffered a neck injury.* (passive)

In the case of *prove*, the noun group is often a reflexive pronoun.

He **has proved** *himself to be a highly skilled politician.*

■ **verbs concerned with intentions, predictions, and expectations**

back	intend	project	schedule	trust
expect	mean	require	tip	

We **expect** *you to show good judgement.*

He **trusted** *her to tell the truth because he knew that she always told the truth.*

He **had been scheduled** *to return to Washington, but now he clearly hoped to stay on.* (passive)

In the case of *trust*, the noun group is often a reflexive pronoun.

I **don't trust** *myself to handle this.*

■ **verbs concerned with someone or something being heard or seen to do something**

be heard	be observed	be seen

These verbs occur in this pattern only in the passive: the corresponding active pattern is **V n inf** (see Unit 22).

New mothers **have been observed** *to touch the feet and hands first, then the body, and then the baby's face.*

■ **other common verbs**

be born	do	take	(not) trouble

That woman **was born** *to be a teacher.* (passive)

In the case of *trouble*, the noun group is always a reflexive pronoun.

Nobody **troubled** *himself to tell me that anything was happening*.

In the case of *do*, the noun group is always an **amount**.

We've **done** *a lot to improve results, and a lot more will be done.*

In the case of *take*, the noun group indicates a period of time.

The treatment **takes** *up to twelve months to produce worthwhile improvement.*

Different forms of the pattern

Who **do** *you* **trust** *to lead this country?*

Michelle and Mark cheer on **the horse** *they* **want to win***.*

I'd **die for her** *if she* **asked** *me to.*

Some verbs, especially *tell*, are sometimes used in a pattern with *as*.

He did as he **was told**.

A Make these statements less direct or definite by rewriting them using the verb given in brackets with the passive of the pattern **V n to-inf**.

1 The Queen is deeply sensitive about the whole issue. (know)
The Queen is known to be deeply sensitive about the whole issue.

2 The two officers were poisoned 25 days ago. (believe)
....

3 The accused is a member of an extreme right-wing gang. (allege)
....

4 The round shape represents the sun. (be said)
....

5 The President favours more negotiations on environmental protection. (know)
....

6 This is one of the most powerful radar systems of its kind in the world. (be said)
....

7 Madonna is planning tours of the Far East and South America later this year. (be rumoured)
....

8 The German foreign minister is very annoyed that he was not consulted about the visit in advance.
(understand)
....

B Match up the two halves of each sentence.

1 The management will require each employee ...   a ... to win the European Championship.
2 You could always trust them ...   b ... to fill in a questionnaire.
3 Paul Gascoigne last night tipped England ...   c ... to do what was necessary.
4 He intended the book ...   d ... to continue.
5 We expect the recovery ...   e ... to reflect ordinary American life.

C Rewrite these sentences using the passive of the pattern **V n to-inf**.

1 Someone heard her say he was 'madly attractive'.
She was heard to say he was 'madly attractive'.

2 People saw her weep during the Hungarian anthem.
....

3 People have observed that cats show strong maternal instincts.
....

4 In one outburst, the spectators heard him yell: 'You're so bloody wrong!'
....

5 Bystanders saw two other men shoot at him.
....

6 When he attended the summit earlier this week, people observed he was suffering from a heavy
cold.
....

Verbs used with a bare infinitive

1 A few verbs are followed by a clause beginning with a **bare infinitive**, that is, an infinitive without *to*. For example, in *He didn't dare disagree with me*, the verb *dare* is followed by the infinitive clause *disagree with me*. This pattern is **V inf**.

	Verb group	infinitive clause
I	didn't dare	leave him.
He	helped	make her a star.

There are only three verbs with this pattern.

dare	help	need

*It was some hours before she **need start preparations for the children's supper**.*

*The United Nations Security Council has taken another step to **help bring about a peaceful settlement to the conflict**.*

Note that the negative of *dare* in this pattern is either *do not dare* or *dare not*, while the negative of *need* is always *need not*. Both verbs are also frequently followed by a to-infinitive clause (see Units 16 and 17) where their negatives are like any normal verb.

*My blood boiled at the sight, but I **dared not speak**.*

*You **needn't worry about whether he will cope**.*

2 Some verbs are followed by a noun group and a clause beginning with a bare infinitive. For example, in *I saw him leave the room*, the verb *see* is followed by the noun group *him* and the infinitive clause *leave the room*. This pattern is **V n inf**.

	Verb group	noun group	infinitive clause
She	heard	the man	laugh.
She	made	him	stop.

Verbs with this pattern belong to the following meaning groups:

- verbs concerned with seeing, hearing, or feeling someone or something perform an action

feel	notice	see
hear	observe	watch

*Chandler **did not notice him enter**.*

*When I turned back to **watch him close the door**, he seemed so utterly alone.*

In the case of *feel*, the noun group is often a reflexive pronoun.

*I **felt myself grow cold** and my hands trembled as I read: We have your son. He is safe so far. If you obey orders he will soon be back with you.*

- verbs concerned with making or letting someone do something, or making or letting something happen

have	let	make

*Let's see what people want, and **make it happen**.*

*Angel eagerly awaited him, anxious to **have him meet Lara**.*

*She **let her head rest on his shoulder**.*

*They threatened him and **made him open the safe**.*

In the case of *let*, the noun group is often a reflexive pronoun.

*I don't think he really **let himself get close to anyone**.*

In the case of many senses of *let*, the noun group is always *me* or *us*. The verb is always in the imperative form.

***Let us look at the evidence**.*

- *Help* also has this pattern.

*The money was an interest-free loan to **help him buy a Paris flat**.*

A In the sentences below, put a dotted line under the verb used with a pattern described in this Unit. Then underline each of the other parts of the pattern.

1 We can't just sit by and watch you throw your life away.
2 Let me say a few more words about economic affairs.
3 We had assembled a team of people to help advise us how to deal with the French government.
4 The first requirement for the undergraduate college is to help students achieve proficiency in written and oral language.
5 They whisper to me that James Hopper likes me, but I don't dare believe them.
6 But you do so much already and, really, you needn't do anything at all.

B Fill in the gaps in the sentences below using the phrases in this list.

   didn't dare   did not help   needn't

1 I .... tell my mother where I was going for fear of her having a heart attack.
2 You .... worry, Mrs Dayton. We'll bring you back safely.
3 Sanctions .... stop the war.
4 We .... eat straightaway. You can read your paper.
5 He feared that the tradition would disappear if he .... keep it alive.
6 For a terrible second I froze. I .... turn around.

C Rewrite each of the following pairs of sentences as one sentence.

1 He went out of the tent. She heard him. _She heard him go out of the tent._
2 A woman picked something up and handed it to another woman. Only one man noticed her.
   ....
3 The students taught and conducted conferences. The university supervisor observed them.
   ....
4 He dived into the deep end. I saw him. ....
5 The police car left the village. From her bedroom window, Jessica watched it.
   ....

D Rewrite these sentences using the verb given in brackets with the pattern **V n inf**.

1 She took her daughter home and persuaded her to lie down on the couch. (have)
   She took her daughter home and had her lie down on the couch.
2 She forced me to promise that I would not tell the others anything about it. (make)
   ....
3 Don't accept a situation where you are overcharged. (let)
   ....
4 Most women say that after using face masks their skin feels very smooth. (make)
   ....

Verbs used with an '-ed' clause

Some verbs are followed by a noun group and an '-ed' clause, which usually consists of just an '-ed' form. For example, in *I had my car repaired*, the verb *have* is followed by the noun group *my car* and the '-ed' clause *repaired*. This pattern is **V n -ed**.

	Verb group	noun group	-ed clause
I	must get	the car	serviced.
I	want	him	found.

The verbs which most frequently have this pattern are *have* and *get*.

One use of these verbs is to indicate that you arrange for someone to do something or perform a service for you. In the case of medical procedures, the action is usually done because it is necessary rather than because you want it to happen, and the verb used is *have*.

Here are some of the more frequent combinations of *have* or *get*, a noun group, and an '-ed' clause:

have a limb amputated	get/have your hair permed
get/have your hair cut	get/have your ears pierced
get/have your house decorated	get/have something repaired
get/have your house done up	get/have your house rewired
have a tooth extracted	get/have your car serviced
get/have something fixed	have someone tailed
have someone followed	have a tooth taken out
get/have someone immunized	get/have someone vaccinated
get/have something made	get/have something valued
get/have something mended	

We **ought to get** the roof repaired before the house gets any damper.

You really **ought to get** your hair cut. It's starting to look ridiculous.

Before a purchaser can make a formal offer to buy, he **must have** the property valued.

At least 1 in 20 parents choose not to **have** their children immunised.

Have is also used to indicate that something happens to you which is caused by someone else.

Did I tell you Hazel**'s had** her car stolen again?

Press photographers on the scene **had** their exposed film confiscated by police.

Get is also used to indicate that someone or something causes something to happen.

Walsh made a determined effort to **get** me fired from my job at the Department of Justice.

'Anything at all that **can get** you noticed is good news in this business,' said Ms Swan.

Get is also used to indicate that someone achieves something.

How **will** I ever **get** all that cooking done?

Here are some more groups of verbs which have this pattern:

■ **verbs concerned with wanting or needing something to be done**

(would) like	need	want

The teachers' union says it **would like** the school shut down.

I **want** this murder investigated.

She came into the shop with a package saying: 'I **don't need** it changed, only re-wrapped.'

■ **verbs concerned with seeing, hearing, or feeling something happen**

feel	hear	see	watch

In the morning, everyone came out to **see** Nick carried into the ambulance.

It was the first time he **had heard** the name spoken in five years.

In the case of *feel*, the noun group is often a reflexive pronoun.

Watching her, Ellis **felt** himself overcome by love.

■ **other common verbs**

find	keep	make	order	report

Please **keep** me informed of your progress.

There's no way he **could have ordered** anyone killed, he says.

Find, *keep*, and *report* are sometimes used in the passive.

A man **was** last night **found** shot dead in the back of his car.

At least three people **were reported** killed when police opened fire in three areas of the capital.

In the case of *make*, the noun group is often a reflexive pronoun.

He had taught me a few words of his language and I **was able to make** myself understood now and then.

Different forms of the pattern

It is a resource **which** the Majorcan authorities wish to **see** used by a larger proportion of the island's visitors.

A In the sentences below, put a dotted line under the verb used with an '-ed' form. Then underline each of the other parts of the pattern.

1 Readers who want a question answered should write to us.
2 Does the boss like to hear three possible courses of action discussed before a recommendation gets offered?
3 A search is going on after a yacht was found abandoned about eighty miles off Shetland.
4 The group would like EC laws changed to allow motorists to 'shop around' for cheaper deals abroad.
5 The door is kept locked at night, and they didn't come into the building.
6 To get you started, we've provided some favorite recipes.

B Fill in the gaps in these sentences using a form of *have* or *get* with the words given in brackets. Sometimes both *have* and *get* are possible.

1 I need to ...*get my amplifier fixed.*.. (my amplifier / fix)
2 Alison says she wants to .... (her ears / pierce)
3 He made a mental note to .... (the car / service)
4 I asked him if he would .... for insurance purposes. (my jewellery / value)
5 Henry eventually married Anne Boleyn and later .... (her / behead)
6 Kevin was unfairly dismissed for refusing to .... (his hair / cut)
7 Six months after the baby was born in 1964, Pauline .... (her / adopt)
8 .... you .... against whooping cough? (your child / vaccinate)

C Rewrite the following sentences using *have*.

1 My friend's bike was stolen last week. ....*My friend had his bike stolen last week.*...............
2 Their salaries should be increased. ....
3 For the third time in three weeks my car's been vandalized.
   ....
4 My first novel was accepted for publication that year.
   ....
5 The driver's sentence has been reduced by the court of appeal.
   ....
6 Then I rang Doc and my suspicions were confirmed.
   ....
7 This is the second time Ms McInnes' work has been screened at Cannes.
   ....
8 His teaching certificate ought to be taken away from him.
   ....
9 Under the scheme, teachers' work will be reviewed by a senior colleague every two years
   ....

Verbs used with a that-clause: 1

Some verbs are followed by a that-clause. For example, in *I said that I would do it*, the verb *say* is followed by the that-clause *that I would do it*. This pattern is **V that**.

After the more frequent verbs such as *say*, *think*, and *notice*, the word *that* is often left out, especially in speech.

	Verb group	that-clause
He I	said agree	he knew nothing about it. that some progress has been made.

Verbs with this pattern belong to the following meaning groups:

■ **verbs concerned with speaking, writing, and other forms of communication**

accept	comment	grant	point out	say
acknowledge	complain	guarantee	pray	signal
admit	concede	hint	predict	specify
advise	conclude	imply	proclaim	speculate
advocate	confess	indicate	promise	state
agree	declare	insist	propose	stress
allege	demand	(not) let on	protest	submit
announce	deny	maintain	recall	suggest
argue	dictate	make out	recommend	swear
ask	direct	mention	regret	testify
assert	disclose	note	remark	threaten
beg	emphasize	observe	report	urge
boast	estimate	order	request	warn
claim	explain	plead	reveal	write
command	forecast	pledge	rule	

*Taylor **said** he was delighted to be at the festival.*

*She **claims** she paid no money for it.*

*We **agreed** that she was not to be told.*

*Ordinary people **complain** that price rises have caused their standard of living to decline.*

*Western aid workers **point out** that the UN offer has come too late.*

*He **predicted** that the terms would be rejected and the war would continue.*

*George Orwell **wrote** that the great enemy of clear language is insincerity.*

Verbs indicating that someone makes a request or suggestion can have *should* or a subjunctive in the that-clause.

*The government **has ordered** that people should not gather in groups of more than two on the streets.*

*We all felt hungry, so I **suggested** that we stop for an early lunch.*

■ **verbs indicating that someone says something after something else has been said**

add	confirm	dispute	reply
agree	counter	object	respond
answer	disagree	repeat	

*She said he was in good health, and **added** that he had given up smoking.*

*I said: 'What a lovely morning,' and he **replied** that it would be very hot later.*

■ **verbs indicating how loudly something is said**

cry	murmur	scream	whisper
cry out	mutter	shout	yell

*Francis **murmured** that he would do anything he could and left the room.*

*She **screamed** that they'd killed her sons.*

■ **verbs concerned with thinking, feeling, knowing, and understanding**

accept	disagree	hold	resolve
acknowledge	doubt	hope	see
agree	dream	imagine	speculate
anticipate	estimate	intend	suppose
appreciate	expect	know	suspect
assume	fancy	(not) mind	think
believe	fear	pray	trust
bet	feel	realize	understand
calculate	figure	reckon	wish
consider	forget	reflect	worry
decide	gather	regret	
determine	guess	remember	

*I **thought** you were dead.*

*He was fantastically short of money, so everyone just **assumed** he sold the pictures.*

*I **decided** that nothing would be done in a hurry.*

*Officials **fear** that crop failure early next year will lead to serious food shortages.*

*'I **didn't know** you owned a camera,' said Michael.*

UNIT 24 Practice

A Fill in the gaps in the sentences below using the verbs in this list. Use each verb once.

advise   boast   complain   dream   forecast   forget   pray   repeat

1 The report .... that up to 250,000 jobs could be lost in the industry.
2 He had never .... that his enemy would dare show his face in the town again.
3 She had .... that he was to leave so soon.
4 Hongkongers like to .... that there are more Rolls-Royces in their city than rickshaws.
5 The computer game market leaders .... that players should take regular breaks.
6 He .... again that the statement on independence was not negotiable.
7 I just .... that everything will come out all right in the end.
8 He .... that she never paid attention to him any more.

B Rewrite these sentences using the pattern **V that**.

1 'I'm from a small town in Vermont,' she explained.
   She explained that she was from a small town in Vermont.
2 'I'm going to call the police!' I shouted. ....
3 'I'd like an ice-cream,' she replied. ....
4 'I had no knowledge of the espionage operation,' insisted the officer.
   ....
5 The President announced: 'The government will be lifting controls on the prices of luxury goods.'
   ....
6 'I'm sorry I cannot reveal the decision yet,' he added.
   ....

C Use a variety of verbs from this list to express your feelings on each of the issues mentioned below.

agree   believe   disagree   doubt   hope   wish   worry

1 Poverty should be eradicated from a civilized, affluent society.
   I believe that poverty should be eradicated from a civilized, affluent society.
2 People could easily be replaced by computers in the workplace.
   ....
3 I won't be one of those parents who try to live their lives through their children.
   ....
4 Racism is on the increase. ....
5 Brazil are the best football team in the world. ....
6 People form their own lives, and experience is the best teacher.
   ....
7 More young people could be brought into the government.
   ....

1 Here are some more groups of verbs which are followed by a that-clause:

■ **verbs concerned with finding out and remembering**

calculate	establish	hear	read	see
conclude	figure out	learn	realize	sense
decide	find	note	recall	(can) tell
deduce	find out	notice	recognize	work out
determine	gather	observe	register	
discover	guess	perceive	remember	

*I **noticed** that a pane of glass was missing.*

*My boyfriend left me as soon as he **found out** I was pregnant.*

*Rigid with fear, Jessica **remembered** that the window was open.*

*Oh, I **see** you've already started.*

■ **verbs concerned with indicating a fact or situation**

confirm	illustrate	indicate	prove	show
demonstrate	imply	mean	reveal	signal

*Research **shows** that more young women are taking up smoking.*

*An argument with a friend or relative **doesn't mean** that you don't get on with anyone.*

■ **verbs concerned with making arrangements for the future, or influencing a situation**

arrange	ensure	guarantee	mind
dictate	fix	mean	see

*He **had arranged** that all calls from there would be charged to the police.*

*I worked hard to **ensure** that everything would go smoothly.*

*The Argonne was one of the better small hotels, but not the best. This **meant** that at off-peak seasons they often had it nearly to themselves.*

Mind is used only in the imperative, usually without the word *that*.

***Mind** you don't slip.*

■ **other common verbs**

check	gamble	pretend	require

*Anastasia **pretended** she hadn't heard his question.*

*She went upstairs and **checked** that her mother's bedside light was out.*

*The law **requires** that one-fifth of the apartments in large cities go to low-income families.*

Different forms of the pattern

*Things didn't, he **admitted**, look good in Russia.*

Some verbs are sometimes used in a pattern with *as* or *than*.

*As Eamonn McCabe **says**, now it's up to the industry to prove him wrong.*

*The meeting lasted longer than he **had anticipated**.*

2 A small number of verbs with the pattern **V that** can also be followed by *so*, when referring back to a statement or thought. These verbs are *assume, believe, fear, hope, imagine, presume, say, suspect,* and *think*.

*Janet considered the general incompetence appalling and **said so**.*

With *believe, imagine, say,* and *think*, the negative can be expressed as in *I don't think* so, or as in *I think not*. With *assume, fear, hope, presume,* and *suspect*, the negative is always expressed by *not* after the verb.

*'So for you it's not going to be a problem.' 'I **don't think** so. I **hope not**.'*

3 Some verbs cannot be followed by *that* alone, but are followed by *the fact that*.

*But then the moment comes when they **have to face the fact that** they will never, ever see their child again.*

*I decided to give up smoking because I **can** no longer ignore the fact that it is bad for my health.*

Some verbs with the pattern **V that** can also be followed by *the fact that*, for extra emphasis.

*You **must accept** the fact that you are older than you used to be.*

A In the sentences below, put a dotted line under the verb used with a pattern described in this Unit.

1 She noticed that the car was almost out of gasoline.
2 Mind you don't let the cat out.
3 I'd be surprised to find out that Spitt ever stole a penny from anybody.
4 As this example illustrates, people enjoy the sense of exercising control in difficult situations.
5 She also regrets the fact that modern children lack freedom.
6 He didn't think much of Goldstone's argument and said so.
7 As I walked back to the car, I decided I would say nothing to Bertie Owen and Charlie Hughes.
8 The papers confirm the fact that the murdered man was also a serving police officer.
9 The regulations will require that labels show the nutritional contents of every food product sold.
10 The audience, I noted, found it hilarious.

B Rewrite these sentences so that the underlined verb is followed by a that-clause.

1 My supervisor was, I realized, a second cousin.
I realized that my supervisor was a second cousin.

2 She was, as you may have guessed, suffering from back pain.
....

3 This would allow more effective planning in the Royal Household, she said.
....

4 Children who take part in competitive sports are more likely to become winners in life, the survey discovered.
....

5 Yul Brynner was an excellent horseman, as he demonstrated in numerous films.
....

6 The intermission for each story would occur at different times, as I had arranged.
....

7 As we revealed in February, the famous Kent complex was sold by Ready Mixed Concrete.
....

8 No rail service, they acknowledged, would mean no future for the village.
....

C Respond to these questions using the verb given in brackets.

1 'Was he meeting someone?' (imagine) *'I imagine so.'* ....
2 'Do you suppose she could have had an accident?' (hope) ....
3 'So Susan will definitely be at the party?' (believe) ....
4 'So you don't think her husband is the murderer?' (suspect) ....
5 'Do all English people speak a foreign language?' (think) ....
6 'That's why Aubrey sent you, isn't it?' (presume) ....

Verbs used with a that-clause: 3

1 Some verbs are followed by a prepositional phrase beginning with *to*, and a that-clause. (The prepositional phrase indicates the hearer or reader.) This pattern is **V to n that**.

admit	demonstrate	point out	reveal	swear
announce	disclose	pray	say	whisper
boast	explain	prove	show	write
comment	hint	recommend	signal	
complain	indicate	remark	stress	
confess	(not) let on	repeat	submit	
declare	mention	report	suggest	

He **admitted** to me that he knew rather little about US law and politics.

I **explained** to him that my mother and father did not speak English.

You **will have to demonstrate** to the court that the repairs are necessary to preserve your property.

2 Some verbs are followed by a noun group and a that-clause. For example, in *I told her that there had been an accident*, the verb *tell* is followed by the noun group *her* and the that-clause *that there had been an accident*. This pattern is **V n that**.

After most of these verbs, the word *that* is often left out, especially in speech.

Active pattern

	Verb group	noun group	that-clause
He	told	me	he loved me.
They	had warned	me	that it would hurt.

Passive pattern

	Verb group	that-clause
He	was informed	that he had been disqualified.
He	was told	that it could never happen.

Verbs with this pattern are concerned with causing someone to know or think something.

assure	guarantee	promise	satisfy	tell
bet	inform	reassure	show	warn
convince	persuade	remind	teach	

We are pleased to **inform** you that we have been able to accept your application.

I **reminded** her that on several occasions she had remarked on the boy's improvement.

When she called at his studio, she **was told** that he had gone to Biarritz. (passive)

We've **been promised** that the telephone will be working in an hour. (passive)

Convince, remind, show, teach, and *tell* sometimes have an inanimate Subject.

By the time he was eighteen years old, something happened which **convinced** him that he was destined for great things.

Something **told** me she wasn't quite dead.

In the case of the following verbs, the noun group is often a reflexive pronoun: *assure, convince, persuade, promise, reassure, remind, satisfy,* and *tell.* When used with a reflexive pronoun, these verbs indicate that someone has a particular idea or thought, often a comforting or confident one.

I **told** myself I'd do better next time.

Remind yourself that the feelings will not last forever, and will become easier to cope with.

Different forms of the pattern

Bobbie needed help, she told him.

Some verbs are sometimes used in a pattern with *as.*

*The world, as Mr Hurd **reminded us**, is indeed entering a crucial period.*

A In the sentences below, put a dotted line under the verb used with a pattern described in this Unit. Then underline each of the other parts of the pattern.

1 They will prove to the world that they are serious about peace.
2 She promised herself that she would pay Granny back someday.
3 He persuaded the court that his basement was used exclusively as an office.
4 She'd been taught that when you said a word often enough, you understood its true meaning.
5 I could still convince myself that I was the victim of a subversive organisation.
6 I had to point out to him that gasoline was cascading down the side of the car.
7 A couple of editors mentioned to Kate that a research job was coming up.
8 Later that evening, I was informed that my father wished me to come to his study.
9 Sometimes I think he just needs to reassure himself that the place hasn't burnt down while he looked the other way.
10 She started hinting to him that he should take a course in business management.

B Rewrite these sentences using the pattern **V to n that** or **V n that**. The tense may have to change.

1 'The entire incident depresses me horribly,' I confessed to Stanley.

   ....

2 'We have a wedding to go to on Saturday,' I reminded him.

   ....

3 'My doctors have warned me to take care,' he said to me at lunch.

   ....

4 The President promises the people: 'The worst is over!'

   ....

5 'It's really not my business,' she told herself.

   ....

6 'He's Amanda's editor,' Mary Sweeny whispered to me.

   ....

C Rewrite these sentences in the passive.

1 They warned the directors that funds for new equipment were limited.

   ....

2 The beautician told me that my skin lacked moisture.

   ....

3 Our bosses promised us that there would be enough work for everyone.

   ....

4 However, when he arrived at the airport, a colleague informed him that the meeting was off.

   ....

5 The US navy has assured the Japanese government that there is no risk of further accidents.

   ....

Verbs used with a wh-clause: 1

Some verbs are followed by a finite wh-clause. For example, in *Can you suggest what I should say to her?*, the verb *suggest* is followed by the wh-clause *what I should say to her*. This pattern is **V wh**.

Many of these verbs can also be followed by a wh-clause consisting of a wh-word and a to-infinitive clause. For example, in *I knew what to do*, the verb *know* is followed by the clause *what to do*. This pattern is **V wh-to-inf**.

	Verb group	wh-clause
I People We	can understand don't notice have to discuss	why your kids are worrying. whether it's winter or summer. how to divide the land.

Verbs with this pattern belong to the following meaning groups:

■ **verbs concerned with speaking or writing, for example asking questions, discussing things, and giving information**

acknowledge	describe	guarantee	point out	set out
advise	detail	hint	proclaim	specify
agree	dictate	illustrate	put down	state
announce	disclose	indicate	recall	stress
ask	discuss	inquire	recommend	suggest
confess	dispute	let on	remark	warn
confirm	emphasize	mention	report	
debate	explain	note	reveal	
declare	forecast	note down	say	

Don't ask who my informant was, because I'm not going to tell you.

*Handing over the bag, she **explained** what had happened.*

*Did he **say** where he was taking the children?*

*A passer-by **inquired** why the television cameras were there.*

These verbs can be followed by a wh-word and a to-infinitive clause: *advise, ask, describe, discuss, explain, illustrate, indicate, reveal, say, specify,* and *suggest*.

*The book **describes** how to set up a self-help group.*

*Are your cosmetics past their sell-by date? We **reveal** how to make them last longer.*

■ **verbs concerned with thinking or having an opinion about something**

accept	consider	imagine	resolve
acknowledge	debate	know	see
agree	decide	(not) mind	suspect
anticipate	determine	plan	think
appreciate	doubt	predict	understand
(cannot) believe	figure	recall	wonder
care	forget	reflect	worry
(cannot) conceive	guess	remember	

*I **doubt** whether my parents said one unnecessary word to each other all their lives.*

*They don't stop to **think** who's going to do the actual basic work.*

*Brand **wondered** what thoughts were going through her mind.*

These verbs can be followed by a wh-word and a to-infinitive clause: *consider, debate, decide, determine, figure, forget, imagine, know, plan, recall, remember, see, think,* and *understand*.

*She began to **plan** how to get out of town without being caught.*

*Kemp **didn't know** whether to believe her or not.*

*I just **couldn't remember** how to spell the most simple of words.*

■ **verbs concerned with finding something out, realizing something, or working something out**

analyse	establish	investigate	piece together	(can) tell
assess	estimate	judge	prove	think
calculate	feel	learn	puzzle out	weigh up
check	figure out	make out	read	work out
decide	find	note	realize	
detect	find out	notice	recognize	
determine	guess	observe	see	
discover	hear	perceive	sense	

*Investigators were last night trying to **discover** why the two planes had been flying so close.*

*I wanted to have a look at the book on my own to **find out** what was going on.*

These verbs can be followed by a wh-word and a to-infinitive clause: *assess, calculate, check, determine, discover, establish, figure out, find out, guess, investigate, judge, learn, puzzle out, realize, see, think, weigh up,* and *work out*.

*People **discovered** how to cultivate cereals thousands of years ago.*

*I **couldn't see** how to make money.*

A In the sentences below, put a dotted line under the verb used with a wh-clause. Then underline the other part of the pattern.

1 I worried how I would cope mentally as well as financially.
2 You can easily guess what to expect from him.
3 Conservative MPs have until next Tuesday to decide who to vote for.
4 Bank customers found out why there were no staff when they heard cries coming from an office.
5 Most voters do not mind whether their representative is a man or a woman.
6 I won't ask why you've suddenly decided to write a book about him.

B Fill in the gaps in the sentences below using the wh-words in this list.

how   what   when   whether   who   why

1 Dr Fitzpatrick suggests .... to get the best from your family doctor.
2 How do you judge .... the significance of all this might be?
3 Simon wasn't in, and his flatmate didn't know exactly .... he'd be back.
4 Welles has said that he couldn't remember .... first thought of the idea.
5 Check that all students understand .... to use the answer books.
6 She didn't actually ever say .... she didn't want to do that.
7 I was trying to work out .... to run away from school or not.
8 David could not imagine .... anyone would wish to make such an ugly thing.
9 The newspaper has not yet decided .... to devote a full page every day to referendum coverage.

C Complete the sentences below using wh-clauses based on the questions. The tense may have to change.

1 How does it feel to live through that shock and pain?
   He appreciates *how it feels to live through that shock and pain.*
2 Why are some men aggressive?
   Scientists have discovered ....
3 How would the room have looked to Jill?
   He could see ....
4 Where did Mr Young find the ornament?
   Mr Young has refused to reveal ....
5 Who were the fans shouting for?
   They wondered ....
6 Why do you sometimes come to see us here?
   I've guessed ....
7 How should children be tested?
   The committee recommended ....
8 What will the proposed changes mean?
   We investigated ....

Verbs used with a wh-clause: 2

1 Here are some more groups of verbs which are followed by a wh-clause:

■ **verbs concerned with showing something**

confirm	illustrate	prove	show
demonstrate	indicate	reveal	signal

You'll be given the chance to __show__ what you can do.

The records __do not indicate__ whether they followed up their enquiries.

Demonstrate and *show* can be followed by a wh-clause consisting of a wh-word and a to-infinitive clause.

He __will show__ how to make some of the restaurant's most popular dishes.

■ **verbs indicating that something influences a situation**

decide	define	determine	dictate	influence

The final exam __determines__ whether you can sit for university entrance or not.

These factors affect costs and __influence__ what can be built.

Different forms of the pattern

Why anybody should be interested, I __do not know__.

2 Some verbs are followed by a prepositional phrase beginning with *to*, and a wh-clause. The prepositional phrase indicates the hearer or reader. This pattern is **V to n wh**.

admit	dictate	indicate	prove	suggest
confess	disclose	let on	reveal	
demonstrate	explain	mention	show	

I don't like people __dictating__ to me what I should do and what I shouldn't do.

Let me __explain__ to you how this works.

3 Some verbs are followed by a noun group and a finite wh-clause. For example, in *He showed me where I should go*, the verb *show* is followed by the noun group *me* and the wh-clause *where I should go*. This pattern is **V n wh**.

The same verbs can also be followed by a to-infinitive clause introduced by a wh-word. For example, in *I'll show you how to do it*, the verb *show* is followed by the noun group *you* and the clause *how to do it*. This pattern is **V n wh-to-inf**.

Active pattern

	Verb group	noun group	wh-clause
He	asked	Paul	what he wanted.
I	'll show	you	what to watch out for.

Passive pattern

	Verb group	wh-clause
We	were shown	how beer is made.
They	were told	what to do.

Verbs with this pattern are concerned with asking, telling, teaching, or showing someone something. The Subject may be human or inanimate, with the exception of *advise* and *ask*, which always have human Subjects.

advise	inform	show	tell
ask	remind	teach	warn

About seven years ago she felt she __had to ask__ herself whether she really wanted to spend her life teaching.

The authors wrote to them last week to __warn__ them what was about to come out in the press.

It's time to __remind__ people why they should feel good about the president.

She thinks it's her job to __tell__ me how to run my life.

You'll also __be shown__ how to check your baby's breathing pattern. (passive)

A In the sentences below, put a dotted line under the verb used with a pattern described in this Unit. Then underline each of the other parts of the pattern.

1 They have proved to me how the system can work.
2 The video will show you what to eat on a food-combining diet.
3 Riddick Bowe has already warned Bruno what to expect.
4 Jurors are told who the key participants are.
5 Nancy was tempted to reveal to Mrs Struthers what she had learned.
6 They did not want to be advised what to do.
7 There are many other factors which influence what we choose to eat.
8 The producer mentioned to her who he was having dinner with.
9 Please indicate whether you require CD or vinyl.
10 Several times a day she would remind herself how lucky she was.

B Rewrite each of the following pairs of sentences as one sentence, using the wh-word given in brackets.

1 Personal computers let everyone explore their own ideas. He had explained that to me. (how)
   He had explained to me how personal computers let everyone explore their own ideas.

2 I never abandon my patients. This incident reminded me why. (why)
   ....

3 My attitude has changed over the years. I told her how. (how)
   ....

4 Something has happened. It's difficult for him to admit it to anyone. (what)
   ....

5 Who planted the bomb? The police hope the security system video recording will show them. (who)
   ....

6 John had taken his shoes off. Shelley asked him why. (why)
   ....

7 On a boat, meals are served in different places. The weather determines the place. (where)
   ....

8 What steps should you take next? Our staff will advise you! (what)
   ....

C Fill in the gaps in the sentences below using the verbs in this list. Use each verb once.

demonstrate   dictate   disclose   inform   suggest

1 The climate .... which grapes will grow best in certain areas.
2 He did not .... anyone there what he was looking for.
3 The banks will have to .... to each other how much they lent the company.
4 Rick .... how to put long hair up into a casual style.
5 We're far too keen to .... to people how they might improve their lives.

Verbs used with a quote: 1

Some verbs are used with a quote. For example, in *'I'm leaving,' he said*, the verb *say* is used with the quote *'I'm leaving'*. This pattern is **V with quote**.

The Subject, verb, and quote can be ordered in five different ways. Note, however, that if the Subject is a pronoun, it comes before the verb, not after it.

quote	Verb group	
'Don't be silly, Dawn!'	said	Quaver.
'But the blood on the back seat?'	objected	Parslow.

quote		Verb group
'Someone in your family?'	Browne	suggested.
'No, no, no,'	she	cried.

quote...	Verb group		...quote
'This,'	said	Dan,	'is Mr Freelove.'
'Yes,'	replied	the man,	'I am.'

quote...		Verb group	...quote
'Yes,'	she	admitted,	'it will.'
'So why,'	he	asked,	'don't they just leave?'

	Verb group	quote
A police spokesman	said:	'It is a mystery.'
He	replied:	'It's nothing.'

The only verb that is frequently used with this pattern in conversation is *say*.

Verbs with this pattern belong to the following meaning groups:

■ **verbs concerned with speaking, writing, and other forms of communication**

admit	command	guess	proclaim	state
advise	comment	insist	promise	stress
allege	complain	maintain	protest	suggest
announce	concede	note	put	urge
argue	conclude	observe	read	warn
ask	confess	offer	recall	wonder
assert	declare	order	remark	write
beg	demand	plead	report	
boast	estimate	pray	request	
claim	explain	predict	say	

'Perhaps I should get the others,' he said, and made for the door.

'What's the matter?' she asked, backing away a step.

'Mr McClintock,' she announced, 'has decided to go and visit the bank in London.'

'We have been told nothing,' claims Mr Matveyev.

'How he lost, I shall never know,' remarked Lord Howard somewhat wistfully.

'Where the hell did these guys come from?' Kravis wondered aloud.

'How depressed I am,' he wrote in his diary.

When *say* is used in conversation, the Subject and verb nearly always come before the quote.

I called Lynda, and I said 'Lynda, how can you do this to me?'

■ **verbs indicating the relationship of something that is said to something else that is said**

add	continue	finish	prompt	resume
agree	correct	go on	put in	
answer	counter	interrupt	repeat	
begin	echo	intervene	reply	
conclude	end	object	respond	

He added: 'The important thing is to go out and win.'

'The fire seems to be behind that door,' Judy began.

'You knew her?' he asked. 'Of course,' she replied.

■ **verbs indicating how something is said, for example how loudly or quickly, or at what pitch**

breathe	cry	exclaim	mutter	shout out
call	cry out	mumble	scream	sing
call out	drawl	murmur	shout	whisper

She called out, 'Nina, come in here and look at this.'

'I guess you guys don't mind if I smoke?' he drawled.

When he came back I asked him whether it was still raining. *'Don't know,' he muttered. 'I didn't notice.'*

'Traitor!' she screamed.

'He's coming,' Egan whispered.

A Fill in the gaps in the sentences below using the verbs in this list. Use each verb once. Use the past simple tense.

admit   ask   boast   echo   exclaim   insist   interrupt   order   pray   predict   reply   suggest

1 'I've done lots of big projects,' he ...., 'hospitals, office blocks, all sorts of things.'

2 'Start turning the car around,' he ...., 'and drive it out of here.'

3 'Oh, God,' she ...., 'don't let there be a war.'

4 'What do you suppose the board would think of the plan?' I .... 'Not much,' he ....

5 'Things aren't going too well at the moment,' Robyn ....

6 'Let's go to a midnight movie,' she ....

7 'I must see him. I must!' I ....

8 Frank felt confused. 'I still don't see -' 'Take a look at this,' Joe ....

9 'The fans will take the place over,' he .... 'They'll hold lots of parties and come dressed up for the occasion.'

10 Mr. Anders strode over and knelt down. Dipping a finger in the liquid, he sniffed it. 'Paint!' he ...., astonished. 'Paint?' Sharon ....

B These sentences show the pattern **V that**. Rewrite them using the pattern **V with quote**. In each answer, choose one of the ways of ordering the Subject, verb, and quote.

1 She confessed that she was terrified of heights.
'I'm terrified of heights,' she confessed.

2 John announced that he had come to a decision.
....

3 He predicted that they would start making a profit next year.
....

4 She promised she would wait for me.
....

5 Steve said he'd never seen anything like it before.
....

6 The cab-driver complained that he had been out all night.
....

7 Agnes murmured that Kathryn was acting strangely.
....

8 Alice remarked that it was good to breathe fresh air again.
....

C In the list of verbs which indicate how something is said, find:

1 five verbs which indicate that something is said softly
....

2 seven verbs which indicate that something is said loudly
....

Verbs used with a quote: 2

1 Here are some more groups of verbs which are used with a quote:

■ **verbs indicating speech accompanied by an expression, gesture, or non-verbal sound**

gasp	nod	smile
laugh	sigh	sob

'Do you know what this means?' I **gasped**, laying a hand on Sauter's shoulder.

'Go ahead,' she **smiled**.

■ **verbs indicating the feeling expressed or felt by the person speaking, for example anger, scorn, or unhappiness**

explode	groan	rage	sneer
fume	jeer	snap	sniff

'Can you believe that?' Terry **fumed**.

'Have you lost it, General?' she **sneered**.

■ **verbs concerned with thinking**

muse	think	wonder

Often quotation marks are not used around the quote.

Someday, I **thought**, *I'll be grown up and have my own car.*

About her hung a strong scent of Chanel No. 5. Where did she get it, **wondered** *Stella.*

■ **verbs which are used when quoting a piece of writing or something such as a song or poem**

go	read	run	say

'You can't kill the spirit, she is like a mountain,' **went** the women's chant.

The sign **read**: *SPEED ZONE AHEAD 35 MPH.*

2 When they are used with a quote, some verbs are sometimes followed by a prepositional phrase beginning with *at*. This pattern is **V at n with quote**. The Subject usually comes before the verb.

These verbs indicate that someone is speaking loudly, angrily, or forcefully. The prepositional phrase indicates who is being addressed.

scream	shout	snap	yell

'Hey, do something!' Bobby **shouted** at them.

'Don't panic,' I **yelled** at him.

3 When they are used with a quote, some verbs are sometimes followed by a prepositional phrase beginning with *to*. This pattern is **V to n with quote**. The Subject usually comes before the verb.

Verbs with this pattern belong to the following meaning groups:

■ **verbs indicating that someone says something to someone else**

admit	comment	explain	observe	scream
announce	complain	insist	proclaim	shout
boast	confess	mumble	protest	suggest
call	cry	murmur	remark	whisper
call out	declare	mutter	say	write

I **said** to Al, *'Wait a minute. What time did Steve call you?'*

'This is all very well,' he **muttered** to himself, *'but what about my dinner?'*

'Your cat isn't very friendly,' a woman **complained** to Reggie.

■ **verbs indicating that someone thinks something**

muse	reason	say	think	wonder

The noun group following the preposition is always a reflexive pronoun. Sometimes quotation marks are not used around the quote.

Just what I was afraid of, Tatiana **thought** to herself.

'No,' he **said** to himself. *'It's not going to be like that.'*

A In the sentences below, put a dotted line under the verb used with a pattern described in this Unit. Then underline each of the other parts of the pattern.

1 'I don't know for sure,' Claire sighed, 'but I do keep wondering about it.'
2 'I'm a very selfish person on some levels,' he confesses to me.
3 'He's got a knife!' Jacky screamed at me, terror contorting her face.
4 'My dog eats anything that doesn't eat him first,' she remarked to John, who smiled.
5 'I feel sick!' Chet groaned, supporting himself against the cupboard.
6 'Relax, will you,' he snapped at her.
7 'We are eating vegetarian,' Mrs McCartney announced to the waiter in an officious manner.
8 'I wonder where the gang found that wreck?' Joe mused.
9 'I think I'd better go now,' she whispered to her table companions.
10 I said to myself, 'Settle down. Try to enjoy this.'

B Fill in the gaps in the sentences below using the verbs in this list. Use each verb once.

admit   explain   fume   go   mutter   nod   read   sob   think   wonder   write   yell

1 If you don't like the message kill the messenger, the old saying ....
2 'Help!' I .... at them at the top of my voice.
3 'What he did was scandalous – I'm furious with him,' she ....
4 He .... to The Sun newspaper: 'Yes, I am broke.'
5 They were wasting time, he .... to himself.
6 A notice ....: Please do not lean out of the windows.
7 I did .... to myself, why not just go into an embassy and get political asylum and leave the country?
8 'No such luck,' Lettie .... to me under her breath.
9 'Dearest, I shall be back soon,' she .... to Solita in early January 1969.
10 'Do you understand me?' 'Oh, yes,' she .... , 'I understand you very well.'
11 'Ali and I were once very good friends,' he .... to Izzy.
12 'Oh Dennis,' she .... 'I'm sorry, I really am.'

C In the lists in this Unit, find:

1 two verbs which indicate that someone is unhappy or dissatisfied ....
2 three verbs which indicate that someone feels contempt ....
3 four verbs which indicate that someone is angry ....

1 Some verbs are followed by a noun group and are used with a quote. For example, in *'I'm used to it,' I told him*, the verb *tell* is followed by the noun group *him*, and is used with the quote *'I'm used to it.'* This pattern is **V n with quote**.

Active patterns

The Subject, verb, and noun group can come after, within, or before the quote.

quote		Verb group	noun group
'Absolutely,' 'We'll do it,'	Cross she	assured promised	her. him.

quote...		Verb group	noun group	...quote
'Why,' 'Doreen,'	I she	asked told	him, me,	'are you here?' 'something's wrong!'

	Verb group	noun group	quote
He She	asked had warned	me, me:	'Who are these people?' 'This guy means business.'

Passive patterns

The Subject and Verb can come after, within, or before the quote. They most frequently come after it, as shown below.

quote		Verb group
'Only include relevant achievements,' 'This is considered unacceptable,'	I he	was advised. was told.

Verbs with this pattern are all concerned with telling and asking. The person being addressed is indicated by the noun group.

advise	beg	inform	promise	urge
ask	command	interrupt	remind	warn
assure	correct	order	tell	

'A suite is always kept ready for me,' Loveday **informed him** with a little laugh.

'It changed me,' she **told me**.

'Don't move,' I **warned him** and took out my clasp knife.

*After a while she **asked me**, 'Do you want to hear one of my songs?'*

'Nothing to worry about,' he **was assured**. (passive)

Tell is sometimes used with a reflexive pronoun following the verb to indicate that someone thinks something, usually something encouraging.

'I am going to make it,' I **told myself**.

Most of the verbs with this pattern also have the pattern **V with quote**. The exceptions are *assure*, *inform*, *remind*, and *tell*.

2 With some verbs, the quote always comes after the noun group, or, when the verb is passive, after the verb. This pattern is **V n quote**.

Verbs with this pattern belong to the following meaning groups:

■ **verbs used when indicating the way a word is pronounced or spelled**

pronounce	spell

'This is your own Tuesday phone-in,' the DJ intoned, **pronouncing it Chewsday**.

*Jimmy Savile, you see, **spells his name S A V I L E**.*

■ **verbs concerned with labelling or inscribing**

be captioned	be headed	be inscribed	mark
be entitled	be headlined	label	be subtitled

*Too often he merely read a report, **marked it 'seen'** and took no action.*

*The photograph **is captioned 'Farnborough, Friday, 5th September 1952'**.* (passive)

The quote often occurs after an '-ed' form used to qualify a noun.

*It was a silver cigarette case **inscribed 'To Laura, with all my love, Leonard'**.*

A In the sentences below, put a dotted line under the verb used with a quote (see this Unit and Units 29 and 30). Then underline each of the other parts of the pattern.

1 'Do you think I should call the police?' 'I'd wait a day or two,' Dad advised her.
2 'You'll need proof,' Frank reminded her. 'Then I'll get proof!' Miss Hardy declared.
3 One energetic 90-year-old was told by her doctor, 'You have the heart of a 20-year-old.'
4 'Come, eat!' the old woman urged.
5 'Bob and I were sitting around at Headquarters discussing the case and...' 'Headquarters?' the director interrupted him sharply.
6 I used to pronounce your name 'Bo-shomp' instead of 'Beechum'.
7 Even foods that are labelled 'additive-free' may have hidden preservatives.
8 'Get a doctor!' Eva begged. 'Somebody do something, quick!'
9 'But I know...' She corrected herself: '*We* know that you've seen Lily.'
10 'Look in that room,' the major ordered Hubert.

B Fill in the gaps in the sentences below using the verbs in this list. Use each verb once. Use the past simple tense.

ask assure beg correct be entitled tell

1 'Everything will be all right,' he .... her.
2 'Just lay there,' said Joy. '*Lie* there,' Mr Abbott .... her and then passed out.
3 Her column .... 'Can this marriage be saved?'
4 'Was it crowded on the beach?' Kay .... her brother.
5 'Please forgive me,' he .... her.
6 'You're doing very well for a beginner,' I .... myself.

C Rewrite these sentences using the pattern **V n with quote**, putting the different parts in an appropriate order. The tense may have to change.

1 He reminded her that he had given up that kind of work.
'I've given up that kind of work,' he reminded her.
2 He told himself that everything would look different tomorrow.
....
3 She warned him that they would be late if he didn't hurry up.
....
4 Joe advised her to go and get some sleep.
....
5 Her secretary informed her that Mr Watson was on the line.
....
6 Jay promised her that he would take care of everything.
....
7 He urged her to smile for the camera.
....

Verbs used with prepositions and adverbs: 1

1 Some verbs are always or typically followed by a prepositional phrase or adverb group. For example, in *She walked across the room*, the verb *walk* is followed by the prepositional phrase *across the room*; in *She walked away*, it is followed by the adverb *away*. This pattern is **V prep/adv**.

	Verb group	prep. phrase/adverb group
I	hurried	home.
He	ran	down the path.

Verbs with this pattern belong to the following meaning groups:

■ **verbs indicating that someone or something moves, goes somewhere, or arrives somewhere**

arrive	fall	head	push	slide
climb	fit	hurry	return	speed
come	flee	jump	roll	spread
continue	float	land	rush	swim
dive	flow	leap	set off	travel
drift	fly	move	set out	turn
drop	get	pass	sit	wander
end up	go	pour	sit down	

*She didn't want to **go home**.*

*Haig **arrived in Bombay** on 22 October 1909.*

***Turn right** at the lights.*

*The sound of a printer **drifted through the open door**.*

*Ron became so ill with worry that he **ended up in hospital**.*

■ **verbs indicating that someone walks or runs somewhere**

bound	leap	shuffle	storm	walk
burst	limp	slip	stroll	
charge	march	sneak	stumble	
crawl	race	stagger	sweep	
dance	run	step	tear	

*She **walked to the window** and looked out.*

*We **had to sneak out** because it was after nine at night.*

*He **stormed out of the apartment**, slamming the door furiously behind him.*

■ **verbs indicating that a form of transport, or someone using a form of transport, goes or arrives somewhere**

cycle	fly	park	pull in	sail
drive	land	pedal	ride	

*They **drove to Heathrow airport**, with Cathy sitting between them.*

*After the plane **landed in Miami**, the man surrendered peacefully.*

■ **verbs used to indicate where someone or something is**

be	lie	remain	sit	stop
hang	live	rest	stand	
keep	occur	settle	stay	

*The restaurant **was in Cork Street, Mayfair**.*

*He **lives in the same village as me**.*

*She **was sitting at the kitchen table** when I came in.*

Live is sometimes used in the passive, with *in*.

*The cottage **has not been lived in** for several years.*

■ **verbs indicating the shape of something, or where it is in relation to something else**

extend	lead	pass	stick
face	look	point	stretch
go	look out	run	wind

*My garden **faces south**.*

*The pool and terrace **look out** over the sea.*

*The road **wound through the mountains**.*

Different forms of the pattern

*Where **did** they **go**?*

*Which way **do** you **go**?*

*Where **is** it?*

*They asked me **where** my money **was**.*

*But one day, she had to say goodbye to **the house** she **had lived in** all her life.*

*I had to find **somewhere** to **stay**.*

*We were having a chat when **in walked** Stanley.*

2 Most verbs with the pattern **V prep/adv** can also be followed by an adverb and a prepositional phrase, or by two prepositional phrases.

*They **drove off into the desert**.*

*He **walked over to his desk**.*

*He **ran down the stairs to the living room**.*

A In the sentences below, put a dotted line under the verb used with a prepositional phrase or an adverb. Then underline the other part of the pattern.

1 She ran down the stairs.
2 Where are you going?
3 She tried to read his face, but he turned away and busied himself with the dishes.
4 Inside were half a dozen pill bottles she'd never seen before.
5 He put down the phone and sat there thinking for a bit.
6 She left the house and followed the moonlit path that led to the clearing beside the river.

B Now do the same with these longer pieces of text. The verb may be followed by an adverb and then a prepositional phrase.

1 'Well, I should probably go inside,' Erin said. 'Uh, sure. Well, see you at school tomorrow.' Zack turned and started to walk down the path. Erin went back into the house. She was shocked to find her whole family waiting for her. Her father was standing near the couch with his arms crossed. Her mother was sitting on the couch.
2 The sheriff turned right at the only traffic light, led him through the business district, turned left and headed up a low hill. On the left was an area of trees that might have been a park. A white church stood at the top of the hill.
3 I was walking down the hill near Crinan Bottom when a man with a parachute on his back suddenly dropped out of the skies and landed at our feet, having jumped off the summit a few moments earlier. 'Far more exciting than walking down,' he told us.

C Below are instructions on how to get from the post office to the police station shown on the map. Fill in the gaps using the words in these lists.

arrive   come   continue   get   passing   turn   along   at   left   out of   under

1 When you .... the post office, turn .... up Bread Street. When you
.... to the traffic lights, ... right and go .... the High Street. ....
down the High Street, ... the railway bridge, until you ....
the police station.
2 Now write similar instructions on how to get from the police station to the post office.

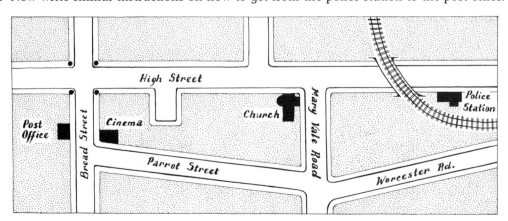

33 Verbs used with prepositions and adverbs: 2

1 Here are some more groups of verbs which are followed by a prepositional phrase or an adverb group:

■ **verbs used to describe people's behaviour**

act	dress	live	think
behave	eat	react	

They *were behaving like animals*.

It's important to *eat sensibly* during pregnancy.

■ **verbs used when talking about how successful something or someone is**

be coming along	fit	progress	sell
come off	go off	read	work
be coming on	handle	run	work out

Her English *is coming along well*.

For once, the show *went off without technical problems*.

This book *will* probably *sell well* in Japan.

■ **verbs concerned with beginning or ending**

begin	conclude	finish	start
close	end	open	

Clinton's campaign *began well*.

The first full day of discussions *ended on a note of optimism*.

■ **verbs used when indicating how long something lasts**

keep	last	live	run

The mixture *will keep for 2-3 days* in the fridge.

The strike *did not last* long.

Different forms of the pattern

How *are* things *working out* there?

How long *does* this effect *last*?

2 Some verbs are always or typically followed by an adverb. This pattern is **V adv**.

	Verb group	adverb group
She	is doing	well.
Wood	marks	easily.

Verbs with this pattern belong to the following meaning groups:

■ **verbs concerned with success or failure**

do	fare	go	perform

The operation *went well*.

The Republicans *did badly* in the election.

■ **verbs used to indicate that something has a desirable quality, such as being easily cleaned, prepared, or used**

clean	cut	fold	wash	wear

His favorite wood is pine because it's perfect for carving and *cuts easily*.

■ **verbs used to indicate that something is damaged**

break	burn	mark	tear
bruise	crack	scratch	

Be sure to store bananas carefully, as they *bruise easily*.

Sarah has typically British fair skin that *burns easily*.

■ **verbs indicating that two or more people live together or spend time with each other**

get	knock around	move in	run off
hang around	live	run away	sleep

The adverb is always *together*.

They usually *hung around together* most of the time.

They decided to *live together* the following year.

■ **verbs indicating that people form a group, do something together, or support each other**

band	club	pull	stick

The adverb is always *together*.

Christian charities *have banded together* to call for action to stop the conflict in Southern Sudan.

A In the sentences below, put a dotted line under the verb used with a prepositional phrase or an adverb group. Then underline the other part of the pattern.

1 The concert went very well.
2 Why are you acting like this?
3 Cosmetics will last longer if stored in a cool, dark place.
4 Despite Mr Neil's nerves, the actual launch went off perfectly.
5 The cover is easy to remove and washes well.
6 An oak tree may live for hundreds of years.
7 Des and Raquel have moved in together.
8 She always dresses in black and I've started to copy her because it makes life so easy.
9 Flat owners now club together to hire security guards to police their blocks.
10 The other republics, increasingly pre-occupied with their own economic and political problems, have so far reacted cautiously.

B Fill in the gaps in the sentences below using the prepositions in this list. Two of the prepositions will be used twice.

by   in   on   with

1 She began .... telling me what the exhibition was about.
2 The meal ended .... toffee bananas and Chinese tea.
3 The conference began .... a debate on broadcasting.
4 Over the last few years, almost everything I've done has ended .... failure.
5 Today's opening round of peace talks ended .... a high note.
6 He ended .... saying, 'Long live the Brazilian people.'

C Match up the two halves of these dictionary definitions.

1 If someone performs well ...   a ... it stays fresh and suitable to eat for a long time.
2 If something wears well ...   b ... he or she works well or achieves a good result.
3 If something fits well ...   c ... it is operating well.
4 If a vehicle handles well ...   d ... it appears quite new or useful after a long time.
5 If a situation works out well ...   e ... it is the right size and shape.
6 If food keeps well ...   f ... what happens is satisfactory.
7 If a system is running smoothly ...   g ... it is easy to drive.

D Put the different parts of these sentences in the right order.

1 for / an hour / the interview / lasted / about ....
2 nicely / were coming / the arrangements / along ....
3 women / behave / why / do / in this way ....
4 with / the company / predictable outrage / has reacted ....
5 well / never / sold / his books ....
6 and / badly / got / started / the tour / worse ....

Verbs used with prepositions and adverbs: 3

Some verbs are always or typically followed by a noun group and a prepositional phrase or adverb group, or by an adverb group and a noun group. For example, in *I buried the box in the garden*, the verb *bury* is followed by the noun group *the box* and the prepositional phrase *in the garden*. These patterns are **V n prep/adv** and **V adv n**. With phrasal verbs, the particle comes either after the noun group or after the verb.

Active patterns

	Verb group	noun group	prep. phrase/adverb
He	threw	a blanket	over my head.
The smoke	drove	the mosquitoes	away.

	Verb group	adverb	noun group
He	Screw knocked	down over	any loose floorboards. a glass of milk.

Passive pattern

	Verb group	prep. phrase/adverb
The sacks	were loaded	onto sixteen army lorries.
The protesters	were dragged	away.

Verbs with this pattern belong to the following meaning groups:

■ verbs concerned with putting something somewhere

arrange	hang	plunge	put	spread
bury	lay	pop	replace	stand
drop	lean	position	rest	stuff
dump	load	pour	set	thrust
fit	place	press	slip	

*He **put** his cup **down**.*

***Place** the mixture in a saucepan* and boil for 1 minute.

*She **slipped** the photograph into her bag.*

■ verbs concerned with attaching one thing to another

bind	join	nail	screw	tie
fix	link	pin	stick	

*Apply glue to the back of this piece and **nail** it to the wall.*

*He **had pinned** up a map of Finland.*

■ verbs concerned with moving or sending something somewhere

blow	knock	push	slide	transfer
brush	lift	raise	spill	turn
divert	lower	roll	sweep	
draw	move	scatter	throw	
drive	pass	send	tip	
kick	pull	shift	toss	

*He **kicked** the ball into the crowd.*

*The boy **pulled** out a pistol and shot another boy in the leg.*

*He accidentally **knocked** his glass off the table.*

■ verbs concerned with carrying something or someone somewhere or accompanying someone

accompany	drag	lead	see	transfer
bear	drive	lift	ship	walk
bring	fly	run	show	
carry	guide	rush	take	

*The plane **was carrying** relief supplies to Sarajevo.*

*Carl **drove** him home at 12.15 and I **saw** him in.*

*The suspects **have** now **been brought** to London.* (passive)

■ verbs concerned with causing someone to go somewhere

allow	drive	kick	post	tempt
ask	force	let	put	transfer
assign	get	march	settle	urge
call	help	move	sit	warn
direct	hurry	order	sit down	wave
drag	invite	persuade	steer	

*His men **have driven** government troops from a number of towns.*

*This was the man who **put** me in hospital for four days.*

*They **were invited** there by the government.* (passive)

■ verbs indicating that someone takes a vehicle somewhere

drive	fly	ride	sail	steer

*He **drove** the truck into the barn and parked it.*

*He **flew** the helicopter back last night.*

Different forms of the pattern

*Where **did** you **take** her?*

*She showed me where to **put** my jacket.*

*John **placed** on the table a jam jar full of worms.*

*You need a case to **put** your clothes in.*

*In the centre of her garden she **placed** a marble statue of a boy.*

A In the sentences below, put a dotted line under the verb used with a prepositional phrase or adverb group. Then underline each of the other parts of the pattern.

1 Natasha fixed the star to the top of the tree.
2 The authorities might kick her out of Barbados.
3 Davenport removed his coat and brushed off the snow.
4 Let me show you to your rooms.
5 We know many more people have died but the army has taken the bodies away.
6 The cage was knocked over and the bird escaped.
7 On Mondays, Rachel often brought to school things she had made at the weekend.
8 Then you have to remember where you buried it.
9 There is no jail to put him in.
10 Within hours of the accident, Mr Graff had been flown to Brisbane for specialist treatment.

B Fill in the gaps in the sentences below using the prepositional phrases in this list. Use each phrase once.

| across the Atlantic | at the dining table | behind the shop | from the town |
| in a semi-circle | over the meat | to the wall | under Carl's nose |

1 The computers were arranged ....
2 Pour the sauce .... and garnish with the onions and herbs.
3 Bookcases and cabinets should be screwed ....
4 The rebels have been driven ....
5 He sailed the catamaran single-handed .... in 1934.
6 He sat himself down ....
7 He lifted the man and dragged the body ....
8 Microphones were pushed .... and flashbulbs popped.

C Put the different parts of these sentences in the right order.

1 into / he / the banknotes / stuffed / his wallet ....
2 a slice of wholemeal bread / spread / peanut butter / on / she
....
3 was shipped / the furniture / three huge containers / over / in
....
4 into / Wren / dropped / her purse / her lipstick ....
5 they / away / the UN trucks / sent ....
6 sheets of wood / the windows / I / over / nailed ....
7 put / on / the tray / the table / she ....
8 her / Christopher / offered / home / to drive ....

Verbs used with prepositions and adverbs: 4

1 Here are some more groups of verbs which are followed by a noun group and a prepositional phrase or adverb group, or by an adverb group and a noun group:

■ **verbs indicating that someone moves a part of their body**

fling	pull	stamp	toss	wave
hide	rub	stretch out	turn	
hold	run	throw	twist	

*Turning to Henry, she **flung** her arms round his neck and **hid** her face on his shoulder.*

With *pull*, *stretch out*, and *throw*, the noun group following the verb is often a reflexive pronoun. This indicates that someone moves their whole body.

*Moira **stretched** herself **out** on the lower bench, lying on her side.*

■ **verbs concerned with keeping or holding someone or something in a particular place**

have	keep	shut
hold	leave	store

*She sat rigidly upright, **holding** her handbag to her chest.*

*He **left** his bike there.*

■ **verbs concerned with seeing, finding, or meeting someone or something in a particular place**

catch	feel	find	meet	see

*I **found** the tape in a garage in Kingston.*

*Martin **met** us at the station.*

■ **verbs concerned with causing something or someone to be or stay in a particular state**

bring	keep	place	put	throw
get	leave	push	set	

*Cover the soup and **bring** it to the boil slowly.*

*They **kept** us out of trouble.*

*He **was placed** under arrest.* (passive)

■ **verbs indicating that one person hits or injures another**

bash	hit	slap
batter	knife	strike

*He **knifed** his attacker through the heart.*

*He **was slapping** a woman around and I objected.*

■ **verbs concerned with starting, passing, or finishing a period of time in a particular way**

begin	finish	pass	start
end	live out	spend	

*Philip **begins** each day with half an hour's meditation.*

■ **other common verbs**

approach	be found	regard	treat
bring up	handle	take	

*When I'm tired – that's when I **handle** everything least well.*

*Michael broke the news to Brian. He **took** it well.*

*I **was brought up** in Shanghai.* (passive)

*Protein **is found** in a wide variety of both animal and plant foods.* (passive)

2 Some verbs have the patterns **V n adv** and **V adv n** but not the pattern **V n prep** – that is, they are used with an adverb but not with a preposition.

Active patterns

	Verb group	noun group	adverb
He	switched	the television	on.

	Verb group	adverb	noun group
Howard	took	off	his jacket.

Passive pattern

		Verb group	adverb
Street lighting		has been switched	off.

Verbs with this pattern belong to the following meaning groups:

■ **verbs indicating that someone puts clothing on or takes it off**

put	rip	slip	take	tear

*She **put** her slippers **on** and shuffled into the kitchen.*

*He **tore off** his shirt and threw it to the ground.*

■ **verbs indicating that someone turns machinery or equipment on or off**

click	flick	put	switch	turn

*He **clicked** on the lamp.*

*Are you **going to turn** the machine off now?*

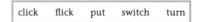

A Fill in the gaps in the sentences below using the noun groups and the prepositional phrases and adverbs in these lists. Use each phrase once.

| his arms | her face | her feet | her hair | his hands | himself |
| around his wife | away from him | back | on the pavement | to his feet | together |

1 She stamped .... to keep out the cold.

2 He threw .... and told her not to worry.

3 She tossed .... with a jerk of her head.

4 Larry rubbed .... with satisfaction.

5 She turned ....

6 Very slowly he pulled ...., using the table as an aid.

B Fill in the gaps in the sentences below using the verbs in this list. Use each verb once.

bring get keep place push throw

1 He's the one that .... me out of trouble.

2 After releasing her, the doctors had .... her on anti-depressants.

3 Any emotional crisis could have .... either of them over the edge.

4 This was a campaign deliberately designed to .... me into disrepute.

5 Britain's Heathrow Airport was .... into chaos again last night after the third bomb attack in less than a week.

6 These relatives are .... in the awkward position of speaking on behalf of the person in a coma.

C The sentences below all contain the verb *run*. Identify the verb pattern (**V prep/adv** or **V n prep/adv**) and write it in the gap at the end of each sentence. Then select from the list the verb that means the same as *run* in that sentence.

flow go last pass race take

1 The show was an instant success and ran for 300 days. .... *V prep, last* ....

2 I was relieved to get home and find everything running smoothly. ....

3 I'll run you back after the show. ....

4 Leo ran his fingers through his thick, graying hair. ....

5 The river runs past the town of Guben. ....

6 Chivers got out of the car and ran home but was later arrested. ....

D Fill in the gaps in the sentences below using the nouns in this list. Use each noun once.

coat cooker dressing-gown light switch tee-shirts

1 They ripped off their .... and started waving them above their heads.

2 Then he flicked down the .... on the office intercom.

4 Just bring the peas to the boil, then turn the .... off.

5 Robina put on her ...., took a shopping basket and went out.

6 He saw that a .... had been clicked on in the office next to him.

Verbs used with *way*

The verb is followed by a noun group which consists of a possessive determiner, such as *my, his, her,* or *their,* and the noun *way.* This is followed by a prepositional phrase or adverb group. For example, in *He pushed his way through the crowd,* the verb *push* is followed by the possessive determiner *his,* the noun *way,* and the prepositional phrase *through the crowd.* This pattern is **V way prep/adv**.

	Verb group	*way*	prep. phrase/adverb group
I	groped	my way	out.
She	ate	her way	through a pound of chocolate.

This pattern is very productive: any verb indicating an action can be used with this pattern. Here we give the most typical.

Verbs with this pattern belong to the following meaning groups:

■ verbs which are used with *way* to indicate that someone or something manages to get somewhere

find	make	wend

Shirley and Boris **made their way home** *in thoughtful silence.*

■ verbs indicating that someone moves or gets somewhere with difficulty or using force

barge	claw	fight	push	steamroller
battle	cut	force	shoot	tear
blast	dig	hack	shoulder	thrust
bore	drill	jostle	shove	
burrow	elbow	power	smash	

They're trying to **fight** *their way towards the besieged army camp.*

Four gunmen **forced** *their way into the house and opened fire.*

■ verbs indicating that someone moves carefully or avoids obstacles

ease	grope	navigate	thread
edge	inch	pick	weave
feel	manoeuvre	squeeze	worm

We **edged** *our way past the soldiers and turned up the staircase.*

She turned her back on him and began to **thread** *her way through the dancers.*

■ verbs indicating that someone or something moves or travels in a particular way

bump	hitchhike	pedal	splash
crawl	limp	shuffle	wing
flap	meander	sneak	zigzag

Ordinary Japanese people **had to pedal** *their way about on bicycles.*

They **splashed** *their way along the stream.*

She **zigzagged** *her way to the far corner of the cemetery and stood at last at the foot of her father's grave.*

■ verbs concerned with talking persuasively or lying in order to get into or out of a situation or place

bluff	con	negotiate	sweet talk
charm	lie	reason	talk

I just **bluffed** *my way in.*

He **lied** *his way into power.*

He'd **talked** *his way out of awkward corners before, but none like this.*

■ verbs which are used with *way* to indicate that someone achieves something by means of a legitimate activity

borrow	export	spend	work
buy	play	trade	

I do not believe governments **can spend** *their way out of recession.*

■ verbs which are used with *way* to indicate that someone achieves something by doing something illegal or immoral

bribe	cheat	murder	wangle
bully	insinuate	trick	worm

He **has cheated** *his way to the title.*

He **tricked** *his way into a senior management job at Guy's Hospital.*

■ verbs used with *way* to indicate that someone eats or drinks the whole of something

chew	drink	eat	munch	work

Mrs Lorimer **chewed** *her way through a large helping of apple tart.*

Work is also used more generally to indicate that someone deals with all of a set of things.

She **was working** *her way through a pile of correspondence.*

■ verbs indicating that someone says, sings, or plays the whole of something

croon	mumble	shout	stammer	whistle
grunt	mutter	slur	strum	yell

Our chairman **mumbled** *his way through a couple of prayers.*

A Match up the two halves of each sentence.

1 She elbowed ...	a ... her way through a tomato salad.
2 The police smashed ...	b ... their way home.
3 He inched ...	c ... his way out of jail.
4 We charmed ...	d ... our way through the litter-strewn streets.
5 Anne is munching ...	e ... her way through the crowd.
6 They couldn't find ...	f ... their way through the front door.
7 We picked ...	g ... our way out of trouble.
8 He bribed ...	h ... his way to the window.

B These sentences show the pattern **V prep/adv**. Rewrite them using the pattern **V *way* prep/adv**.

1 He limped along the corridor. .....*He limped his way along the corridor.*......................

2 She pushed to the front of the queue. ....

3 They zigzagged across the snow. ....

4 We edged past the soldiers. ....

5 Jack was working through a mountain of paperwork.

....

6 When the larvae hatch, they bore into the beans.

....

Now rewrite these sentences using the verb given in brackets.

7 William went to the door. (make) ....

8 Somehow the news got into the Italian newspapers. (find)

....

C The ends of ten sentences are given below. Provide beginnings for them using verbs from this list with the pattern **V *way* prep/adv**. Use each verb once.

bluff   borrow   eat   hack   hitchhike   inch   murder   shoulder   stammer   whistle

1 .... through the crowd.

2 .... along the narrow ledge.

3 .... through the National Anthem.

4 .... round Europe.

5 .... into the job.

6 .... through a bag of crisps.

7 .... out of the recession.

8 .... through the poem.

9 .... to the throne.

10 .... through the undergrowth.

Verbs used with *about*: 1

1 Some verbs are followed by a prepositional phrase which consists of *about* and a noun group. For example, in *I lied about my age*, the verb *lie* is followed by the preposition *about* and the noun group *my age*. This pattern is **V about n**. With most verbs, the preposition is sometimes followed by an '-ing' clause or a wh-clause.

	Verb group	*about*	noun group/-ing/wh
Other players	are grumbling	about	unpaid wages.
We	don't care	about	what you think.
I	dream	about	winning the 100 meters.

Verbs with this pattern belong to the following meaning groups:

■ **verbs indicating that someone speaks or writes about something**

argue	complain	inquire	quarrel	speak
ask	drone on	joke	rabbit on	talk
bang on	enthuse	keep on	rant	waffle on
boast	generalize	lie	rant on	whinge
brag	go on	moan	rave	witter on
burble on	grumble	mutter	sing	write
chat	harp on	protest	sound off	

*He **talked** about all kinds of things.*

*Some of them could be heard **muttering** about the high prices of the clothes.*

*He **had boasted** about stabbing a woman.*

Note that the phrasal verbs in this list are fairly informal.

*'For God's sake, stop **going on** about Fate!' Alex shouted.*

In the case of the following verbs, the preposition *about* is sometimes followed by a wh-clause: *argue, ask, chat, inquire, joke, lie, quarrel,* and *talk*.

*He and Patra **argued** about what to wear.*

The more frequent verbs are sometimes used in the passive.

*This is an idea that **has been talked** about before.*

■ **verbs indicating that someone phones or writes to someone**

call	phone up	ring up
phone	ring	write in

*Hello? I'**m calling** about the ad for the car.*

*I hope many more people **write in** about this.*

■ **verbs concerned with thought or feeling**

agree	care	dream	speculate	worry
bother	differ	forget	think	
brood	disagree	know	wonder	

*For the most part, people **think** about themselves rather than others.*

*He told me he **had** always **dreamed** about being a star when he was a kid.*

*Different psychiatrists **might disagree** about what causes the condition.*

Forget, know, and *think* are sometimes used in the passive.

*It's a problem that **has been known** about for years.*

■ **verbs concerned with acquiring knowledge**

find out	hear	learn	read

*We **found out** about these changes by pure accident.*

*I **heard** about the trouble on the television early this morning, so I hurried on over.*

*The players **learned** about competing against quality opposition and improved each game.*

In the case of *learn*, the preposition *about* is sometimes followed by a wh-clause.

*Even in school, Hewitt **was learning** about how to use time.*

Different forms of the pattern

*So **what** exactly **is** he **complaining** about?*

*I asked Pollard **what** he **was thinking** about.*

*That's **the man** you **were talking** about, isn't it?*

*Racism is quite difficult to **talk** about.*

*It's **a good subject** to **write** about.*

***All** you **care** about is money.*

2 A number of verbs with the pattern **V about n** are sometimes followed by *about*, a noun group, and an '-ing' clause. These verbs include *complain, joke, go on, know, think, worry, hear,* and *read*.

*Terrified residents **complained** about aircraft flying low over their homes.*

*I think he still **worries** about me being the youngest.*

*And that's how you **heard** about Ron Hythe fighting with Doyle?*

A **Put the different parts of these sentences in the right order.**

1 about / the girls / were chatting / fashion ....

2 my father / about / her / worries / being so tired ....

3 the woman / her daughter / I / about / and / asked ....

4 do / how / you / know / the kidnapping / about ....

5 always / how ugly she was / about / going on / she / was ....

6 write / know / about / about / something / you ....

B **Fill in the gaps in the sentences below using the verbs in this list. Use each verb once.**

disagree   forget   hear   phone   read   worry   write in

1 Hello Doctor, it's Mrs Jones again. I'm .... about my daughter.

2 They .... about her death in the newspapers.

3 We agreed about much more than we .... about.

4 I didn't tell her about my problem because I didn't want her to .... about it.

5 Our mail this week included a letter from George Farmer of Westchester, Ohio, who
.... about a number of things.

6 I went into the attic and there I found something I had .... about.

7 The day after I wrote about a character falling down a lift shaft I .... about a
similar tragedy on the radio.

C **In the sentences below, put a dotted line under the verb used with *about*. Then underline each
of the other parts of the pattern.**

1 In other words he does not care about you.

2 He seemed not to understand what I was talking about.

3 What have we got to worry about?

4 He shouldn't be a doctor if all he thinks about is money.

5 They are useful earplugs, and reasonably comfortable and easy to forget about.

6 Antonio's favourite dishes include mushrooms, about which he has written extensively.

D **In each of the sentences below, one of the verbs from this list is missing. Mark where it goes
and say what it is. Use each verb once.**

complain   dream   find out   joke   know   lie   read

1 He'd / about his parents being friends of the owner. ......*lied*......

2 Despite her enormous wealth, she was always about one thing or another. ....

3 My sister is the only one who about my eating problem. ....

4 How did the press about it? ....

5 I know several players got really upset when they about him criticising the team. ....

6 My mother and I about the fact that whatever she loves I'll hate, and vice versa. ....

7 He was living the life that others only dared to about. ....

Verbs used with *about*: 2

Some verbs are followed by a noun group and a prepositional phrase which consists of *about* and a noun group. For example, in *She told him about her plan*, the verb *tell* is followed by the noun group *him*, the preposition *about*, and the noun group *her plan*. This pattern is **V n *about* n**. With some verbs, the preposition is sometimes followed by an '-ing' clause or a wh-clause.

Active pattern

	Verb group	noun group	*about*	noun group/-ing/wh
She	warned	me	about	people like you.
They	tease	me	about	being overweight.
He	was telling	her	about	what had happened.

Passive pattern

	Verb group	*about*	noun group/-ing/wh
He	was grilled	about	his personal life.
They	were lectured	about	how to beat crime.
Nothing	can be done	about	changing it.

Verbs with this pattern belong to the following meaning groups:

■ **verbs indicating that someone talks to someone else**

advise	inform	nag	remind	warn
ask	interrogate	press	teach	
consult	interview	question	tease	
grill	lecture	reassure	tell	

Tell me about your skiing holiday.

*MPs were indignant that the government **had not consulted** them about starting price reforms.*

*They ruthlessly **questioned** him about why he hadn't bothered to see Christopher or even find out our address.*

*About 25 army officers **are** currently **being interrogated** about their part in the coup.* (passive)

With *teach* and *tell*, the prepositional phrase sometimes has an **amount** before it.

*She **taught** me a lot about plants.*

■ **verbs concerned with approaching or challenging someone about something**

approach	challenge	confront	contact	tackle

*I **could** never **confront** people about the things that annoyed me.*

*One of the networks **approached** him about hosting a science show.*

*I **tackled** him about how one could live amidst so much poverty.*

■ **verbs concerned with thoughts or feelings**

dislike	feel	hate	like	love	think

These verbs usually occur in clauses and questions beginning with *what*.

*What do you **think** about this threatened strike by professional footballers, then?*

*What I **loved** about Gloria was her talent and her independence.*

■ **verbs indicating that someone knows or finds out about something**

find out	hear	know	learn

The noun group following the verb is always an **amount**.

*She frequented the library to **find out** all she could about the disease.*

*He may be a brilliant 'personality', but he **knows** nothing about producing a play.*

*We've **learned** a lot about how to travel with kids and how not to.*

*Very little **is known** about him.* (passive)

The preposition *about* is sometimes followed by a noun group and an '-ing' clause.

*I heard Wally **didn't know** anything about me going to Canberra and that he was upset about it.*

■ *Do* and *say* also have this pattern.

*My doctor kept telling me to **do something about my weight**, but I never bothered.*

*Did he **say** anything about being shot at?*

The preposition *about* is sometimes followed by a noun group and an '-ing' clause.

*Did he **say** anything about anyone stealing anything from him?*

Different forms of the pattern

*What **do** you **know** about his family?*

*Joe asked his aunt what she **had found out** about Dr Montrose.*

*Remember the guys I **told** you about?*

A In the sentences below, put a dotted line under the verb used with *about*. Then underline each of the other parts of the pattern.

1 I never asked her about ghosts again.
2 Dr. Miller has been advising the government about milk production.
3 What do people think about your policy?
4 I didn't know what to do about it.
5 A senior lawyer said that several people had been contacted about taking part in the trial.
6 But what did he say about us?
7 Harry was questioned about where his father got the money.
8 As usual, they told me nothing about the case.
9 I reminded him about changing the name on the box.
10 Artie was probably one of the rogues Molly had warned her about.

B Match up the two halves of each sentence.

1 Parents should warn their children ...   a ... about my home life.
2 Her father teased her ...   b ... about what he eats.
3 He kept asking me ...   c ... about how much she is loved.
4 The president reminded reporters ...   d ... about the dangers of talking to strangers.
5 I still nag him ...   e ... about her weight.
6 I try to reassure her ...   f ... about his statement two days ago.

C Rewrite these sentences using the noun group in brackets in a clause beginning with *what*.

1 I like the fact that there are heaps of trees. (this school)
   What I like about this school is that there are heaps of trees.

2 I like the day-to-day contact with clients. (my job)

3 I like his evident determination to think things out for himself. (him)

4 I hate the uncomfortable seats. (my car)

5 I love the fact that you never know what you'll find. (these shops)

6 I love the fact that the people really love sport. (Australia)

7 I dislike the fact that it takes itself so seriously. (the fashion world)

Verbs used with *against*: 1

Some verbs are followed by a prepositional phrase which consists of *against* and a noun group. For example, in *He voted against the proposal*, the verb *vote* is followed by the preposition *against* and the noun group *the proposal*. This pattern is **V** *against* **n**.

	Verb group	*against*	noun group
You	're competing	against	younger workers.
The bottle	smashed	against	a wall.

Verbs with this pattern belong to the following meaning groups:

■ **verbs concerned with opposing someone, competing with someone, or doing something to harm someone**

battle	fight back	plot	rise up	win
compete	gang up	prevail	run	
draw	lose	race	stand	
fight	play	rise	testify	

*The competition gave junior players the chance to **compete against members of other clubs**.*

*When I started at college, all the girls in my class seemed to **gang up against me** and talk and laugh about me.*

*He began to believe that colleagues and his wife **were plotting against him**.*

■ **verbs concerned with trying to stop something that is happening or is planned**

campaign	fight	protest	vote
demonstrate	lobby	strike	

*He **has campaigned against apartheid** all his life.*

*They **were protesting against government plans** to cut public spending.*

*Only twelve members **voted against the plan**.*

■ **verbs concerned with saying that something is bad in some way**

advise	argue	hit out	protest	speak out
appeal	come out	lash out	rule	warn

*Church leaders **have** also **spoken out against the killings**.*

*The prime minister **warned against an excess of nationalism**.*

The preposition *against* is sometimes followed by an '-ing' clause.

*Doctors **advise against putting a thermometer into your child's mouth** because it may cause him to choke.*

■ **verbs indicating that something hits or touches something else**

beat	bump	rest	slam	strike
brush	knock	rub	smash	

*They reversed until they **bumped against a wall**.*

*Something **brushed against her leg**.*

■ **other common verbs**

battle	decide	react	rebel	struggle

*She is portrayed as a near saint who **struggled against impossible odds**.*

*Not surprisingly, she **reacted against this treatment**.*

In the case of *decide* and *react*, the preposition *against* is sometimes followed by an '-ing' clause.

*We **decided against having a midday meal** so as to save time.*

Different forms of the pattern

*He tied the boat to the sturdy post **against which** it **was resting**.*

*I want **my team** to be difficult to **play against**.*

*I didn't have **any structure** to **rebel against**.*

*That is **what** we **are fighting against**.*

A In the sentences below, put a dotted line under the verb used with *against*. Then underline each of the other parts of the pattern.

1 An iron bed rested against the far wall.
2 He was the strongest man I have ever played against.
3 The victim refused to testify against him.
4 He was offered a place at the Royal College, but he'd already decided against becoming a classical musician.
5 There are a lot of young, fit guys out there to compete against.

B Match up the two halves of each sentence.

1 Reeves had been battling ...   a ... against his own brother?
2 What kind of man would testify ...   b ... against a corner of the table.
3 These magazines have campaigned ...   c ... against a referendum.
4 His head smashed ...   d ... against me!
5 Everyone is plotting ...   e ... against everything her mother represented.
6 There was a time when she rebelled ...   f ... against a knee injury.
7 The government has decided ...   g ... against high level corruption.

C Fill in the gaps in the sentences below using the verbs in this list. Use each verb once.

advise   appeal   protest   race   react   win

1 Mr Drew wanted to take Nancy home, but the doctor .... against this.
2 In the quarter-finals, Worcestershire beat Glamorgan, and Somerset .... against Middlesex.
3 I've .... against champions all over the world and Michael is one of the best.
4 The negative campaigns of the '80s won't work in the '90s because voters will .... against them.
5 He has said he will .... against the decision in the Supreme Court.
6 Hundreds of people took to the streets to .... against the continued detention of political prisoners.

D Put the different parts of these sentences in the right order.

1 beat / the rain / against / the windows ....
2 a wall / a glass ornament / against / smashed ....
3 against / you / rebelling / what / are ....
4 stood / against / he / the president / in the 1990 election

....

5 the government / more than forty Conservatives / voted / against

....

6 worth / this / is / against / something / fighting ....
7 its mistress's legs / came / rubbed / and / against / into the room / a cat

....

Verbs used with *against*: 2

Some verbs are followed by a noun group and a prepositional phrase which consists of *against* and a noun group. For example, in *We insured the house against fire*, the verb *insure* is followed by the noun group *the house*, the preposition *against*, and the noun group *fire*. This pattern is **V n *against* n**.

Active pattern

	Verb group	noun group	*against*	noun group
Your policy	insures	you	against	redundancy.
She	pressed	her back	against	the door.

Passive pattern

	Verb group	*against*	noun group
Children	should be vaccinated	against	measles.
My gain	must be balanced	against	your loss.

(With phrasal verbs, the particle comes either after the noun group or after the verb.)

Verbs with this pattern belong to the following meaning groups:

■ **verbs concerned with protecting someone or something**

cover	defend	insulate	protect	vaccinate
cushion	immunize	insure	spray	

We **couldn't protect** ourselves against attack.

In normal times, the federal government has the means to **cushion** the nation against a recession.

Record numbers of children **were immunised** against infectious diseases last year. (passive)

■ **verbs concerned with striking or putting one thing against another**

bang	lean	press	prop	slam	strike

The Commissioner **propped** his cane against the bed and sat down.

Dean fell and **struck** his head against the bannister.

■ **verbs concerned with attacking someone or being hostile towards someone**

direct	level	perpetrate

The violence **has been directed** against foreigners who've come to Germany as refugees or guest workers. (passive)

He claimed he was not well enough to answer the charges that **have been levelled** against him. (passive)

■ **verbs concerned with considering or dealing with two or more different things, people, or groups**

balance	match	play off	set	weigh

Union leaders **have been playing off** one bid against another to try to secure the best possible deal.

You **have to weigh** the responsibilities against the rewards.

■ *Turn* and *warn* also have this pattern.

She feared that he **would turn** her daughter against her.

In the case of *warn*, the preposition *against* is sometimes followed by an '-ing' clause.

When this business first started I **warned** him against staying there.

Different forms of the pattern

They are criminals of the worst sort, **against whom** society **must be protected**.

Sieg closed **the book** he **had propped** against his glass.

A Fill in the gaps in the sentences below using the verbs in this list. Use each verb once. The sentences show the pattern **V n *against* n** or its passive, or the pattern **V *against* n** (see Unit 39). Say which pattern is shown in each sentence.

brush   campaign   insulate   insure   lean   play
press   protect   spray   turn   vaccinate   warn

1 One in four homes is not ......*insured*...... against theft, fire or flood. *V n against n (passive)*

2 She .... her bike against a tree. ....

3 The two men were arrested frequently as they .... against racial segregation. ....

4 The government has to .... its citizens against terrorists. ....

5 She .... a finger against her lips, signaling him to remain silent. ....

6 Hungary were the best team I .... against. ....

7 Try to see that the living room is well .... against draughts. ....

8 These new taxes have helped .... public opinion against the government. ....

9 If your bare hand or arm .... against one of the stone walls carelessly, the stone would draw blood. ....

10 It would do no good at all to .... this boy against any danger. ....

11 They wanted to be sure that everybody was .... against cholera. ....

12 Mist the foliage twice daily on hot days and .... the plants against pests. ....

B Rewrite these sentences using the verb given in brackets with *against* and a noun group or '-ing' clause.

1 She attacked the vice president. (direct)
She directed an attack against the vice president.

2 Regular physical exercise also helps prevent you getting heart disease. (protect)
....

3 You have to compare the advantages and the disadvantages before you begin. (weigh)
....

4 Because of her father's wealth, she did not suffer the effect of several disasters. (cushion)
....

5 Before I set off, Mother would tell me not to go anywhere dangerous. (warn)
....

6 He hit the edge of the desk with his hand. (bang)
....

7 The same criticism can hardly be made about James Baker, the former Secretary of State. (level)
....

Verbs used with *as*: 1

1 Some verbs are followed by a prepositional phrase which consists of *as* and a noun group. For example, in *She works as a designer*, the verb *work* is followed by the preposition *as* and the noun group *a designer*. This pattern is **V *as* n**.

	Verb group	*as*	noun group
She	trained	as	a teacher.
The scandal	began	as	a family feud.

Verbs with this pattern belong to the following meaning groups:

■ **verbs concerned with doing a job, getting or leaving a job, or training for a job**

practise	run	stand	train
qualify	serve	stand down	work
resign	sign up	step down	

He **worked** *as a kitchen assistant* for the Ministry of Defence.

She **has** recently **qualified** *as a doctor* and is hoping to practise in Pakistan.

He intends to **step down** *as chairman* in 1997.

■ **verbs concerned with having a role or a function**

act	double up	operate
double	function	serve

Always breathe through your nose: it **acts** *as a filter*.

The room **had to double up** *as my studio*.

■ **verbs concerned with beginning, continuing, and ending**

begin	end	finish	remain	start off
continue	end up	finish up	start	start out

The camp **began** *as a maze of tents*, but over 14 years it has grown into a proper village.

Mr. Barker **will continue** *as chairman of the company's corporate finance division*.

When we were together at Liverpool, I never thought Kevin **would end up** *as a manager*.

■ **verbs indicating that someone or something is perceived as a particular thing**

come across	count	go down	qualify	rate
come over	emerge	pass	rank	shape up

Moving home **ranks** *as one of life's most stressful events*.

The MP **came across** *as a genuine, committed socialist*.

The work barely **qualifies** *as opera* at all.

■ **verbs indicating that someone is trying to be perceived as something they are not, or that something is intended to be perceived as something it is not**

dress up	masquerade	pose

Jones and his accomplice **posed** *as police officers* to gain entry to the house.

As a youngster he loved **dressing up** *as Superman*.

Productive use: Many other verbs are sometimes followed by a prepositional phrase beginning with *as* which indicates the role of the Subject. For example, someone can *compete* *as an amateur*, *live* *as a recluse*, or *testify* *as a witness*.

2 A few verbs are followed by a prepositional phrase which consists of *as* and an adjective group. For example, in *That counts as old*, the verb *count* is followed by the preposition *as* and the adjective *old*. This pattern is **V *as* adj**.

	Verb group	*as*	adjective group
A large number of plants	qualify	as	medicinal.

Verbs with this pattern indicate that someone or something is perceived as having a particular quality or status.

come across	count	pass
come over	emerge	qualify

I'm told that I **come across** *as hard and intimidating* but I don't feel hard and intimidating.

In Italy, many women **count** *as unemployed* even if they have a perfectly respectable 'black market' job.

A Rewrite these sentences using the verb given in brackets with the pattern **V *as* n**.

1 In 1976, Harold Wilson announced that he would no longer be Prime Minister. (resign)
In 1976, Harold Wilson resigned as Prime Minister.

2 She had to put on men's clothes. (dress up)

3 She became a chemical engineer. (qualify)

4 She studied to become a commercial artist. (train)

5 He was Minister of Agriculture for four years. (serve)

6 In the early 1960s he was a Labour candidate in local elections. (stand)

7 Henry will still be chairman and chief executive officer. (continue)

8 He was conscripted into the German army and eventually became a prisoner of war. (end up)

B Fill in the gaps in the sentences below using the noun groups in this list. Use each noun group once.

| a great cricketer | females | a lawyer | a lorry driver |
| an office | a single person | women | a world power |

1 He took two degrees and practised as .... in Durham.
2 My brother had two or three odd jobs and he finished up as ....
3 These men are said to have masqueraded as ....
4 The grant is quite good as I'm not married and so I count as ....
5 There are lots and lots of fish that change gender. Mostly they start off as .... and later they become males.
6 Like Japan, China has emerged as ....
7 We met in her comfortable North London home, which doubles as ....
8 I believe he will go down as ....

C In the sentences below, put a dotted line under the verb used with *as* and an adjective group. Then underline each of the other parts of the pattern.

1 In many of the books science comes across as interesting, exciting, fun.
2 These works emerge as more complex and more interesting than you might expect.
3 A train has to be one hour behind schedule to count as late compared with five minutes in 1986.
4 13 percent of American households qualify as poor.
5 They come over as nice but characterless.

Verbs used with *as*: 2

Some verbs are followed by a noun group and a prepositional phrase which consists of *as* and a noun group. For example, in *They chose her as their representative*, the verb *choose* is followed by the noun group *her*, the preposition *as*, and the noun group *their representative*. This pattern is **V n *as* n**. With some verbs, the preposition is sometimes followed by an '-ing' clause.

Active pattern

	Verb group	noun group	*as*	noun group/-ing
They	regard	him	as	a real friend.
She	perceived	Jean	as	being ungrateful.
She	began	her career	as	a model.

Passive pattern

	Verb group	*as*	noun group/-ing
A life sentence	is defined	as	being twenty-five years.
Ellen	was chosen	as	a tour leader.

(With phrasal verbs, the particle comes either after the noun group or after the verb.)

Verbs with this pattern belong to the following meaning groups:

■ **verbs concerned with labelling or describing someone or something in a particular way**

address	classify	denounce	identify	mention
attack	condemn	describe	know	name
cite	define	dismiss	label	

*A Home Office spokesman **has described** reports of deaths inside the prison **as speculation**.*

*Do you want to **be labelled** as a woman playwright?* (passive)

■ **verbs concerned with having a particular idea regarding someone or something**

accept	fancy	put down	regard	write off
acknowledge	intend	rank	remember	
consider	interpret	rate	see	
count	perceive	recognize	view	

*Like most exporters, it **regards** China **as the next great target in Asia**.*

*Carter **is remembered** as the president who wore a heavy wool sweater in the White House.* (passive)

*I think it's too easy for bands to **be written off** as sounding like other people.* (passive)

In the case of *fancy*, the noun group following the verb is always a reflexive pronoun.

*Like most joyriders, Stuart **fancied** himself as an expert driver and a match for the police.*

■ **verbs concerned with nominating or choosing someone for a particular position**

adopt	cast	elect	name	proclaim
appoint	choose	install	nominate	select

*The president is likely to **appoint** a woman as secretary of the navy.*

■ **verbs concerned with representing or presenting someone or something in a particular way**

express	pass off	present	promote
market	portray	project	represent

*The group tended to **represent** its interests as those of society as a whole.*

■ **verbs concerned with showing someone or something to be a particular thing**

confirm	establish	expose	mark out	reveal

*In 1876 he **had been exposed** as a fraud and jailed.* (passive)

■ **verbs concerned with using or treating someone or something in a particular way**

employ	keep	train	treat	use

*He **could use** his shirt as a rope, and tie one end to the branch.*

*Men need to **treat** women as equals.*

■ **verbs concerned with beginning, continuing, or ending something**

begin	continue	end	finish	start

*Lloyd Wright **began** his career as a landscape architect.*

■ *Strike* also has this pattern.

*He **struck** me as being a very healthy young man.*

Different forms of the pattern

*It had become obvious that Mrs Thatcher and **the man** she **had appointed** as her deputy did not see eye to eye.*

*He **dismissed** as scare stories reports that teachers were being sacked because schools couldn't pay them.*

*Journalists have expressed concern at **what** they **see** as a sinister new development.*

UNIT 42 Practice

A In the sentences below, put a dotted line under the verb used with *as*. Then underline each of the other parts of the pattern.

1 The board named Allan Gilmour as vice chairman for financial services.
2 When he reached the back porch, he met an officer, whom he addressed as captain.
3 His views have been widely denounced as being racist.
4 We should not dismiss as lies the incredible stories that children may tell us about themselves.
5 In 1960, John Fitzgerald Kennedy was elected as the 37th US President.
6 He had been cast as the king in Shaw's 'The Apple Cart'.
7 Manchester United are the team that have the best chance of finishing the season as Premier League champions.
8 He regarded Harry as being still solidly part of the family.
9 It was a long time before anyone recognised him as the great driver he is.
10 Top executives around the country have rated Atlanta as the nation's best city for business.

B Rewrite these sentences using the verb given in brackets with the pattern **V n *as* n** or its passive.

1 He seemed to me a serious but friendly person. (strike)
He struck me as a serious but friendly person.

2 Joe thought his stress was an inevitable part of his job. (perceive)
....

3 His peers said he was the best rider Australia had produced. (acknowledge)
....

4 The refugees were called 'vagabonds and escaped prisoners'. (label)
....

5 His irreverence for authority indicates that he is a troublemaker. (mark out)
....

6 Tilefish is a beautifully colored fish which is often sold under the name golden bass. (market)
....

7 The market became flooded with fake watches. People pretended they were originals. (pass off)
....

8 I often wondered why this band wanted me to be their singer. (choose)
....

9 He declared that the tape was a fake. (denounce)
....

10 The documentary suggests that Los Angeles is a city about to explode. (portray)
....

Verbs used with *as*: 3

Some verbs are followed by a noun group and a prepositional phrase which consists of *as* and an adjective group. For example, in *I saw the question as crucial*, the verb *see* is followed by the noun group *the question*, the preposition *as*, and the adjective *crucial*. This pattern is **V n *as* adj**.

Active pattern

	Verb group	noun group	*as*	adjective group
We	can't dismiss	it	as	trivial.
She	perceived	him	as	stupid.

Passive pattern

	Verb group	*as*	adjective group
The talks	were described	as	frank and friendly.
The area	can be considered	as	safe from attack.

(With phrasal verbs, the particle comes either after the noun group or after the verb.)

Verbs with this pattern belong to the following meaning groups:

■ **verbs concerned with labelling or describing someone or something in a particular way**

attack	condemn	describe	label
cite	denounce	dismiss	

*Eyewitnesses **described** the attack as savage.*

*He **attacked** the governors' decision as 'ludicrous'.*

*The Australian government **has condemned** the killings as outrageous and cowardly.*

■ **verbs concerned with having a particular view of someone or something**

accept	interpret	rate	remember	write off
acknowledge	perceive	recognize	see	
consider	rank	regard	view	

*He refused to **accept** the judgement as final.*

*Depending upon your circumstances, you **might interpret** redundancy as welcome or unwelcome.*

*One man **regards** a glass of water as half full while another **views** it as half empty.*

*The state **was** still **recognized** as independent in 1925.* (passive)

■ **verbs concerned with representing or presenting someone or something in a particular way**

pass off	portray	present	represent

*The four denied trying to **pass** the notes **off** as genuine.*

*Abraham's death **is presented** as good.* (passive)

■ **verbs concerned with showing someone or something to have a particular characteristic or quality**

confirm	expose	mark out	reveal

*The whole idea **was exposed** as stupid and naive.* (passive)

*Her diamond rings **marked** her **out** as seriously rich.*

■ *Strike* also has this pattern.

*The answering machine wasn't on and that **struck** her as strange.*

Different forms of the pattern

*I do not intend to cause distress to its members by publishing the texts of rituals **which** they **perceive** as sacred.*

*Dr Cato **described** as 'disgusting' a proposal to build a restaurant in the park.*

Practice

A In the sentences below, put a dotted line under the verb used with *as*. Then underline each of the other parts of the pattern.

1 They rate themselves as ambitious and strong-willed.
2 The doctors wrote him off as incurable eight years ago, but he is still alive.
3 The separation and eventual divorce were presented as amicable.
4 Adorno set out to expose as false all claims that the 'good' or 'just' society had been achieved.
5 The demonstrators were trying to draw attention to the export of live sheep to France, which they denounced as cruel.
6 With healthy self-esteem we perceive ourselves as lovable and capable.
7 In the UK all babies who weigh less than 5lb 8oz (2.5kg) at birth are labelled as premature.
8 It's a suggestion that officials dismiss as misleading.
9 The company admitted to re-finishing surplus airplane parts and then passing them off as new.

B These sentences show the pattern **V n *as* n** or its passive. Rewrite them using the pattern **V n *as* adj** or its passive.

1 He remembers her as an exceptional beauty.
He remembers her as exceptionally beautiful.
2 The book was condemned as blasphemy by many people.
....
3 The atmosphere inside the House of Commons was described as absolute chaos.
....
4 Her story was beginning to be widely accepted as the truth.
....
5 He denied that he was trying to portray himself as a madman.
....

C Fill in the gaps in the sentences below using the adjective groups in this list. Use each adjective group once.

dead   more important   satisfactory   timid and tearful   too violent   unfair

1 The British Airways pilot is today recovering at Southampton General Hospital. His condition is described as ....
2 The movie has been attacked by many critics as ....
3 This tax was regarded as .... because it meant millions of people made no direct financial contribution to local services.
4 We rank pets as .... to us than issues like the British economy, our personal hobbies and exercise, and holidays.
5 Then he'd been noble and heroic and now he was revealed as ....
6 Six government soldiers are confirmed as .... after the six hour battle.

Verbs used with *at*: 1

Some verbs are followed by a prepositional phrase which consists of *at* and a noun group. For example, in *They swore at him*, the verb *swear* is followed by the preposition *at* and the noun group *him*. This pattern is **V *at* n.**

	Verb group	*at*	noun group
The rivals	shouted	at	each other.
He	glanced	at	his watch.

Verbs with this pattern belong to the following meaning groups:

■ **verbs indicating that one person speaks loudly or unpleasantly to someone else, or laughs at them**

go on	scream	snap
laugh	shout	swear

He **used to shout** at people and sometimes even hit his assistants.

Most of these verbs are sometimes used in the passive.

*I didn't want him to look foolish and **be laughed** at.*

Go on, *scream* and *shout* are sometimes followed by a prepositional phrase beginning with *at*, and a to-infinitive clause.

*They were firing. I **screamed** at them to stop.*

■ **verbs indicating that someone communicates using a facial expression or a gesture**

grin	smile	wave	wink

*Michael just **grinned** at her, maddeningly.*

*I saw my parents **waving** at me through the window.*

■ **verbs indicating that someone looks at something or someone**

glance	glare	look	stare

Look at the holes in the walls!

*Betty **glared** at her in disgust.*

These verbs are sometimes used in the passive.

*I often realise I **am being stared** at just because my clothes are unusual.*

■ **verbs indicating that someone expresses a bad opinion of something**

grumble	lash out	protest
hit out	laugh	scoff

*They **scoffed** at my suggestion.*

They **are protesting** at conditions in the jail.

■ **verbs indicating that someone hits or touches something or tries to do so**

beat	hack away	pull	stab	tap
grab	knock	slash	swing	tear

*I **knocked** at the front door.*

*'Maria?' he said again and **pulled** at her wrist.*

■ **verbs indicating that a person or animal bites, eats, or drinks something**

chew	nibble	peck	sip	suck
gnaw	nip	pick	snap	

*He **chewed** at the end of his pencil, thinking out the next problem.*

*Near the garden gate a hen and her chicks **peck** at corn.*

■ **verbs indicating that someone attacks someone else**

aim	fire	rush
come	fly	shoot

*The soldiers **were shooting** at anything that moved now.*

■ **verbs used when indicating the size, level, weight, or price of something**

average out	level off	run	stand
bottom out	peak	sell	work out

*The cost of the fighter programme now **stands** at more than four thousand million dollars.*

*The average rise **works out** at 6.5 per cent.*

■ **other common verbs**

aim	guess	hint	point

*The girl **pointed** at the blackboard on the wall.*

In the case of *aim* and *hint*, the preposition *at* is sometimes followed by an '-ing' clause.

*The Government **must aim** at getting Britain back to work.*

Different forms of the pattern

*What **are** you **looking** at?*

*He looked for some clue about **what** the doctor **was hinting** at.*

*She set **a standard of excellence** for me to **aim** at.*

Practice

A In the sentences below, put a dotted line under the verb used with *at*. Then underline each of the other parts of the pattern.

1 He nibbled at his bottom lip and shook his head slowly.
2 It's hoped that the game will sell at less than a pound.
3 People complained they'd been sworn at for failing to park according to the rules.
4 Then he gave a cry and the two officers turned to see what he was staring at.
5 They sped off, firing at random at people in the streets.
6 If you can't laugh at yourself, who can you laugh at?
7 Skylark is a temperamental horse and doesn't like being shouted at.
8 Provide interesting pictures, books and mobiles to look at.

B Rewrite these sentences using the pattern **V *at* n**.

1 Mahoney gave him an angry look.
   Mahoney looked at him angrily.
2 Arnold took a few sips of his beer.
   ....
3 She turned to Frank and gave him a triumphant grin.
   ....
4 The police can only make a guess about the scale of the problem.
   ....
5 I gave Sandy a casual wave.
   ....

C Complete the questions below using the words given in brackets with *at*. Then rewrite them as reported questions, starting with the words provided.

1 a) What ....*are they pointing at?*.. (they / are / pointing)
   b) I asked someone ......*what they were pointing at.*..

2 a) What .... ? (you / are / looking)
   b) I asked him ....

3 a) Who .... ? (you / are / waving)
   b) I asked her ....

4 a) Who .... ? (they / are / shooting)
   b) I asked him ....

6 a) What .... ? (you / are / hinting)
   b) I asked her ....

7 a) Who . ... ? (he / was / shouting)
   b) I asked someone ....

Verbs used with *at*: 2

Some verbs are followed by a noun group and a prepositional phrase which consists of *at* and a noun group. For example, in *She shouted insults at him*, the verb *shout* is followed by the noun group *insults*, the preposition *at*, and the noun group *him*. This pattern is **V n *at* n.**

Active pattern

	Verb group	noun group	*at*	noun group
I	shook	my fist	at	him.
Estimates	put the	death toll	at	about 200.

Passive pattern

	Verb group	*at*	noun group
Bombs	were thrown	at	shops in the capital.
The share price	was set	at	£1.75.

Verbs with this pattern belong to the following meaning groups:

■ **verbs indicating that someone points or aims something at someone or something**

aim	point	stab
direct	shake	swing

*She **pointed** the gun at him.*

*He **swung** a hammer at her head but missed.*

■ **verbs indicating that someone throws an object at someone or something**

chuck	fling	hurl	throw

*She **threw** a pillow at him.*

*A gang who nearly killed a policeman by **hurling** a brick at his car have been jailed for a total of sixty years.*

■ **verbs indicating that someone speaks to someone, often in a hostile way**

aim	direct	hurl	scream	shout

*They stood there and **shouted** abuse at me as I walked down the street.*

*Accusations about stealing money **were hurled** at her by her husband.* (passive)

■ **verbs indicating that someone looks or smiles at someone or something**

direct	flash	shoot	throw

*He turns to **flash** a loving smile at his new bride.*

*The maid backed out, **throwing** one last cautionary look at her mistress.*

■ **verbs indicating that someone buys, sells, or puts a value on some property**

buy	price	quote	sell	value

*Estates **may sell** property at a discount to raise money quickly for taxes.*

*One day Carret **was able to buy** some bonds at $89, which he then sold at a profit.*

■ **verbs indicating that someone estimates, fixes, or maintains a number or amount**

estimate	maintain	put	reckon	set

*The number of child workers **was put** at more than 4.8 million.* (passive)

*The cost **is estimated** at more than twelve thousand million dollars.* (passive)

*In winter, **maintain** the temperature at 36 degrees F or higher.*

Different forms of the pattern

*But his words clearly carry no weight at all with those at whom they **were directed**.*

*The authorities now **put** at twenty the number of dead in the recent unrest.*

*His suit was spattered with the eggs that students **had thrown** at him.*

A In the sentences below, put a dotted line under the verb used with *at*. Then underline each of the other parts of the pattern.

1 Norma aimed the gun at them.

2 After a few moments I realised that her question was directed at me.

3 Angrily, the woman shook her fist at Bragg's departing back.

4 Michael shot a quick glance at him, then turned back to Miss Treves.

5 He flashed a handsome smile at the television cameras.

6 In early trading in Hong Kong, gold was quoted at $366.50 an ounce.

7 Casualties were estimated at over 1,000.

8 Groups of people threw stones at us throughout the journey.

9 In the end I couldn't take the violence and the insults she would hurl at me.

10 The bombs hit the targets they were aimed at about 25 percent of the time.

B Fill in the gaps in these sentences. For each pair, one verb from this Unit goes in both sentences.

1 I had abuse .... at me by supporters of the hunt.

Rocks were .... at the police.

2 A procession of haughty and accusing looks were .... at the interviewer.

The Blackburn manager is alleged to have .... improper comments at Stockport referee William Flood.

3 He .... his rifle at me.

But he denied his comments were .... at Liberal Party colleagues.

4 For some reason I just cracked and .... my drink at this guy.

One reporter noted the angry glares Desiree .... at Tyson yesterday.

C Write sentences about these amounts, using the verb given in brackets with the passive of the pattern **V n *at* n**.

1 The number of birds: one billion. (estimate)
The number of birds was estimated at one billion.

2 The number of people out of work: more than thirty-eight thousand. (put)
....

3 The cost of repairs: £1 million. (estimate)
....

4 The turnout in the election: sixty percent. (put)
....

5 The number of victims: around three percent of the population. (reckon)
....

6 The dividend: 9.2 pence. (maintain)
....

7 The exchange rate: 39 pesos to the US dollar. (set)
....

Verbs used with *between* or *among*

1 Some verbs are followed by a prepositional phrase which consists of *between* and a **plural noun group**. For example, in *She alternated between anger and depression*, the verb *alternate* is followed by the preposition *between* and the plural noun group *anger and depression*. This pattern is **V *between* pl-n**.

	Verb group	*between*	plural noun group
I	liaise	between	these groups.
They	can't distinguish	between	right and wrong.

Verbs with this pattern belong to the following meaning groups:

■ **verbs indicating that someone sorts out or helps the relationship between two people or groups**

adjudicate	arbitrate	liaise	mediate

*I've been instructed to **liaise between my chief and the Branch** and to assist where I can.*

■ **verbs concerned with recognizing the difference between two or more things**

differentiate	discriminate	distinguish

*It's difficult to **differentiate between chemical weapons and chemicals for peaceful industrial use**.*

■ **verbs concerned with doing, being, or using two things alternately**

alternate	oscillate	vacillate	waver

*In the winter he started to have constant back pain. He **had to alternate between work and lying down**.*

*She **oscillated between anger and guilt**.*

■ **verbs indicating that something has a range of values**

hover	oscillate	range	vary

*Prices **range between $30 and $50**.*

■ *Choose* also has this pattern.

*Why **should** women **have to choose between a job and a family**?*

2 Some verbs are followed by a noun group and a prepositional phrase which consists of *between* or *among* and a **plural noun group**. For example, in *He divided his money among his children*, the verb *divide* is followed by the noun group *his money*, the preposition *among* and the plural noun group *his children*. This pattern is **V n *between/among* pl-n**. With phrasal verbs, the particle comes either after the noun group or after the verb.

Active pattern

	Verb group	noun group	*between/among*	pl. noun group
I	Split	the wages	between	you.
	would rate	him	among	the top players.

Passive pattern

	Verb group	*between/among*	pl. noun group
The cash	will be shared	between	the two charities.
The food	was distributed	among	the refugees.

Verbs with this pattern belong to the following meaning groups:

■ **verbs concerned with dividing something between two or more people or groups**

distribute	divide up	share out	split up
divide	share	split	

When only two people or groups are involved, the preposition is usually *between* rather than *among*. When more than two people or groups are involved, you can use either *between* or *among*.

*Drain the noodles and **divide them among the individual serving bowls**.*

*The tips **are divided up equally between the staff**, and then added on to their wage packet. (passive)*

■ **verbs indicating that someone considers someone or something to be in a particular group**

number	rank	rate

Only the preposition *among* is used with these verbs.

*He **numbered several Americans among his friends**.*

Rank is sometimes used with an ordinal number in this pattern, as shown below.

*One survey **ranked her fifth among preferred presidential candidates**.*

Different forms of the pattern

*He even **numbered among his connections certain lords**.*

*Heads of schools that improved would be given cash bonuses to **distribute among teaching staff**.*

A In the sentences below, put a dotted line under the verb used with a pattern described in this Unit. Then underline each of the other parts of the pattern.

1 A prominent government supporter has promised to <u>mediate</u> <u>between</u> <u>the two sides.</u>
2 Always try and alternate between two or three tasks.
3 The sheep farmers have 120 million dollars of government hand-outs to share out between them.
4 For general daylight use, these two cameras are difficult to choose between.
5 With album releases of this quality he'll soon be rated among the top reggae producers.
6 The group numbers among its members some of the most influential women in Sweden.
7 Last year they raised £22,000, which was split between several charities.
8 The money will be split up between the three of them.

B Fill in the gaps in these sentences using *between* or *among*.

1 Temperatures on the coast vary .... 25 and 30 degrees Celsius all year round.
2 Eskimo hunters are trained to discriminate .... dozens of types of snow.
3 My school is ranked .... the high achievers in Brisbane.
4 Payments are expected to range .... $9 billion and $12 billion this year.
5 He vacillated .... republican and monarchist sentiments.
6 The new president numbers building and joinery .... his hobbies.

C Fill in the gaps in the sentences below using the nouns in this list. Use each noun once.

death   doubt   family   football   women

1 As a youngster he'd had to choose between athletics and ....
2 The whole question is about how we divide our lives between work and ....
3 He was in intensive care, hovering between life and ....
4 The Koran does not discriminate between men and ....
5 She stood there worrying, vacillating between happiness and ....

D Rewrite these sentences using the verb given in brackets with *between* or *among*.

1 Her brown eyes were sometimes amused and sometimes embarrassed. (waver)
   Her brown eyes wavered between amusement and embarrassment.
2 The President thinks that economic and political refugees are different. (distinguish)
   ....
3 He was willing to help the government and the workers come to an agreement. (arbitrate)
   ....
4 He gave pennies to all the neighbourhood children. (distribute)
   ....
5 I think he is one of the fastest bowlers in the world. (rate)
   ....

Verbs used with *by*: 1

1 Some verbs are followed by a prepositional phrase which consists of *by* and an '-ing' clause. For example, in *They responded by ordering him to go home*, the verb *respond* is followed by the preposition *by* and the '-ing' clause *ordering him to go home*. This pattern is **V *by* -ing**.

	Verb group	by	-ing clause
He	began	by	asking me about my house.
Protesters	retaliated	by	throwing stones.

Verbs with this pattern belong to the following meaning groups:

■ **verbs concerned with starting or finishing a task, session, or period of time in a particular way**

begin	end	finish off	start	start out
close	finish	finish up	start off	

Start off by exercising for five to ten minutes every day.

*She **ended** by inviting her listeners to send their own experiences to her.*

■ **verbs concerned with responding to something that has been done, or compensating for it**

atone	counter	reciprocate	respond
compensate	react	reply	retaliate

*Pollack **responded** by calling the police.*

*The company tried to **compensate** by expanding sales at home.*

Productive use: Many other verbs which involve a response to an action or situation sometimes have this pattern.

2 Some verbs are followed by a noun group and a prepositional phrase which consists of *by* and an '-ing' clause. For example, in *He ended his speech by saying that there would be elections soon*, the verb *end* is followed by the noun group *his speech*, the preposition *by*, and the clause *saying that there would be elections soon*. This pattern is **V n *by* -ing**. With phrasal verbs, the particle comes either after the noun group or after the verb.

	Verb group	noun group	by	-ing clause
They	started	the day	by	having a cup of coffee.
He	opened	the session	by	calling for reforms.

Verbs with this pattern are concerned with beginning or ending a session, career, or period of time in a particular way.

begin	end	finish up	preface	start off
close	finish	open	start	start out

*When my father's education finished, he **began** his engineering career by building ice factories.*

*The South Korean president **has ended** his visit to Japan by inviting Emperor Akihito to pay a return visit to South Korea.*

*He **started off** this particular interview by saying, 'Yes, I think you're on to a good idea.'*

Productive use: You can use this pattern with a wide range of verbs. The prepositional phrase indicates the means by which something is done, as in *He **escaped** the law by fleeing the country.*

3 Some verbs are followed by a noun group and a prepositional phrase which consists of *by* and a noun group. For example, in *He took her by the arm*, the verb *take* is followed by the noun group *her*, the preposition *by*, and the noun group *the arm*. This pattern is **V n *by* n**.

	Verb group	noun group	by	noun group
He	grabbed	me	by	the hair.
I	held	her	by	the waist.

Verbs with this pattern indicate that someone holds or takes hold of part of someone's body.

catch	grab	have	hold	take

The noun group after *by* usually begins with *the*.

*He **grabbed** Rivers by the shoulders and dragged him out of the car.*

A In the sentences below, put a dotted line under the verb used with a pattern described in this Unit. Then underline each of the other parts of the pattern.

1 He started his career by shortening his name.
2 She started off by accusing him of blackmail but he just ignored her.
3 I'd like to begin by asking about the system of management in the school and how you fit into that.
4 They finished the day by reaching the final of the Queen Mother Challenge Cup.
5 Bake the pudding in the oven for 7 minutes. Finish by browning it under a grill.
6 He opened the meeting by quoting lyrics from Bob Dylan's 'The Times They Are A-Changin'.'

B Rewrite the second sentence in each pair using the verb given in brackets with the pattern **V by -ing**.

1 Furness shivered and stepped closer to Mace. He put an arm around her. (respond)
   He responded by putting an arm around her.
2 He stepped on the cat. The cat scratched his leg. (react)
   ....
3 Again the police charged to separate rival groups. The fans pelted them with plastic chairs. (retaliate)
   ....
4 When Caroline was five she scribbled on a wall. Her father threw her toys on the fire. (respond)
   ....
5 I told them I could not possibly pay the sum demanded. They reduced the demand to £730. (reply)
   ....

C Rewrite these sentences using the verb given in brackets with the pattern **V n by n**.

1 Shelley took hold of his ankles and dragged him down. (grab)
   Shelley grabbed him by the ankles and dragged him down.
2 He took hold of my hair and pushed me roughly up the trailer steps. (grab)
   ....
3 Then she stepped toward the door, but George took hold of her wrist. (catch)
   ....
4 He took her hand and led her into the next room. (take)
   ....
5 I was holding his ears and I was beating his head against the pavement. (have)
   ....
6 She stood there, holding Sofia's hand but not looking her in the face. (hold)
   ....

Verbs used with *by*: 2

1 Some verbs are followed by a prepositional phrase which consists of *by* and a noun group indicating an amount. For example, in *Their incomes have dropped by 30 per cent*, the verb *drop* is followed by the preposition *by* and the noun group *30 per cent*. This pattern is **V *by* amount**.

	Verb group	*by*	amount
The overall number of jobs	decreased	by	1000.
The Reds	were leading	by	two runs.

Verbs with this pattern belong to the following meaning groups:

■ **verbs indicating that a quantity or level increases or decreases.** The prepositional phrase indicates the size of the increase or decrease.

climb	dive	increase	shoot up	slump
come down	drop	jump	shrink	soar
decline	fall	plummet	sink	tumble
decrease	go down	plunge	slide	
dip	go up	rise	slip	

*Queensland's population **has increased** by 13 percent in that period.*

*The price of petrol at Shell garages **is coming down** by more than four pence a gallon.*

*Sales **went up** by 0.1 per cent last month as consumers began to shop early for Christmas.*

■ **verbs concerned with winning and losing.** The prepositional phrase indicates either the difference in the scores, or the actual scores.

lead	lose	win

*In the event, Cambridge **won** by fifteen points.*

*The government **lost** by one vote.*

*Popov **is leading** by 11 points to nine.*

■ **verbs indicating that an amount that was set is exceeded**

overrun	overspend

*The reception **overran** by forty-five minutes.*

*Guy's hospital and Lewisham hospital **have** already **overspent** by £800,000.*

2 Some verbs are followed by a noun group and a prepositional phrase which consists of *by* and a noun group indicating an amount. For example, in *It is cutting its prices by a third*, the verb *cut* is followed by the noun group *its prices*, the preposition *by*, and the noun group *a third*. This pattern is **V n *by* amount**.

Active pattern

	Verb group	noun group	*by*	amount
The company	has cut	its workforce	by	3,000.
	Multiply	each figure	by	five.

Passive pattern

	Verb group	*by*	amount
Fares	were raised	by	10 per cent.

Verbs with this pattern are concerned with increasing or decreasing an amount.

cut	devalue	increase	multiply	reduce
decrease	divide	lower	raise	

*The government plans to **raise** petrol prices by thirty six per cent.*

*You need to **divide** the total by six to work out your income.*

Different forms of the pattern

*He announced that France **will cut** by half the rate of interest it charges on loans to most countries in Africa.*

Practice

A In the sentences below, put a dotted line under the verb used with a pattern described in this Unit. Then underline each of the other parts of the pattern.

1 Beer prices have shot up by 10 per cent or so over the past 12 months.
2 Its shares slumped by a third after the crash of BCCI.
3 Economists have forecast that employment will fall by between 10,000 and 30,000.
4 Sterling has been devalued by some 17 per cent and interest rates have been cut by four points.
5 The World Health Organisation says the number of cases of cholera reported worldwide has increased by ten per cent.
6 This historic treaty will reduce by two-thirds current nuclear arsenals.
7 The Argentine Agriculture Minister rejected EC proposals to cut farm subsidies by thirty percent as totally unacceptable.
8 The average family spent a third of its budget on food back then, so the cost of the diet was multiplied by three to determine the poverty line.

B Divide the list of verbs beginning with *climb* into two smaller groups:

1 verbs indicating that a quantity or level increases

....

2 verbs indicating that a quantity or level decreases

....

....

C Fill in the replies using the pattern **V *by amount***.

1 Who won the Test match? (Pakistan scored 217 runs. New Zealand scored 150 runs.)
   Pakistan won by 217 runs to 150. or *Pakistan won by 67 runs.*
2 Who won the rugby? (Ireland scored nine points. France scored 25 points.)

....

3 Who's winning? (Fiji have 13 points. England have 17 points.)

....

4 Who's leading at the moment? (Edberg has won two sets. Krickstein hasn't won any sets.)

....

5 How many votes did he lose by? (He got 34 votes. His opponent got 46 votes.)

....

6 Are Manchester winning or losing? (Manchester United have scored one goal. Aston Villa have scored three goals.)

....

Verbs used with *for*: 1

Some verbs are followed by a prepositional phrase which consists of *for* and a noun group. For example, in *He asked for a pay rise*, the verb *ask* is followed by the preposition *for* and the noun group *a pay rise*. This pattern is **V for n**.

	Verb group	for	noun group
He	pleaded	for	mercy.
We	are hoping	for	a happy ending.

Verbs with this pattern belong to the following meaning groups:

■ **verbs indicating that someone asks for something or tries to get something**

advertise	call	fish	push	send off
aim	campaign	hold out	put in	shout
appeal	claim	lobby	register	stand
apply	compete	negotiate	ring	strike
ask	demonstrate	plead	run	try
beg	fight	pray	scream	vote
bid	file	press	send	wish

I'm asking for your protection.

They are campaigning for multi-party democracy.

Send off for your free tickets now!

Michel Rocard first stood for the presidency in 1969.

Some of these verbs, especially *apply* and *send*, are sometimes used in the passive.

The doctor was sent for and arrived surprisingly quickly.

■ **verbs indicating that someone looks for something or is alert for something**

check	feel	listen out	search	watch out
dig	hunt	look	shop	
explore	listen	look out	watch	

Always look for other ways of managing difficult situations.

Meanwhile, the band are searching for an appropriate venue for a special festive show.

Watch out for pests and disease.

With many of these verbs, the prepositional phrase beginning with *for* can come after or before another prepositional phrase, or an adverb, which indicates where someone is searching.

He felt in his pockets for a coin.

I've been looking for you everywhere.

■ **verbs indicating that someone wants something**

be dying	hope	long	pray	wish

I'm dying for a breath of fresh air.

Hope and *pray* are sometimes used in the passive.

It's probably the best that can be hoped for in the circumstances.

■ **verbs indicating that someone chooses something**

go	opt	plump	settle

None of the children has opted for farming as a career.

Go for products with the lowest amount of fat.

The preposition *for* is sometimes followed by an '-ing' clause.

I wanted to be a dancer but my father said I couldn't possibly do that, so instead I settled for getting married and having children.

■ **verbs indicating that someone goes towards a particular destination**

depart	head	leave	make	run

He spun around and headed for the door.

My wife and I are leaving for Mexico next month.

A In the sentences below, put a dotted line under the verb used with *for*. Then underline each of the other parts of the pattern. (For different forms of the pattern, see Unit 50.)

1 The Socialist Democrats are still pressing for a boycott of the elections.
2 What level of responsibility are you aiming for?
3 Ingrid tried to file for a Swedish divorce, but the technical difficulties made it impossible.
4 He persuaded the Duchess to hold out for the best deal possible.
5 She doubted he really checked the instruments or even really knew what to check for.
6 These are all good points to look for.
7 You can send off for the competition details by cutting the coupon.

B Fill in the gaps in the sentences below using the verbs in this list. Use each verb once.

aim   feel   fight   listen   plead   pray   run   scream   search   shop

1 Shop fronts were smashed and tourists .... for cover as a short, sharp street battle erupted.
2 For weeks she lay in her hospital bed as her devoted husband .... for a miracle.
3 We should unite and .... for our rights.
4 While he .... for his own apartment they were roommates.
5 The major was alert in a second, ... for his revolver deep inside his fur pocket.
6 Every fifty meters, he'd stop and .... for those behind him.
7 Women .... for them and run to the stage and kiss them and hand them flowers.
8 In its original targets Euro Disney .... for an average daily attendance of 30,000.
9 Relief workers are .... for further international help to alleviate the conditions.
10 When you .... for food, how frequently do you go to a large supermarket?

C Rewrite these sentences using the verb given in brackets with the pattern **V** *for* **n**.

1 Cross saw Brown come through the door and move towards the bed. (head)
   Cross saw Brown come through the door and head for the bed.
2 Most university students choose the straight three-year course. (opt)
   ....
3 The officials said two of them have requested political asylum. (ask)
   ....
4 His father, Tony, told him not to be satisfied with second best. (settle)
   ....
5 I'm not sure that the people demanding this change have thought through its implications. (push)
   ....
6 First, the police must be asked to come. (send)
   ....

1 Here are some more groups of verbs which are followed by the preposition *for* and a noun group or an '-ing' clause:

■ verbs indicating that someone works for someone or does something for them

act	fight	play	work
cover	fill in	speak	write
cover up	model	stand in	

He **works** *for a local heavy engineering firm*.

I'm always **having to cover up** *for her* and lie to my father.

Then someone rang and asked if I **would stand in** *for Frank Bough* and do the Sunday cricket on BBC2.

■ verbs indicating that someone is training or preparing for something

gear up	prepare	revise	study	train

The crew of the space shuttle Atlantis **is preparing** *for the ride back to Earth tomorrow*.

Janet **has been revising** *for her exams* this week.

■ verbs concerned with compensating for an action or situation in some way

apologize	compensate	make up	pay

The government has always said that it will raise salaries to try to **compensate** *for the price increases*.

The preposition *for* is sometimes followed by an '-ing' clause.

I **apologized** *for wasting his time*.

■ other common verbs

care	go	live	qualify	sell
enter	last	pay	save up	wait

Come on, Frank, let's **go** *for a walk*.

This effect **can last** *for several days* after the treatment session.

They want us to **pay** *for services we don't use*.

I **was waiting** *for you* at the crossroads.

Care and pay are sometimes used in the passive.

For some weeks the baby **was cared** *for* in the Convent of St Sulpice.

Different forms of the pattern

What **are** you **waiting** *for*?

She showed no surprise when he explained what he **was looking** *for*.

The concessions it **has asked** *for* would cost us money.

I have **nothing** to **apologize** *for*.

The new atmosphere of spontaneity was exactly **what** we **had hoped** *for*.

Some verbs are sometimes used in a pattern with *than*.

They are giving us much more than we **have asked** *for*.

2 Some verbs are followed by a prepositional phrase beginning with *for*, and a to-infinitive clause. This pattern is **V *for* n to-inf**.

	Verb group	*for*	noun group	to-infinitive clause
The director	asked	for	him	to be removed.
She	's longing	for	Mark	to come home.

Verbs with this pattern belong to the following meaning groups:

■ verbs indicating that someone asks for something to be done or to happen

appeal	call	plead	press	shout
ask	campaign	pray	push	

The CBI **is pressing** *for firms to invest more cash in training*.

In the case of *ask* and *campaign*, the to-infinitive is usually passive.

They **asked** *for their identities to be kept secret*.

■ verbs indicating that someone wants something to happen or be done

be dying	long	pray

All the women **will be dying** *for you to make a mistake*.

He **longed** *for the winter to be over*.

■ *Arrange* and *wait* also have this pattern.

We **can arrange** *for you to be picked up at the airport and transferred to your hotel*.

I don't want to sit around **waiting** *for the phone to ring*.

A Match up the two halves of each sentence.

1 At 15 she was modelling ...

2 I was filling in ...

3 It's taken me a year to save up ...

4 The demonstrators were calling ...

5 He decided to begin studying ...

6 Nine teams entered ...

7 You'll never know how very much I longed ...

8 They will pay ...

9 He wasn't very handsome, but he made up ...

10 His photographs sell ...

a ... for letting him escape.

b ... for my bike.

c ... for $2,000 each.

d ... for it in enthusiasm and charm.

e ... for the tournament.

f ... for the injured Graham Gooch.

g ... for him to resign.

h ... for us to be friends.

i ... for Elle magazine.

j ... for the Vermont bar exams.

B In each of the sentences below, one of the verbs from this list is missing. Mark where it goes and say what it is. Use each verb once.

apologize   care   fight   last   live   pay   stand in   train   wait   work

1 Her future husband will be / for her at Sydney. .....*waiting*..............

2 Teresa has been for the 2.7km walk by walking the 1.5km to her local shop. ....

3 The rainy season has just begun and will for several more months. ....

4 She has been for the company for 16 years and says that she is still learning. ....

5 Can we afford the luxury of what you propose? Who will for it? ....

6 The baby is for from 9.30 to 6.30 by an extremely capable 27-year-old trained nanny.

   ....

7 He for his work and he would have gone on for ever if he could. ....

8 I have done nothing for which I should. ....

9 His big break come when he for another dentist who had been taken ill. ....

10 He went on to say he was proud that he had for his country. ....

C These sentences show the pattern **V *for* n to-inf**. Fill in the first gap using the verbs in this list. Then think of a way to fill in the second gap.

campaign   plead   pray   press   shout   wait

1 For four years he had ......*campaigned*...... for disabled athletes *to be allowed to compete in*

   the Games.

2 The father of a girl who disappeared from her home a month ago .... for her to

   ....

3 We'll .... for somebody to ...., then grab him before he

   can close the door behind him.

4 She eyed the phone, ... for it to ....

5 The hostages' relatives have been .... for more action to

   ....

6 Graham hurried after the porter, ... for him to ....

Verbs used with *for*: 3

Some verbs are followed by a noun group and a prepositional phrase which consists of *for* and a noun group. For example, in *He asked his father for the money*, the verb *ask* is followed by the noun group *his father*, the preposition *for*, and the noun group *the money*. This pattern is **V n *for* n**. With some verbs, the preposition is sometimes followed by an '-ing' clause.

Active pattern

	Verb group	noun group	*for*	noun group/-ing
She	has brought	a nice present	for	you.
I	don't blame	you	for	being upset.

Passive pattern

	Verb group	*for*	noun group/-ing
A room	has been booked	for	him.
He	was arrested	for	stealing a car.

(With phrasal verbs, the particle comes either after the noun group or after the verb.)

Verbs with this pattern belong to the following meaning groups:

■ verbs indicating that someone does something for someone else

book	cook	find	leave	play
bring	do	fix	make	pour
buy	fetch	get	order	prepare

I followed her to the kitchen where she **was making coffee for all of them.**

My father took me into town one day and **bought the record for me.**

In the case of *do*, the noun group following the verb is often an **amount**.

The nurses **can't do much for her**, *apart from make her comfortable.*

Productive use: Any verb concerned with doing something for someone can be used with this pattern.

■ verbs concerned with exchanging one thing for another

barter	substitute	trade
exchange	swap	trade in

Someone **swapped the blank for a real bullet.** *He is lucky to be alive.*

■ verbs indicating that someone asks someone for something

ask	beg	press

They **asked me for fresh ideas**, *but I had none.*

■ verbs indicating that someone has or expresses a good or bad opinion of someone else. The prepositional phrase indicates the reason.

admire	blame	congratulate	(cannot) fault	tell off
attack	condemn	criticize	praise	tick off

I **admire them for their independent attitudes.**

The whole world seems to **condemn you for being overweight.**

Adam **ticked him off for smoking too much.**

The air force and navy **are being praised** *for the rescue operation.* (passive)

■ verbs concerned with treating someone in a particular way because of what they have done

arrest	forgive	punish	sue	want
compensate	pay back	report	thank	
execute	prosecute	reward	try	

I **had** *generously* **rewarded** *her for her services*, *which had delighted her.*

They **could sue** *him for breach of contract.*

I **must thank** *you for being so kind to me.*

He told officers he wanted to **pay them back** *for locking him up three weeks earlier.*

He's **wanted** *for murder.* (passive)

Productive use: Any verb concerned with treating someone in a particular way can be used with this pattern.

A In the sentences below, put a dotted line under the verb used with *for* (see this Unit and Units 49 and 50). Then underline each of the other parts of the pattern.

1 I admire him tremendously for his efforts.
2 He listened for sounds inside as he climbed the stairs.
3 He studied engineering and went to work for the telephone company.
4 I ordered a birthday gift for my mother last month.
5 We'll trade in the Buick for another car.
6 They made a home for him in the nursery.
7 Was he covering up for Grace? Or was he telling the truth?
8 Some day I'll pay you back for this!
9 He was warmly congratulated by his five colleagues for hosting the first meeting.

B Rewrite each of the following pairs of sentences as one sentence, using *for* and a noun group or '-ing' clause.

1 Her daughter had taken control of her own finances. Sissie had never forgiven her.
   Sissie had never forgiven her daughter for taking control of her own finances.
2 I just want some money from Gil. I've begged him again and again.
   ....
3 He was drunk on duty. A crew member reported him.
   ....
4 He wanted hot water. I picked up a bucket to fetch some.
   ....
5 Both leaders were wanted in France. They were to be questioned in connection with an alleged plot.
   ....

C These sentences show the pattern **V n n** (see Units 8 and 9). Rewrite them using the pattern **V n for n**, if possible. If it is not possible, leave the space blank.

1 Perhaps you might cook him dinner.
   Perhaps you might cook dinner for him.
2 She forgave Lisette her deception because she knew what a desperate position she was in.
   ....
3 We will send you a letter which will tell you the day you are expected to come into hospital.
   ....
4 I always wondered why they named him Stanley.
   ....
5 Shirley had bought him a double espresso to thank him for taking her to Baton Rouge.
   ....
6 They asked me some sensible questions.
   ....
7 Devlin got him his coat and took him out to the car.
   ....

Verbs used with *for*: 4

Here are some more groups of verbs which are followed by a noun group and a prepositional phrase beginning with *for*:

■ **verbs concerned with preparing someone or something for a particular task, purpose, or situation**

equip	intend	prepare	qualify	train

We're preparing our children for the 21st century.

The course is designed to equip students for a career in radio or magazines.

■ **verbs concerned with considering or choosing someone or something for a particular role or purpose**

choose	nominate	recruit	select
interview	recommend	seek	

President Clinton had originally nominated Ms Guinier for the job.

Amanda Saranah and Michelle Taylor have been chosen for the regional netball team. (passive)

This remedy is toxic in large doses and is not recommended for use by untrained persons. (passive)

■ **verbs indicating that someone pays or charges for something**

charge	pay

The noun group following the verb may indicate the person who is paid or charged money, or the amount paid.

Pay the gentleman for his services, please.

A collector has paid many thousands of pounds for a pistol used by Winston Churchill.

There is sometimes an **amount** between the noun group and the prepositional phrase.

He was shocked when the bank charged him £110 for the manager's time.

■ **verbs concerned with searching somewhere for something**

comb	explore	scan	scour	search

Police searched the area for other bombs.

Seventy officers and a police helicopter combed the streets for seven-year-old Maria.

■ **other common verbs**

enter	pay	say	sell	treat
hold	put down	schedule	test	wait

The President has scheduled a news conference for this afternoon.

They deserve to pay the penalty for their crimes.

The truck driver was treated for shock. (passive)

Passengers had to wait 40 minutes for another train.

Rough streets hold no fears for her.

In the case of *say*, the noun group following the verb is always an **amount**.

The fact that she had the full support of her husband says much for his courage.

Different forms of the pattern

What can I do for you?

I was trying to work out what to buy for my mother.

She was wearing a dress that her mother had made for her.

This is a real opportunity to go and do the job that we've been trained for.

I chose for these interviews Roger de Grey, Lawrence Gowing, and John Piper.

A **Fill in the gaps in the sentences below using the verbs in this list. Use each verb once.**

charge   interview   prepare   say   scan   select   test

1 He .... the horizon anxiously for his camera crew.
2 Flasks are .... for their ability to keep liquid hot or cold.
3 They never doubted that they had done their best to .... the country for war.
4 That the Escort is still the nation's bestselling car .... a lot for the power of Ford's marketing people.
5 Space engineers meet today to .... a launch date for the next space mission.
6 They .... high prices for admission and keep details of the venues secret until the last minute.
7 If you are being .... for an executive position, a dark suit and a conservative shirt and tie are essential.

B **Rewrite these sentences, using the verb given in brackets with the pattern V n *for* n or its passive. In some cases the beginning of the sentence is provided.**

1 The car probably cost him about £7,900. (pay)
   He *probably paid about £7,900 for the car.*
2 The course did not give her the skills needed for a new career. (equip)
   ....
3 Ashton decided that Diana Adams should dance the ballerina role. (choose)
   ....
4 A child's admission is $4 and an adult admission is $7 at all of our local cinemas. (charge)
   All of our local cinemas ....
5 I think we should go all over the house, looking for clues. (search)
   ....
6 She was not interested in the magazine. (hold)
   The magazine ....
7 It has been decided that the next meeting will be held on Monday. (schedule)
   The next meeting ....

C **Put the different parts of these sentences in the right order.**

1 an ambulance / waited / for / 53 minutes / she ....
2 I / for / interesting pieces of clothing / scour / second-hand shops ....
3 was nominated / for / Ingrid / an Academy Award as best actress ....
4 this product / I / for / don't recommend / long hair ....
5 my doctor / wants / for / me / diabetes / to be tested ....
6 for / this is / what / not / was intended / the grant ....

Verbs used with *from*: 1

1 Some verbs are followed by a prepositional phrase which consists of *from* and a noun group. For example, in *We will all benefit from this change*, the verb *benefit* is followed by the preposition *from* and the noun group *this change*. This pattern is **V *from* n**. With some verbs, the preposition is sometimes followed by an '-ing' clause.

	Verb group	*from*	noun group/-ing clause
They	could not escape	from	the country.
Fitness	comes	from	working against gravity.
She	could borrow	from	her family.

Verbs with this pattern belong to the following meaning groups:

■ **verbs indicating that someone or something leaves or comes from a place, thing, or person**

back away	emerge	issue	run away	vanish
break away	escape	return	separate	withdraw
depart	fall	rise	split off	
drain	get away	rise up	transfer	

*The last bus **will depart** from the stadium at 9.30pm.*

*She's going to destroy me. I **have to get away** from her.*

■ **verbs used when indicating the cause, source, or origin of something**

arise	derive	flow	result	stem
come	develop	follow	spring	

*Heavy drinking often **results** from feeling stressed or overworked.*

*They will enjoy the sense of security which **stems** from knowing how to deal with emergencies when they occur.*

In the case of *arise*, *come*, and *result*, the preposition *from* is sometimes followed by a noun group and an '-ing' clause.

*Conflict **results** from A trying to grab something belonging to B.*

■ **verbs indicating that someone gets something from a source.** The thing that is obtained is not explicitly mentioned.

borrow	import	quote

*That's why it's so expensive to **borrow** from finance companies.*

■ **verbs indicating that someone gets a benefit of some kind from something**

benefit	gain	learn

*Many areas of the world **would** actually **gain** from global warming.*

*I'm sure our players **would benefit** from having fewer matches.*

■ **verbs concerned with not doing something, stopping doing something, or not wanting to do something**

keep	retire	shy away
refrain	shrink	withdraw

*But he stressed he had no intention of **retiring** from politics yet.*

*He never **shrank** from a fight, and he actively sought new challenges.*

*We **refrain** from giving advice unless it is asked for.*

With *keep*, the preposition *from* is always followed by an '-ing' clause.

*She bit her lip to **keep** from crying out.*

■ **verbs concerned with having something such as an illness or a shock**

die	recover	suffer

*He **is suffering** from cancer.*

■ **verbs concerned with being or becoming different**

differ	evolve	stand out

*The culture of the south **differs** from that of the north in many ways.*

Different forms of the pattern

*They are sure that the illness **from which** they **are suffering** is a purely physical illness.*

A Match up the two halves of each sentence.

1 It is good to be able to learn ...
2 The hydrogen, being light, will escape ...
3 Most of these settlements developed ...
4 In 1975, John Lennon withdrew ...
5 They can't borrow ...
6 Each year 35,000 British smokers die ...
7 Whales evolved ...
8 I saw Andrew emerge ...

a ... from heart disease.
b ... from the doorway.
c ... from his career altogether.
d ... from banks any more.
e ... from agricultural centres.
f ... from a crisis.
g ... from the atmosphere.
h ... from four-legged mammals.

B Fill in the gaps in the sentences below using the verbs in this list. Use each verb once.

benefit   come   flow   import   keep   recover   refrain   retire   stand out   vanish

1 She is going to have to work hard to .... from the crowd.
2 All grief and despair .... from her face as quickly as a summer rain.
3 She may never fully .... from her horrific burn injuries.
4 We .... from a major manufacturer in America, the home of the mountain bike.
5 Ten years from now I expect I will .... from politics.
6 She fell against his shoulder and held on to him to .... from falling.
7 Mrs Hardie .... from making any comment.
8 Most applications .... from people seeking money to cover their rent or mortgages.
9 Large revenue gains .... from relatively modest increases in taxes.
10 It was announced that Kenya will .... from a sixty million dollar grant from Washington.

C Rewrite each of the following pairs of sentences as one sentence, using a relative clause as shown.

1 There was a huge crack in the floor. Puffs of steam issued from it.
   There was a huge crack in the floor, from which puffs of steam issued.
2 Our hero sustained wounds in battle. He later died from them.
   ....
3 They are in the grip of a dreadful power. They cannot escape from it.
   ....
4 Richard has recently had a bad bout of flu. He needs to recover from it.
   ....
5 Education is an investment. Everyone benefits from it.
   ....
6 She has been staying with her husband. She separated from him five months ago.
   ....

1 Here are some more common verbs which are followed by the preposition _from_ and a noun group:

choose	date	deviate	hear	take over

You **will** also **be able to choose** from a range of topics such as Business Language, Language in the Media, and Grammar.

The building **dates** from the middle of the last century.

Lady Thatcher **will take over** from the university's first chancellor, Lord Hailsham.

Hear is sometimes used in the passive.

They **have not been heard** from since.

Choose often has the following form of the pattern.

There are **plenty of designs** to **choose** from.

2 Some verbs are followed by a prepositional phrase beginning with _from_ and another prepositional phrase beginning with _to_. This pattern is **V _from_ n _to_ n**.

Verbs with this pattern belong to the following meaning groups:

■ **verbs indicating that someone stops doing or using one thing and starts doing or using another**

change	change over	move	switch	turn

I find it easy to **switch** from one role to the other.

Health is another reason for **turning** from tap water to mineral water.

■ **verbs indicating that someone or something becomes different**

change	turn

Her attitude to the town **had changed** from resentment to a feeling of belonging and involvement.

With both these verbs, the second preposition is sometimes _into_ instead of _to_.

I watched little Molly **turn** from a baby into a child.

■ **verbs used when indicating a range**

range	vary

Hundreds of them were given expert advice on problems **ranging** from debt to credit card management.

The cost **varies** from £25 to £85 per session.

■ _Last_ and _pass_ also have this pattern.

It has appeared very difficult for such diseases to **pass** from one species to another.

We are now in the peak hay fever season, which **lasts** from May to July.

3 Some verbs are followed by a prepositional phrase which consists of _from_ and a noun group referring to an amount, and another prepositional phrase which consists of _to_ and a noun group referring to an amount. This pattern is **V _from_ amount _to_ amount**.

Verbs with this pattern indicate that a quantity or level increases or decreases.

climb	drop	jump	shrink	soar
come down	fall	plummet	sink	tumble
decline	go down	plunge	slide	widen
dip	go up	rise	slip	
dive	increase	shoot up	slump	

Inflation **has increased** from 8.9 per cent to 9 per cent.

My wages **will come down** from just under £270 a week to about £210.

Practice

A Match up the two halves of each sentence.

1 Guests may choose ...
2 Most ancient fossils date ...
3 It is forbidden to deviate ...
4 I would like to hear ...
5 Civilian leaders took over ...

a ... from about six-hundred-and-fifty-million years ago.
b ... from the military a dozen years ago.
c ... from these rules.
d ... from ten hot dishes and twenty cold dishes.
e ... from boys and girls aged 14-16.

B In the sentences below, put a dotted line under the verb used with *from* and *to*.
Then underline each of the other parts of the pattern.

1 OPEC has seen its share of the the world oil market drop from two thirds to one third.
2 What were the most difficult things about changing over from the one school to the other?
3 Now the labs are attempting to turn from weapons of mass destruction to more peaceful industries.
4 The Multi-Cultural Programmes Department makes a wide range of programmes varying from topical current affairs to popular entertainment.
5 The 93-day event will last from August 7 to November 7.

C Think of a way to complete each sentence.

1 What is required is a job structure in which people can move from part-time to ....
2 The exhibited artists range from established names to ....
3 The beach barbecues last from dusk to ....
4 Our experience of life can change from something approaching hell to ....
5 In the past two weeks, the British have switched from red meat to ....

D Complete these sentences using the verb and figures given in brackets and the pattern **V *from* amount *to* amount**.

1 Despite improved sales, Densitron International's pre-tax profits
   slipped from £550,000 to £376,000 .... (slip / £376,000 / £550,000)

2 Next year, Elland Road Stadium's capacity will temporarily
   .... (fall / 30,000 / 32,728)

3 With imports continuing to rise, the trade deficit has
   .... (widen / $5 billion / $9.3 billion)

4 For the past 25 years, the business has seen its workforce
   .... (shrink / nine / 16 people)

5 Truck production is likely to
   .... (decline / 260,000 / 276,000)

6 Weekly production of Range Rovers
   .... (go up / 350 / 370)

7 Pre-tax profits are expected to
   .... (climb / £98 million / £105 million)

8 Unemployment has
   .... (soar / over 300,000 / near zero)

55 Verbs used with *from*: 3

Some verbs are followed by a noun group and a prepositional phrase which consists of *from* and a noun group. For example, in *I borrowed the money from my father*, the verb *borrow* is followed by the noun group *the money*, the preposition *from*, and the noun group *my father*. This pattern is **V n *from* n**. With some verbs, the preposition is sometimes followed by an '-ing' clause.

Active pattern

	Verb group	noun group	*from*	noun group/-ing clause
He	borrowed	money	from	friends.
He	saved	her	from	having a breakdown.

Passive pattern

	Verb group	*from*	noun group/-ing clause
Egypt	has been eliminated	from	the World Cup.
They	were spared	from	watching England lose.

(With phrasal verbs, the particle comes either after the noun group or after the verb.)

Verbs with this pattern belong to the following meaning groups:

- **verbs indicating that someone gets something from someone or somewhere, or tries to get it**

acquire	collect	draw	inherit	seek
borrow	demand	gain	learn	select
choose	derive	get	obtain	steal

Often they just **cannot get** money **from** anyone.

He says he **has been demanding** more support **from the other agencies**.

A number of documents **were stolen from the building**. (passive)

In the case of *learn*, the noun group following the verb is often an **amount**.

I **learned** a lot **from** him.

- **verbs concerned with removing someone or something from somewhere**

chase	divert	pull	take	wipe
clear	drain	remove	take away	withdraw
dismiss	eliminate	strip	tear away	

He's in a stable condition after having surgery to **remove a blood clot from the brain**.

He **wiped** the sweat **from** his forehead.

She **couldn't tear** herself **away from** the radio.

She **had been dismissed** from her job at the university a year earlier. (passive)

- **verbs concerned with not including someone or something**

exclude	omit

Their names **had been omitted from the voting lists**. (passive)

- **verbs concerned with separating someone or something from something, physically or metaphorically**

distinguish	isolate	mark out	set apart
divide	mark off	separate	

Unfortunately, he appears unable to **distinguish** fantasy **from reality**.

Should the offender **be separated** from her children and sent to prison? (passive)

- **verbs indicating that someone frees or rescues someone from a dangerous or unpleasant situation**

deliver	release	save
free	rescue	spare

The band are currently trying to **free themselves from their contract with their record company**.

Fire-fighting ships are still trying to **save a Norwegian supertanker from sinking** off the coast of Texas.

Three other people **were rescued from the sea** by defence force officers. (passive)

A In the sentences below, put a dotted line under the verb used with *from* (see this Unit and Unit 53). Then underline each of the other parts of the pattern. (For different forms of the pattern, see Unit 56.)

1 The Netherlands differs from other EC states in that there are many English speaking companies.
2 Who did you learn your chess from?
3 Mark has separated from Annette, so he and I will be sharing a place in Studio City.
4 I must watch carefully, and learn from my father's example.
5 The shock was so profound that it seemed to drain all strength from her.
6 You have to choose your basic design from a few previously drawn by the computer.
7 Think about the word RELAX and let the tension drain from your stomach.
8 With the commander's help we separated the police from the journalists.
9 Apart from her professor's salary, she had money that she had inherited from her father.
10 Fired by this motivation, we are likely to eliminate from our behaviour all that is socially unacceptable.

B Fill in the gaps in the sentences below using the verbs in this list. Use each verb once.

borrow   collect   divide   exclude   get   pull   save   take away

1 Many people cease to have migraine attacks if they .... certain foodstuffs from their diets.
2 Ian, from Manchester, was .... unconscious from the water and is now recovering.
3 You can now .... your boarding pass from the domestic Executive Club Lounge.
4 They worked side by side to help .... dolphins from being killed by tuna fishermen.
5 President Juarez .... the Church from the government to reduce its power.
6 The family raised half the price itself and .... the rest from the bank.
7 In a bid to beat the terrorists, litter bins have been .... from airport terminals.
8 He said that he'd .... my name from a newspaper article.

C Rewrite the following sentences using the verb given in brackets with the pattern **V n *from* n** or its passive.

1 Dr. Brandon began to take the fossils out of the trunk. (remove)
   Dr. Brandon began to remove the fossils from the trunk.
2 They need to think of ways in which they can keep the good guys and the bad guys apart. (separate)
   ....
3 He was let out of prison this afternoon after £19,000 bail was paid over. (free)
   ....
4 He was charged with using his influence to take out loans with two government-owned banks. (acquire)
   ....
5 He got the recorder out of his shirt and adjusted it. (take)
   ....

1 Here are some more groups of verbs which are followed by a noun group and a prepositional phrase beginning with *from*:

- **verbs concerned with stopping someone from doing something**

ban	discourage	prevent	restrict
bar	keep	prohibit	stop

The preposition *from* is usually followed by an '-ing' clause rather than a noun group.

*The doctors tried to **stop me from going in** but I ignored them.*

*He **was banned** from driving for three years.* (passive)

- **verbs indicating that someone hides or keeps something, usually information, from someone**

conceal	hide	keep

*She quickly realized that it was virtually impossible to **conceal** her family background from her fellow students.*

- **verbs indicating that someone makes something from a particular material or thing**

carve	create	make	produce
construct	fashion	manufacture	

*Father explained how to **make glass from sand**.*

- *Protect* also has this pattern.

*You **can protect** yourself from attack by using an insect repellent.*

Different forms of the pattern

*Where **did** you **get** that idea from?*

*He knew that he could not pay back the money he **had stolen** from his companies.*

*Their idea is to **exclude** from the election any group that breaks the ceasefire.*

2 Some verbs are followed by a noun group and two prepositional phrases, the first beginning with *from* and the second beginning with *to*. This pattern is **V n *from* n *to* n**.

Verbs with this pattern belong to the following meaning groups:

- **verbs concerned with moving someone or something from one place or level to another**

divert	pass	promote	send	transfer

*A colleague tried to **send** a parcel from Cardiff to London.*

*He **was promoted** from eighth to third place.* (passive)

With these verbs, the second preposition is sometimes *into*.

*We can even arrange for your bank to **transfer** funds from your account into the trust account each month.*

- **verbs indicating that someone increases or lowers an amount**

increase	lower	raise	reduce

*The bank **lowered** its discount rate from 3.75 per cent to 3.25 per cent.*

*The pensionable age for men and women **was raised** from 60 to 65.* (passive)

- **verbs concerned with changing something from one thing to another**

change	transform	translate	turn

*She **changed** her name from Blanca to Bianca.*

With these verbs, the second preposition is sometimes *into*.

*They are attempting to **transform** their country from a totalitarian state into a democracy.*

With *translate*, the second preposition is always *into*.

*His grandfather **translated** science books from German into English.*

A Rewrite these sentences, starting with the words provided. Use the verb given in brackets with *from* and an '-ing' clause.

1 Large crowds surrounded polling booths and people were unable to vote. (prevent)
Large crowds *surrounded polling booths and prevented people from voting.*

2 People are not allowed to ask for money on the city streets at night. (prohibit)
People ....

3 Because of his good manners, he did not tell her what he really thought. (kept)
His good manners ....

4 Some couples don't marry because of the tax and social security laws. (discourage)
The tax and social security laws ....

5 Renaissance artists were highly original, despite the conservative environment. (stop)
The conservative environment ....

6 Shell Australia will not allow its customers to use mobile phones at its service stations. (ban)
Shell Australia's customers ....

B Rewrite these sentences, starting with the words provided. Use the pattern **V n *from* n *to* n**.

1 Nuclear Electric's workforce will fall from 12,394 to just 9,000 over the next three years. (reduce)
Nuclear Electric *will reduce its workforce from 12,394 to just 9,000 over the next three years.*

2 Under the administration plan, the grant would go up from $2,400 to $3,700. (raise)
The administration plan ....

3 The Conservative majority rose from one to thirty-five. (increase)
The Conservatives ....

4 The price has gone down from $115 to $90. (lower)
Wine merchants ....

C Put the different parts of these sentences in the right order.

1 Joey / tried / to hide / she / from / her despondency ....

2 their children / are supposed / harm / from / parents / to protect

....

3 plants / from / are able to manufacture / water / their own food

....

4 from / delegates / entering the hall / were barred ....

5 sheep's teeth / necklaces / Stone Age settlers / fashioned / from

....

6 will pass / to / twenty-six small satellites / simple digital messages / from / place / place

....

7 the president / the highest tax rate / 31 per cent / 28 per cent / is prepared / to increase / from / to

....

8 French / Rachid Boudjedra / translated / Arabic / into / from / his novels

....

Verbs used with *in*: 1

Some verbs are followed by a prepositional phrase which consists of *in* and a noun group. For example, in *They believe in democracy*, the verb *believe* is followed by the preposition *in* and the noun group *democracy*. This pattern is **V *in* n**. With some verbs, the preposition is sometimes followed by an '-ing' clause.

	Verb group	*in*	noun group/-ing clause
She	lectures	in	economics.
Drugs	can help	in	lowering the level of cholesterol.

Verbs with this pattern belong to the following meaning groups:

■ **verbs concerned with being in or entering a thing, group, or situation**

appear	go	lie	rank	sit
belong	land	move	ride	

*Over the past few years, he **has sat** in Parliament as an independent Social Democrat.*

*Fifty-year-olds **don't** really **belong** in the same category as their mothers of 70.*

*World champion Lance Armstrong **is** currently **lying** in third place.*

■ **verbs indicating that someone has a feeling or thought**. The feeling or thought is the Subject.

live	live on	rise	stick	stir

*Panic started to **rise** in my throat.*

*It is something that **will live** in my memory for the rest of my life.*

■ **verbs concerned with being involved in something or taking part in an activity**

act	compete	help	join	star
aid	engage	interfere	participate	
appear	feature	intervene	share	
assist	figure	invest	stand	

*The job gave her a chance to **participate** in sales and product development.*

*The sales staff **can assist** in making selections.*

*He has not yet announced whether he **will stand** in the election.*

*You do not have the right to **interfere** in our internal affairs.*

■ **verbs indicating that someone is successful or unsuccessful**

fail	succeed

*Local residents **had failed** in an attempt to have the march banned.*

In the case of *succeed*, the preposition *in* is often followed by an '-ing' clause.

*I finally **succeeded** in getting him out of the room.*

■ **verbs concerned with learning or teaching a subject**

graduate	lecture	major	qualify	train

*He now **lectures** in crime prevention at various London colleges.*

*He went to a junior college and **majored** in computer programming.*

■ **verbs concerned with trading or work**

deal	specialize	trade

*He **specializes** in treating epileptics and schizophrenics.*

*He **deals** in antiques and fine art.*

UNIT 57 Practice

A In the sentences below, put a dotted line under the verb used with *in*. Then underline each of the other parts of the pattern. (For different forms of the pattern, see Unit 58.)

1 Brought up in the Midlands, she graduated in English and Drama from Manchester University.
2 The negotiators say environmental protection does not belong in a trade agreement.
3 In my feverish state, one image stuck in my mind.
4 Sainsbury's, Tesco and Safeway have between them £1.4 billion of equity capital to assist in their development programmes.
5 He had been warned in writing not to deal in shares between January and March.
6 Okay, so you know what you want out of a fund and what type of fund you want to invest in.
7 The author suggests that this is the area in which future development lies.

B Fill in the gaps in these sentences using *in* or *with* (see Unit 83). Sometimes both are possible.

1 Kendall called me into his office to put together a plan to deal .... the crisis.
2 He had interfered .... the country's internal affairs by criticizing the conduct of local elections.
3 Johnson will be unable to compete .... the world junior championships next year because of her age.
4 She hired two consultants to help .... the search for a new school superintendent.
5 California and Florida were the only states to rank .... the top ten in all three categories.
6 I had ideas and information that belonged .... police hands.

C Rewrite the sentences below using the verbs in this list. Use each verb once. Use *in* with a noun group or an '-ing' clause.

    aid   figure   lecture   star   stick   succeed   trade

1 Piloo was a professor of English Literature at the universities of Bombay and Delhi.
Piloo lectured in English Literature at the universities of Bombay and Delhi.
2 Fred Astaire and Jack Buchanan take the lead roles in this tale of a song-and-dance man.
....
3 He buys and sells vintage posters, brochures, and other memorabilia.
....
4 He did not manage to publish his book.
....
5 Yoga can be helpful in the prevention, cure and management of many diseases.
....
6 Their plans don't include marriage.
Marriage ....
7 I have remembered that incident all these years, and now I know why.
That incident ....

Verbs used with *in*: 2

Here are some more groups of verbs which are followed by the preposition *in* and a noun group or an '-ing' clause:

■ **verbs concerned with enjoying something or feeling good about something**

bask	delight	exult	rejoice	revel

*Soviet journalists **revelled** in their new freedom to probe and to criticize.*

*He **delights** in stirring up controversy and strife.*

■ **verbs concerned with belief**

believe	trust

*I **don't believe** in coincidences.*

■ **verbs indicating what something abstract consists of or involves**

consist	lie

*Most people think that happiness **consists** in experiencing pleasure.*

*As with so many other aspects of a relationship, the solution **lies** in communication.*

■ **verbs indicating that something or someone suddenly starts to be in a different state**

break out	come out	go up

The range of noun groups used after *in* is quite restricted. *Break out* and *come out* are followed by phrases such as *in spots* and *in a sweat*; *go up* is followed by *in flames* and *in smoke*.

*They either **come out** in spots, grow too much hair where they don't want it or go bald!*

*The whole place **went up** in flames.*

■ **verbs concerned with beginning and ending. The prepositional phrase indicates the situation or event at the beginning or end of something.**

begin	culminate	end

*His tenure of office **began** in confusion when his predecessor refused to go.*

*Andrew's first marriage **ended** in disaster.*

In the case of *culminate* and *end*, the preposition *in* is sometimes followed by a noun group and an '-ing' clause.

*They had an argument, which **culminated** in Tom getting drunk and beating her in front of all the customers.*

■ **verbs indicating that something increases, decreases, or is different in some way**

change	decrease	drop	go down	rise
come down	differ	fall	go up	shrink
decline	double	gain	increase	vary

*Gasoline, for instance, **has gone up** in price in the last week.*

*This frees manufacturers from relying on natural supplies, which **can vary** in quality.*

■ **other common verbs**

come	dress	persist
confide	dress up	result

*The badges **come** in 20 different colours and shapes.*

*I wish she **would confide** in me.*

*She always **dresses** in black.*

*It was too beautiful a day to **persist** in such efforts.*

*The operation **resulted** in the arrest of one alleged kidnapper and the death of another from gunshot wounds.*

In the case of *persist*, the preposition *in* is sometimes followed by an '-ing' clause.

*Even though he's happy with her weight, she **persists** in dieting.*

In the case of *result*, the preposition *in* is sometimes followed by a noun group and an '-ing' clause.

*These circumstances **may result** in a child being taken away from its family for good.*

Different forms of the pattern

*What events **did** you **specialize** in?*

*People should be prepared to stand up for **the things** they **believe** in.*

A Fill in the gaps in the sentences below using the verbs in this list. Use each verb once.

believe   consist   double   dress up   end   go up   rejoice   result

1 Thieves watched thousands of pounds .... in smoke after accidentally setting fire to the contents of a shop safe.

2 An international conference on global warming has .... in controversy.

3 Dr. Spock cautioned that a lack of vitamins could .... in reduced body size.

4 Do you .... in love at first sight?

5 The next task .... in listing the questions to be answered.

6 High-street store The Gap intends to .... in size over the next four years.

7 She asked a group of students to .... in different costumes and wigs so that they all looked different from each other.

8 I .... in the simple pleasures that are available all the time.

B Fill in the gaps in these sentences using *in* or *from* (see Unit 54).

1 The Chinese yuan has fallen .... value by 25 per cent this month.

2 Detached houses, however, went up .... price by a multiple of 14.9.

3 The number of horses in his care has risen .... eight to 20.

4 The US dollar has gone down .... value recently and that makes US goods more attractive to foreigners.

5 Wage inflation fell .... 15 to less than four per cent, but unemployment still rose.

6 A course of treatment varies .... length as it depends on your body's needs.

7 The temperature had dropped .... 20 degrees to four, on the coldest May day on record.

8 The response of the audience varied .... outright rejection to warm hospitality.

C Complete the second of each pair of sentences using the information contained in the first sentence. Use the verb with *in*, a noun group, and an '-ing' clause.

1 He left her.
Rumours of problems culminated in ...*him leaving her.*...

2 People will have several occupations during their lifetimes.
These changes will eventually result in ....

3 She was removed from power.
Her policies led to a growing anger against her, which ended in ....

4 He took an overdose of sleeping tablets.
He went through a rebellious phase which culminated in ....

5 He was sued for libel.
His fearless campaigning for racial justice resulted in ....

6 She was attacked by robbers.
He persuaded her to take the trip to Egypt which ended in ....

Verbs used with *in*: 3

Some verbs are followed by a noun group and a prepositional phrase which consists of *in* and a noun group. For example, in *He dipped a biscuit in his tea*, the verb *dip* is followed by the noun group *a biscuit*, the preposition *in*, and the noun group *his tea*. This pattern is **V n *in* n**.

Active pattern

	Verb group	noun group	*in*	noun group
They	threw	him	in	jail.
She	covered	his car	in	paint.
	Include	your partner	in	your activities.

Passive pattern

	Verb group	*in*	noun group
The machine	will be encased	in	concrete.
The biscuits	were packed	in	airtight tins.

Verbs with this pattern belong to the following meaning groups:

■ **verbs concerned with putting, moving, or keeping something somewhere, either physically or metaphorically**

concentrate	immerse	keep	place	stick
dip	include	land	put	throw
enter	insert	lock	settle	
fix	invest	pack	shut	

*Wash the fish fillets and dry them, then **dip them in the beaten egg**.*

*We **locked** her in the bathroom.*

*Several of them **could be placed** in the category of 'high flyer'.* (passive)

*More than 100 stitches **were inserted** in her head during the surgery.* (passive)

■ **verbs concerned with covering or enclosing something in something**

coat	cover	encase	enclose	wrap

__Wrap the chicken in foil__ and bake for 2 hours.

■ **verbs concerned with someone becoming involved in an activity**

be caught up	employ	engage	include	involve

*He has already started to **involve** himself in the country's domestic political issues.*

*I went and **engaged** her in conversation.*

The preposition *in* is sometimes followed by an '-ing' clause.

*Riding in the car offers a wonderful opportunity to **engage** your child in observing the surroundings.*

■ **verbs indicating that someone takes part in an activity along with someone else**

assist	help	join	lead

*We **assist** students in their search for employment.*

*Why **do** you **not join** your friends in the fight against Fascism?*

The preposition *in* is sometimes followed by an '-ing' clause.

*The leader strikes a bell three times and **leads** the others in chanting something in a foreign language.*

■ **verbs indicating that someone concentrates very hard on something**

bury	immerse	lose

The noun group following the verb is always a reflexive pronoun.

*I **immersed** myself in the writings of this remarkable Japanese writer.*

*Imaginative children **lose** themselves in fantasy worlds through stories.*

A Match up the two halves of each sentence.

1 Eden returned to Cairo to join the others ...
2 Please don't keep us ...
3 They covered the armchairs ...
4 The police should throw them ...
5 He packed papers ...
6 These factories employ disabled people ...
7 He said he included his name ...

a ... in prison.
b ... in the bottom of the case and shirts on top.
c ... in the message so he could be contacted.
d ... in keeping an eye on the situation.
e ... in a turquoise-and-white striped material.
f ... in suspense.
g ... in productive work.

B In the sentences below, put a dotted line under the verb used with *in*. Then underline each of the other parts of the pattern. (For different forms of the pattern, see Unit 60.)

1 One delegate said it was important to involve members in policy making.
2 Since her divorce last year, she has buried herself in charity work.
3 The children will be caught up in the excitement.
4 Tommy began carefully folding up the brown paper in which the painting had been wrapped.
5 Maybe she could just shut him in his room while Robert was visiting.
6 Similar devices had been placed in several hotels in the area.
7 The 50,000 brochures we inserted in Cycling Weekly in February were well received.
8 I assisted Phil in getting control of his own life situation.
9 Some recipes tell you to coat the meat in flour first.
10 I would include in this category organizing social events such as the Christmas party.

C Rewrite the sentences using the verb given in brackets with *in* and an '-ing' clause.

1 We must reverse this process if we want the students to learn. (engage)
  We must reverse this process if we want to engage the students in learning.

2 I'm concentrating on writing music. (bury)
  ....

3 She admits helping her boss to shred important documents. (assist)
  ....

4 He and Franklin issued radio messages together. (join)
  ....

5 Some 500 people are currently building the dam. (be employed)
  ....

6 Irving Berlin sang 'God Bless America' and the audience sang with him. (lead)
  ....

Verbs used with *in*: 4

Here are some more groups of verbs which are followed by a noun group and a prepositional phrase beginning with *in*:

■ **verbs indicating that someone hits or injures someone else.** The prepositional phrase indicates the part of the body that is harmed.

| bite | kick | shoot | stab |
| hit | punch | smash | strike |

The noun group after *in* usually begins with *the*.

*He **was stabbed** in the back.* (passive)

*The fiery actress punched him on the nose and **kicked** him in the shins.*

■ **verbs concerned with making a hole in something**

| bore | drill | gouge | punch |

*The researchers **drilled** small holes in the pipes at 1-metre intervals.*

■ **verbs concerned with dividing something into pieces**

| break | cut | slice | split |
| chop | divide | snap | tear |

*I **tore** the letter in pieces.*

The preposition *in* is sometimes followed by a fraction or number.

***Divide** the pastry in half.*

■ **verbs indicating that someone has a particular feeling or attitude with regard to something**

| find | hold | place | put | take |

*Her parents **will find** comfort in the fact that they have been blessed with a large family.*

*He said he **was placing** his faith in prayer.*

The preposition *in* is sometimes followed by an '-ing' clause.

*How **could** anyone **find** pleasure in hunting and killing this beautiful creature?*

With the verb *hold*, the prepositional phrase indicates the person's attitude.

*Little by little you'll come to hate me and **hold** me in contempt.*

■ **verbs indicating that someone or something causes someone to feel an emotion**

| arouse | stir |

*He urged people to avoid any action which **could arouse** fear or passion in others.*

■ **other common verbs**

| interest | be ranked | tie |
| lead | see | train |

*Australia **leads** the world in modern winemaking techniques.*

*Throughout the Seventies she **was ranked** in Britain's top ten.* (passive)

*It **was tied** in a knot.* (passive)

In the case of *interest*, *lead*, *see*, and *train*, the preposition *in* is sometimes followed by an '-ing' clause.

*Some salesmen tried to **interest** me in buying property here.*

*The militants **see** no contradiction in using violence to bring about a religious state.*

The verb *be ranked* is often followed by an ordinal and a prepositional phrase beginning with *in*.

*Gul **is ranked** eighth in the world.*

Different forms of the pattern

*They could probably get back some of **the money** they**'d invested** in the album.*

*The thought **aroused** in Isaacs a sense of excitement.*

Practice

A Fill in the gaps in the sentences below using the verbs in this list. Use each verb once.

divide   drill   hold   be ranked   see   shoot   stir   take

1 The New Yorkers .... delight in explaining the intricacies of their city.
2 Although she .... in the top five, she was relatively little known.
3 It is very difficult to .... somebody in the arm.
4 Soccer can .... great passions in men from all walks of life.
5 The Port Authority wants to .... a hole in the roof above this parking garage.
6 She .... no point in visiting the school now Martin had settled down.
7 They both .... him in great affection and respect.
8 The food is so plentiful you can .... a lunch in two and save half for dinner.

B Rewrite these sentences using the pattern **V n *in* n**.

1 He took a knife from his car and stabbed her neck.
He took a knife from his car and stabbed her in the neck.
2 So I took my lunch box and tried to hit Rab's face with it.
....
3 Get off my property before I come out there and punch your nose.
....
4 Nicky, the singer, tried to kick his face.
....
5 A consultant yesterday admitted he had struck his fiancee's face with a bunch of flowers.
....
6 Dewey's chest was bitten twice by two rattlesnakes.
....

C Rewrite these sentences using the verb and noun group given in brackets. Sometimes the noun group follows the verb and sometimes it follows *in*.

1 They talked a lot and enjoyed each other's company. (find / pleasure)
They talked a lot and found pleasure in each other's company.
2 We may despise him, but he might be the only viable president. (hold / contempt)
....
3 From the outset he had trusted me, the son of his old friend. (put / his trust)
....
4 The public tend to have little respect for architects. (hold / low esteem)
....
5 I am comforted by the fact that earnings are up this year. (find / comfort)
....
6 I always enjoy giving photographers my most radiant smile. (take / delight)
....

Verbs used with *into*: 1

Some verbs are followed by a prepositional phrase which consists of *into* and a noun group. For example, in *He bumped into a chair*, the verb *bump* is followed by the preposition *into* and the noun group *a chair*. This pattern is **V into n**.

	Verb group	*into*	noun group
The plane	broke	into	pieces.
Mike	sank	into	suicidal depression.

Verbs with this pattern belong to the following meaning groups:

■ verbs indicating that something becomes something else

change	develop	evolve	grow	turn
convert	escalate	form	merge	

*With her care, he **grew** into a normal, healthy child.*

*Caterpillars **turn** into butterflies.*

■ verbs indicating that something breaks or divides into pieces or groups

break	divide	shatter	split
crumble	separate	smash	

*The plane hit the ground and **broke** into three pieces.*

■ verbs indicating that one person or thing collides with another

bang	crash	slam
bump	run	smash

*The spokesman said both vehicles **crashed** into a burned-out car.*

■ verbs concerned with someone entering a place

book	check	crowd	move	pile
break	cram	dive	pack	push

*We drove back to Lichfield and **booked** into a hotel.*

*Then we all **crowded** into a small restaurant and ordered a meal.*

*I want you to **move** into my apartment.*

Break is sometimes used in the passive.

*Our house **was broken** into earlier this year.*

■ verbs indicating that someone or something disappears or is not noticeable

blend	fade away	merge
fade	melt	vanish

***Does** the new housing stick out like a sore thumb or **blend** into its surroundings?*

■ verbs concerned with pressing something or making a hole in something

bite	dig	drill	eat	sink

*He **bit** into the bread and chewed slowly.*

■ verbs indicating that someone investigates something

dig	inquire	look	probe	research

*The team **has been researching** into the genetic cause of the disease for more than six years.*

Look is sometimes used in the passive.

*He said that the matter **was being looked** into.*

■ verbs indicating that someone becomes involved in something

break	get	plunge	tumble	walk
enter	go	rush	venture	

*Always seek professional legal advice before **entering** into any agreement.*

*I'd like to **get** into management.*

■ verbs indicating that someone or something starts being in a different state or starts doing something

break	descend	fly	plunge	slip
burst	dissolve	get	retreat	
burst out	erupt	lapse	sink	
come	fall	launch	slide	

*She **burst** into tears.*

*Three days later he **slipped** into a coma and died.*

■ verbs indicating that someone puts on different clothes

change	slip

*I **changed** into my suit.*

■ *Fit* and *tap* also have this pattern.

*It's hard to see how he **would fit** into the team.*

*We'll help you **tap** into your creative energy.*

A Here are some pairs of sentences showing a verb used with the pattern **V** *into* **n** with two different meanings. Write down what each sentence means, using a verb with a different pattern.

1 a) She changed into her nightgown. *She put on her nightgown.*................................

   b) She changed into a snake. ....

2 a) He broke into song. ....

   b) Someone had broken into my house. ....

3 a) Her fingers dug into his arm. ....

   b) I've been digging into Laura's past. ....

4 a) He slipped into his bathrobe. ....

   b) He slipped into a fitful doze. ....

5 a) The plate smashed into pieces. ....

   b) His car smashed into a garden fence at 75 mph. ....

6 a) How did our schools get into this state? ....

   b) The Malloy twins got into the business at age 17. ....

B Fill in the gaps in the sentences below using the verbs in this list. Use each verb once.

bite   dissolve   fly   get   look   melt   pile   run   turn

1 You don't want to .... into trouble again, do you?

2 The nylon rope .... into his wrists.

3 The crew .... into their vehicle.

4 She .... into tears at the mention of Munya's name.

5 'She wants to be able to .... into the background,' one royal source said.

6 The two countries are sure that their border clashes will not .... into full-scale war.

7 35 people died after a commuter train .... into the back of a stationary one at about 56 kilometres per hour.

8 In the meantime, Dorset police are .... into allegations of corruption in the Metropolitan Police in London.

9 One night he plucked up the courage to ask her about it and she .... into a terrible rage.

C Match up the two halves of each sentence.

1 At San Antonio, our destination, we checked ...   a ... into a wider war.
2 The fighting could escalate ...   b ... into several pieces.
3 Sue wants to research ...   c ... into the jungles south of Jaffna.
4 The camera separated ...   d ... into the hotel.
5 Companies are now tapping ...   e ... into the huge potential for advertising.
6 The guerillas vanished ...   f ... into his family background.

Verbs used with *into*: 2

Some verbs are followed by a noun group and a prepositional phrase which consists of *into* and an '-ing' clause. For example, in *He talked me into going with him*, the verb *talk* is followed by the noun group *me*, the preposition *into*, and the clause *going with him*. This pattern is **V n *into* -ing**. The preposition is sometimes followed by a noun group instead of an '-ing' clause.

Active pattern

	Verb group	noun group	*into*	-ing clause/noun group
They	pushed	her	into	resigning.
I	provoked	him	into	a fight.

Passive pattern

	Verb group	*into*	-ing clause/noun group
They	should not be pressured	into	making hasty decisions.
She	was lured	into	a trap.

Verbs with this pattern belong to the following meaning groups:

■ verbs concerned with **making someone do something or get involved in something by using force or pressure**

blackmail	force	panic	rush
bully	frighten	press	scare
coerce	intimidate	pressure	shame
drag	manipulate	provoke	be sucked
embarrass	nag	push	terrify

*He tried to **frighten** people into doing what he wanted.*

*I **bullied** him into taking two days off and coming with me to Paris.*

*The Communist government **forced** Michael into exile in 1947.*

*The intention was to **shame** young drivers into better behaviour on the roads with the threat of a return to L-plates.*

*The British and the French have been very careful not to **be sucked** into the conflict.* (passive)

*They **will not be panicked** into making premature decisions about their tax policy.* (passive)

■ verbs concerned with **making someone do something by tricking or deceiving them**

con	fool	lure	trick
deceive	lull	trap	

*You **trapped** my son into marriage because you wanted a father for your child!*

*They had hidden the money and then **fooled** people into thinking it has been lost for ever.*

*He **may have been tricked** into carrying the explosives onto the plane.* (passive)

■ verbs concerned with **making someone do something by being nice to them in some way or by saying something that pleases them**

charm	coax	sweet talk

*He **has charmed** the local authorities into letting him buy back another family property.*

*Eileen **could be coaxed** into babysitting.* (passive)

■ verbs concerned with **persuading someone to do something, or motivating them to do it**

lure	spur	stir	tempt
persuade	steer	talk	

*He **talked** me into studying philosophy rather than history.*

*They fear that higher prices for wood **may tempt** builders into using substitute materials.*

*Gerald Smith **was spurred** into action by a dramatic television news broadcast earlier this month.* (passive)

A In the sentences below, put a dotted line under the verb used with *into*. Then underline each of the other parts of the pattern.

1 He remained motionless, fearful that any sudden movement <u>might provoke</u> <u>Graham</u> <u>into</u> <u>pulling the trigger</u>.

2 What they did not realise was that they were being lured into a trap.

3 You're not going to trick me into saying things I don't want to.

4 He was so shaken by the heavy lorries roaring past his home he was stirred into action to stop them.

5 For a start, people want to be lulled into a sense of security, false or not.

6 They scramble aboard with knives between their teeth and terrify the crew into surrender.

B These sentences show *make* used with the pattern **V n inf**. Rewrite them using the verb given in brackets with the pattern **V n *into* -ing**.

1 Janet made Ian move house. (nag)
   Janet nagged Ian into moving house.

2 Parents should not make kids take sides. (force)
   ....

3 I've just got to make my dad let me have a season ticket now. (persuade)
   ....

4 He made my parents get him a watch when he was seven. (pressure)
   ....

5 The government was trying to make him testify against my father. (coerce)
   ....

6 We made him tell us everything he knew about the robbery. (pressure)
   ....

7 He sees it as a way to make children take up the guitar. (tempt)
   ....

8 They found out about the magistrate's own wrongdoings and made him step down. (blackmail)
   ....

C These sentences say what someone did or does. Using the passive form of the verb given in brackets, write a sentence saying why they did it or do it.

1 He had changed his mind. (frighten)
   He had been frightened into changing his mind.

2 He renounced his throne after Franco chose Juan Carlos to be his successor. (talk)
   ....

3 The Government has been trying to do something about the problem. (embarrass)
   ....

4 Chinese tourists have been staying home. (scare)
   ....

5 So how did you get involved? (con)
   ....

6 Don't buy stuff just for the sake of it. (rush)
   ....

Verbs used with *into*: 3

Some verbs are followed by a noun group and a prepositional phrase which consists of *into* and a noun group. For example, in *He rolled his socks into a ball*, the verb *roll* is followed by the noun group *his socks*, the preposition *into*, and the noun group *a ball*. This pattern is *V n into n*. (With phrasal verbs, the particle comes either after the noun group or after the verb.)

Active pattern

	Verb group	noun group	*into*	noun group
His first album	Shape sent	the dough critics	into into	an oblong. fits of rapture.

Passive pattern

	Verb group	*into*	noun group
Intent	has to be translated	into	action.
Toxins	are absorbed	into	the blood.

Verbs with this pattern belong to the following meaning groups:

■ **verbs concerned with changing something into something new, or changing its form or shape**

change	make	shape	turn
convert	process	transform	weave
form	roll	translate	

*Music has the power to **change** one mood **into** another.*

*Some of my books **have been made** into movies.* (passive)

■ **verbs concerned with breaking or dividing something into smaller pieces or groups**

break	chop	divide up	slice	split
break down	chop up	resolve	slice up	split up
break up	cut	rip	smash	tear
carve	cut up	separate	smash up	
carve up	divide	shatter	sort	

*The impact **broke** the truck **into** three pieces.*

*Then I take the sausages out and **cut** them **up** into pieces.*

*The basic causes of disease **can be divided** into three groups.* (passive)

■ **verbs concerned with putting something or someone into something, either physically or metaphorically**

be absorbed	feed	lock	pump	throw
book	inject	pack	put	
dip	insert	pay	sink	
draw	introduce	plunge	stick	
enter	load	pour	stir	

*He **had booked** both of us into the local hotel.*

*Graham handed her the card and she **fed** the name **into a computer**.*

*The money **was paid** into a special account.* (passive)

■ **verbs concerned with incorporating or absorbing someone or something into a system or organization**

absorb	accept	build	incorporate	integrate

*The decision to **incorporate** the students **into** the army as a punishment was very much criticised by the independent press.*

*One needs to learn how to **build** enjoyment **into** what happens day in, day out.*

■ **verbs concerned with causing someone or something to be in a particular state or situation**

draw	fling	plunge	talk	work up
drive	get	send	throw	

*The rebels dynamited power lines, **plunging** much of the city **into** darkness.*

*More complicated events, such as speaking or attending a business meeting, **sent** me **into** a panic.*

In the case of *fling*, *throw*, and *work up*, the noun group following the verb is always a reflexive pronoun.

*She **flung** herself **into** anti-racist work.*

*She **worked** herself **up** into a bit of a state.*

■ **verbs concerned with causing something or someone to have a quality or feeling**

breathe	inject	strike

*The massive blast **struck** terror **into** thousands of innocent office workers and tourists.*

*Grace did her best to **inject** a note of welcome **into** her voice.*

Different forms of the pattern

*This created the mould **into** which the molten iron **was poured**.*

*We **must incorporate** into the budgets this possible increase in sales.*

Practice

A These sentences say what someone or something becomes or is used to make. Rewrite them using the passive form of the verb given in brackets.

1 The remaining part of the building became a chapel. (turn)
The remaining part of the building was turned into a chapel.
....

2 That area has become a public parking lot. (convert)
....

3 Everything is capable of becoming something else. (transform)
....

4 A minus can become a plus. (change)
....

5 Our country's become a battlefield. (turn)
....

6 Its fibres can be used to make rope, fabrics and fine paper. (weave)
....

7 Plums and cherries are used to make liqueurs. (make)
....

8 There may be potential for the material to be used to make compost. (process)
....

B Fill in the gaps in the sentences below using the verbs in this list. Use each verb once.

feed   inject   insert   load   pump   stick   stir   throw

1 He threatened to .... poison into her veins.
2 He .... the bayonets into the ground.
3 .... the sugar into the orange juice until it dissolves.
4 Several bags were .... into the car.
5 If he took that course he would simply be .... into prison.
6 First she .... the tape into the player and adjusted a couple of dials.
7 He vowed to .... billions of pounds into the health service, education, housing and pensions.
8 This network provides the raw information that the forecasters .... into the computers that try to predict the weather.

C Match up the two halves of each sentence.

1 This would plunge the country ...   a ... into fits of laughter.
2 My attempt to account for this sent Lawrence ... b ... into chaos.
3 The recession and hospital bills drove them ...   c ... into defeat.
4 His bluntness got him ...   d ... into bankruptcy.
6 The Prime Minister talked himself ...   e ... into an ambush.
7 They drew the police ...   f ... into a fury.
8 He worked himself up ...   g ... into trouble.

Verbs used with *like, as if,* or *as though*

1 Some verbs are followed by a prepositional phrase which consists of *like* and a noun group. For example, in *He looked like a policeman*, the verb *look* is followed by the preposition *like* and the noun group *a policeman*. This pattern is **V like n**.

	Verb group	*like*	noun group
Music	is	like	a living thing.
This place	feels	like	a prison.
He	didn't act	like	a 13-year-old.

Verbs with this pattern belong to the following meaning groups:

■ **verbs used to indicate how someone or something seems**

be	look	smell	taste
feel	seem	sound	

With all these verbs except *be* and *seem*, you may be saying that one person or thing resembles another, as in *She looks like her mother*, or you may be indicating what you think someone or something is, as in *They look like a good team*.

*He **was** like any other kid any of us knew.*

*From a distance, this **looked** like fields of snow.*

*That **sounds** like a good idea.*

*It **feels** like home already.*

Feel sometimes indicates how someone seems to themselves.

*I **feel** like a new person.*

In the case of *be* and *look*, the preposition *like* is sometimes followed by an '-ing' clause. With *look*, the '-ing' clause indicates what someone or something seems likely to do or experience.

*It **was** like being in a dream.*

*He **looks** like being made president for another year.*

■ **verbs concerned with behaviour.** The prepositional phrase indicates whose behaviour it resembles.

act	behave	dress	live	think

*If Sid wanted to **behave** like a lunatic, that was his choice.*

*We **lived** like fugitives.*

Productive use: Any verb which indicates action or behaviour can be used with this pattern.

■ *Go* also has this pattern. The preposition *like* is always followed by *this*.

*The story **goes** like this.*

■ *Feel* also has this pattern when used to indicate what someone would like to have or do.

*I **feel** like a cup of tea.*

*I **don't** really **feel** like doing any work.*

2 Some verbs are followed by a finite clause beginning with *as if* or *as though*. For example, in *I felt as if I'd been hit*, the verb *feel* is followed by the clause *as if I'd been hit*. This pattern is **V as if/as though**. In informal English, the clause sometimes begins with *like*, although some people think this is incorrect.

	Verb group	as if/as though-clause
He	sounds	as though he's enjoying it.
He	acted	as if he was expecting me.

Verbs with this pattern belong to the following meaning groups:

■ **verbs used to indicate how someone or something seems**

appear	look	smell	taste
feel	seem	sound	

*Isabel's voice **sounded** as if she had been crying.*

*You **look** like you need a rest.*

Feel usually indicates how someone seems to themselves.

*He **felt** as though he had run five miles.*

■ **verbs concerned with behaving or speaking**

act	behave	speak	talk

***Act** as if nothing had happened.*

*He **talks** as if he rules the universe.*

Productive use: Any verb which indicates action or behaviour can be used with this pattern.

A Rewrite the sentences below, changing the verb *be* to one of the verbs in this list.

feel   look   sound   taste

1 It's like a desert. ....

2 The roar of battle was like thunder. ....

3 The young leaves are edible: they are like spinach.

   ....

4 She was like a film star. ....

5 Your cotton sheets will be like silk. ....

6 This is like Russian music. ....

7 The grass beneath your feet is like a cushion.

   ....

8 This coffee is like washing-up water! ....

B *Feel* has the pattern **V *like* n** with more than one meaning. For each sentence, say whether the noun group after *like* indicates how someone seems to themselves or indicates what someone wants.

1 I feel like a fool. ...*seem*....

2 I feel like an ice cream. ....

3 I feel like a drive. ....

4 I feel like an old man. ....

5 I feel like a sandwich. ....

6 I feel like a caged lion. ....

C Fill in the gaps in the sentences below using the verbs in this list. Use each verb once.

act   dress   live   think

1 We were .... like outlaws, sleeping in the open, eating on the run.

2 When I started teaching I .... like a student and wore jeans and men's jackets.

3 Will you stop .... like a baby?

4 I can see you've started .... like a politician already.

D Match up the two halves of each sentence.

1 She looked ...	a ... as if I have cheated them.
2 This wine tastes ...	b ... as though it was on fire.
3 The air smells ...	c ... as if it cost at least twice the price.
4 I feel ...	d ... as if someone's been frying goats.
5 The house looked ...	e ... as if he was telling the truth.
6 My skin felt ...	f ... as though it was made for the big screen.
7 He sounded ...	g ... as though she might cry.
8 This film looks ...	h ... as if burglars had ransacked it.

Verbs used with *of*: 1

1 Some verbs are followed by a prepositional phrase which consists of *of* and a noun group. For example, in *She complained of a headache*, the verb *complain* is followed by the preposition *of* and the noun group *a headache*. This pattern is **V of n**. With some verbs, the preposition is sometimes followed by an '-ing' clause.

	Verb group	*of*	noun group/-ing clause
She	talked	of	killing herself.
I	do not approve	of	this change.

Verbs with this pattern belong to the following meaning groups:

■ **verbs indicating that someone talks about something**

boast	speak	tell
complain	talk	warn

He __complained__ of a ringing in his ears.

She __boasted__ of knowing all about sailing and fishing.

All these verbs except *tell* are sometimes used in the passive.

A 30 billion dollar deal __is being spoken__ of.

■ **verbs indicating that someone thinks about something or has a particular opinion of something**

approve	despair	dream
(cannot) conceive	disapprove	think

She's not even trying. I __despair__ of her!

Peter __is thinking__ of giving up teaching to become a full-time politician.

These verbs are sometimes used in the passive.

A recent poll found that the mayor __was approved__ of by 55 per cent of people.

■ **verbs indicating that someone gets or has knowledge about something**

hear	know	learn

They also __knew__ of the link between Lathan and the two journalists.

I've __heard__ of looking on the bright side of life, but this is ridiculous!

Hear is sometimes used in the passive.

They've never __been heard__ of again.

■ **verbs indicating that something smells or tastes like something else**

smell	taste

The water was refrigerated and __tasted__ of metal.

■ **other common verbs**

come	consist	die	dispose	tire

Nothing much ever __comes__ of his efforts.

The crew __consisted__ of pilot, co-pilot, navigator and flight engineer.

It appears he __died__ of natural causes.

Dispose is sometimes used in the passive.

Toxic waste __should be disposed__ of cleanly and efficiently.

In the case of *come*, *consist*, and *tire*, the preposition *of* is sometimes followed by an '-ing' clause.

One of the disembarking passengers __had tired__ of waiting for the coach and set off at a smart pace.

Different forms of the pattern

What __did__ he __die__ of?

What was the 'price' __of which__ he __spoke__?

I have __nothing__ to __complain__ of.

2 A number of verbs with the pattern **V of n** are sometimes followed by *of*, a noun group, and an '-ing' clause. They are concerned with talking, thinking, and knowing.

We __talked__ of him getting a summer job.

She __disapproves__ of me talking to you.

The president admitted that he __did not know__ of any rebels having surrendered so far.

3 Three verbs are followed by a prepositional phrase beginning with *of* and another prepositional phrase which consists of *as* and a noun group, '-ing' clause, or adjective group.

These verbs are concerned with regarding or describing someone or something as a particular thing.

speak	talk	think

She __speaks__ of her family as a 'great support system'.

Some __talk__ of her as being arrogant and unfriendly.

I __don't think__ of myself as abnormal, just unusual.

Practice

A Match up the two halves of each sentence.

1 Did he die ...
2 61 percent of Americans disapprove ...
3 I dream ...
4 Why does Grandma's house always smell ...
5 I wish I'd thought ...
6 It has become commonplace to talk ...
7 Villagers complained ...
8 I was sorry to learn ...

a ... of going to law school.
b ... of suffocation?
c ... of the death of William Towns.
d ... of it twenty years ago.
e ... of the president's handling of the economy.
f ... of flowers being stolen from the churchyard.
g ... of America as the sole remaining superpower.
h ... of cooking?

B In the sentences below, put a dotted line under the verb used with a pattern described in this Unit. Then underline each of the other parts of the pattern.

1 Those who know Mick never tire of his singing.
2 The country talked of nothing else and seemed to watch nothing else.
3 They simply cannot conceive of anyone objecting to the way they work.
4 Analysts warn of the risk in releasing a low-budget film during an economic recession.
5 Do you approve of Britain following this path?
6 Glenn's friends speak of him as a man who always wanted to help other people.
7 90 percent of all the poisonous garbage generated in this country is disposed of on site.
8 Do you have to go out and buy a type of saucepan you've never even heard of?

C Use the first sentence in each pair to complete the second, so that the verb is followed by *of*, a noun group and an '-ing' clause.

1 Sandra gave up her career.
   Matt approved *of Sandra giving up her career.* ....

2 Her son was causing noise.
   Neighbours complained ....

3 Something was wrong at the football match.
   It was the first I knew ....

4 Children are growing up with breathing difficulties.
   He spoke ....

5 Love was her religion.
   At one point she talked ....

6 She had come home.
   She knew others would soon hear ....

7 Perhaps he'll find me.
   I often dream ....

8 People charge absolutely exorbitant prices.
   I have heard ....

Verbs used with *of*: 2

Some verbs are followed by a noun group and a prepositional phrase which consists of *of* and a noun group. For example, in *Mr Goodwin has informed me of your visit*, the verb *inform* is followed by the noun group *me*, the preposition *of*, and the noun group *your visit*. This pattern is **V n *of* n**. With some verbs, the preposition is sometimes followed by an '-ing' clause.

Active pattern

	Verb group	noun group	*of*	noun group/-ing clause
They	Clear	your mind	of	other thoughts.
	suspected	him	of	doing away with Beryl.

Passive pattern

	Verb group	*of*	noun group/-ing clause
People	were cheated	of	their retirement cash.
They	were convicted	of	handling explosives.

Verbs with this pattern belong to the following meaning groups:

■ **verbs concerned with taking something away from someone or something, either physically or metaphorically**

cheat	cure	free	rid	starve
clear	deprive	relieve	rob	strip

The Opposition leaders warned that the Bill **might deprive citizens of fundamental rights**.

I wish I **could rid myself of this uneasy feeling**.

Her brain **was starved of oxygen** for about twenty minutes. (passive)

They **were robbed of their wristwatches** and shot during the course of the robbery. (passive)

■ **verbs indicating that someone talks or writes to someone**

advise	convince	persuade	remind
assure	inform	reassure	warn

It is your duty to **inform him of the danger to his father's life**.

He said Western leaders **had assured him of their commitment to help**.

He **reminded voters of the President's 'No new taxes' pledge**.

■ **verbs concerned with declaring or thinking that someone has or has not committed a crime**

accuse	acquit	clear	convict	suspect

They **convicted Gladys of voluntary manslaughter**.

He **was cleared of threatening to kill Holmes's mother**. (passive)

They **are suspected of being members of an extreme right-wing organisation**. (passive)

■ **other common verbs**

ask	expect	make	require	think
assure	hear	remind	see	

Real Madrid's goalless draw at Valladolid **assured them of the title** for the fifth year running.

Make a feature of glass kitchenware by displaying it on simple, open shelves.

You **remind me of my father**.

In the case of *ask, expect, hear, see,* and *think,* the noun group following the verb is always or often an **amount**.

I **haven't seen much of him** lately.

Little **has been heard of the plan** since then. (passive)

Think and *make* (meaning 'think') often occur in a question or clause beginning with *what*.

'**What did you think of the video?**' 'Well, it's not that bad really.'

I asked him **what he made of the present situation**.

The verb *think* is also sometimes followed by an adverb group and a prepositional phrase beginning with *of*.

Neil **thinks very highly of him** indeed.

Different forms of the pattern

What was he accused of?

She still could not believe that he had been involved in the murders **of which he was suspected**.

All these tests, however, **require of the examinee a moderate command of language**.

I have **a very great favour to ask of you**.

 **Practice**

A In the sentences below, put a dotted line under the verb used with *of*. Then underline each of the other parts of the pattern.

1 The naval court <u>acquitted</u> <u>him</u> of <u>the charge of personal dishonesty.</u>
2 It would be too simple to say I was cured of all my symptoms.
3 Manufacturers failed to warn doctors and consumers of the possible side effects.
4 This is a lot to ask of a partner.
5 Three city employees were accused of playing golf while on duty.
6 I assured the president of our intention to maintain only a minimum nuclear strategic force.
7 The government decided to strip the province of its autonomy.
8 What do you make of our neighbours?
9 That means he was not guilty of the crime of which he was accused.
10 Tell me, David, what does the smell remind you of?

B Fill in the gaps in the sentences below using *of* or *from* (see Unit 55).

1 That night, someone had robbed him .... all his money.
2 His goats strip the leaves .... the few sparse trees.
3 We must clear our minds .... the other versions.
4 Only the seat belt had saved him .... going through the windscreen.
5 A number of documents were stolen .... the building.
6 She stretched her neck this way and that to free it .... the tension.
7 The young political reformer promised to clear corruption .... the halls of government.
8 The World Boxing Association stripped him .... his title and his boxing licence.

C Rewrite these sentences using the pattern **V n *of* n** or its passive.

1 I'll tell them about your generous offer. (inform)
   I'll inform them of your generous offer.
2 I soon made him believe that I was innocent. (convince)
   ....
3 Customs officers are obliged to tell passengers about these rights. (advise)
   ....
4 That story brought to mind one I heard a while ago at college. (remind)
   ....
5 We had been alerted to the danger of pickpockets. (warn)
   ....
6 The authorities have stressed to us their willingness to cooperate. (assure)
   ....

Verbs used with *on*: 1

Some verbs are followed by a prepositional phrase which consists of *on* and a noun group. For example, in *He remarked on the heat*, the verb *remark* is followed by the preposition *on* and the noun group *the heat*. This pattern is **V *on* n**. With some verbs, the preposition is sometimes followed by an '-ing' clause or a wh-clause.

Sometimes *upon* is used instead of *on*. *Upon* is a more formal or literary word.

Active pattern

	Verb group	*on*	noun group/-ing/wh
They	cannot agree	on	what they want done.
Everything	depends	on	the weather.
He	is concentrating	on	getting himself re-elected.

Passive pattern

	Verb group	*on*
This fault	has been commented	on.

Verbs with this pattern belong to the following meaning groups:

■ **verbs concerned with speaking, writing, or expressing views**

advise	remark	rule	touch
comment	report	speak	vote
lecture	report back	talk	write

*The government **has not** yet **commented** on his release.*

*The Parliament is also due to **vote** on lowering the legal voting age from twenty-one to eighteen.*

*Police refused to **comment** on why she had been freed.*

■ **verbs concerned with thought, or the expression of thought**

agree	differ	dwell	ponder	speculate
brood	disagree	muse	reflect	

*It gave me a chance to **reflect** on what I was doing.*

*Even the experts **don't** always **agree** on how much sleep we need.*

■ **verbs concerned with depending or relying on something or someone, or hoping to have something**

bank	depend	hinge	rest	turn
count	hang	rely	ride	

*I hope we **can count** on your support.*

*A great deal **hangs** on the answer to these questions.*

*People **can** no longer **rely** on doing their chosen job for life.*

*Much **will hinge** on how well the Free Democrats do tonight.*

In the case of *bank*, *count*, *depend*, *hinge*, and *rely*, the preposition is sometimes followed by a noun group and an '-ing' clause.

*In the case of spacecraft such as the Space Shuttle, lives **depend** on such systems working properly.*

In the case of *count*, *depend*, and *rely*, there is sometimes a second prepositional phrase beginning with *for*, which indicates what is provided or ensured.

*She, too, **relied** upon him for her safety.*

■ **verbs concerned with working**

collaborate	experiment	operate	work

*After his return to Edinburgh, we **collaborated** on a musical version of Kingsley Amis's 'Lucky Jim'.*

*Mr Waldegrave said British diplomats **were working** on solving these problems.*

*He **has been operated** on for cancer. (passive)*

■ **verbs indicating that someone has or starts to have a particular thing as their focus of attention**

centre	concentrate	focus	home in

***Focus** on your goal.*

*The film **centres** upon two prisoners: Gerry Conlon and his father Giuseppe.*

*He gave up his party duties to **concentrate** on clearing his name.*

■ **verbs concerned with using something as a basis or exploiting it**

act	build	cash in	improve	trade

*Civil servants, **acting** on government instructions, have started to question the financial management of the society.*

*This year we **are building** upon that success to provide an even better and bigger show.*

A In the sentences below, put a dotted line under the verb used with a pattern described in this Unit. Then underline each of the other parts of the pattern. (For different forms of the pattern, see Unit 69.)

1   The Oscar-winning director will collaborate on a series of video-games.
2   She needed to write on what was nearest and most relevant to her life.
3   The accommodation I think could be improved on in many ways.
4   Airlines depend on business travelers for both volume and profit.
5   Computer learning centers focus on teaching children to use computer technology.
6   Many of the papers' lead stories report on the police appeal for help.
7   Even before the agency's first transaction was announced, its every move was speculated on.
8   You're the only person I can count on, Sheppy.
9   Now Paramount is banking on the sequel being another box-office hit.
10 That's what Congress will be voting on.

B Fill in the gaps in these sentences using *on* or *that* (see Unit 24).

1   Everyone agreed .... commerce was important.
2   Chris had relied .... Jeff's knowledge of the movie industry in casting them.
3   Our clients have frequently remarked .... the quality of our staff.
4   Some analysts speculate .... corn prices won't drop much lower.
5   Nutritionists disagree .... whether animal fat is bad for us.
6   I asked if her mother had commented .... her lateness.
7   The repairman reported .... the computer had a virus.
8   He wants to concentrate .... the rehabilitation of his people and the reconstruction of his country.

C Rewrite these sentences using the verb given in brackets with the pattern **V** *on* **n**.

1   The future of the Republic could be determined by the outcome of these elections. (hinge)
    The future of the Republic could hinge on the outcome of these elections.
2   He talked about a variety of social and economic topics. (speak)
    ....
3   It's fascinating to consider how fashions in the home have changed in the last 15 years. (reflect)
    ....
4   They take advantage of the generosity of visitors. (cash in)
    ....
5   Prosecutors in that case didn't mention his fund-raising efforts. (touch)
    ....
6   The legal dispute is likely to revolve around whether or not commitments were made. (centre)
    ....
7   The task is not to break new ground, but to develop what has already been accomplished. (build)
    ....

Verbs used with *on*: 2

Here are some more groups of verbs which are followed by the preposition *on* (or *upon*) and a noun group:

■ **verbs indicating that someone or something hits or touches something**

bear down	knock	pull	stamp	tread
beat	press	rest	tap	

*She **knocked** on the door and waited.*

*His legs were stretched out and his feet **rested** upon a sofa.*

■ **verbs concerned with going towards or onto something or someone**

bear down	close in	descend	move in	sneak up
close	creep up	fall	settle	

*The rebels **are closing in** on the capital.*

*When the news went out that an explosion had occurred, dozens of reporters **descended** on the campus.*

*There was clearly no way to **sneak up** on the house.*

WE CAN SEE YOU!

■ **verbs concerned with visiting someone**

call	call in	drop in	look in

*We'**ll drop in** on him after school and take him out.*

■ **verbs indicating that something affects or begins to affect someone or something, often negatively. The Subject often refers to a worrying thought or situation.**

act	descend	press	tell
creep up	fall	sneak up	weigh

*A gloomy silence once again **descended** on the room.*

*A feeling of responsibility **weighs** on me.*

■ **verbs indicating that someone interrupts or gets involved in something, sometimes when this is unwelcome**

get in	move in	sit in
intrude	muscle in	walk in

*If you **were to walk in** on the man you love, and he was with somebody else, what would you feel?*

*They wrote him letters from time to time, but **did not intrude** on his privacy.*

■ **verbs indicating that someone attacks or harms someone else, or treats them in a bad or hostile way**

clamp down	gang up	lean	stamp
crack down	hang up	run out	tell
dump	inform	set	turn
fire	jump	spy	walk out

*They're urging the government to **crack down** on right-wing extremists.*

*One of their leaders had been helping the secret police for 17 years, **informing** on colleagues.*

*His first wife **walked out** on him.*

*I took the short cut, over the fields, and I **was set** upon by a gang of boys. (passive)*

■ **verbs indicating that someone changes their plans or their attitude to something**

back down	cave in	climb down	compromise	go back

*The government **has backed down** on plans to introduce national tests for seven-year-old children.*

*You **can't go back** on your promise.*

*Neither side is prepared to **compromise** on the issue.*

Practice

A Match up the two halves of each sentence.

1 She tried to stamp ...
2 They all jumped ...
3 At night, the police crept up ...
4 The journalists will come and sit in ...
5 I will be glad to call ...
6 Her spell fell ...
7 The Government wants to clamp down ...
8 A young man and woman knocked ...

a ... on him like a rugby scrum.
b ... on student unions.
c ... on his feet and push him away.
d ... on you at your office.
e ... on the lobby windows a few feet away.
f ... on the interviews.
g ... on the house and surrounded it.
h ... on everyone who came in contact with her.

B Fill in the gaps in the sentences below using the verbs in this list. Use each verb once.

go back   inform   intrude   look in   settle   sneak up   tap   weigh

1 I'm sure he doesn't want to .... on his promise for no new taxes, but I guess he's finding that he just can't keep that promise.
2 He eventually admitted that he'd .... on four people who were later shot.
3 They had no right to .... on my personal life in the way that they did.
4 I stood in a phone booth, holding the receiver, until a guy came by and .... on the glass.
5 A pigeon .... on the window-sill, eyed him uncertainly, then flew off.
6 He wanted to .... on Laura and have another word about Grace.
7 It had .... on his conscience and now he decided to repay the money.
8 I managed to .... on him when you knocked on the door.

C Rewrite the sentences below using the verbs in this list with the pattern **V on n**. Use each verb once.

back down   compromise   descend   drop in   fire   walk in   walk out

1 There are no signs that the republic is prepared to withdraw its declaration of independence.
There are no signs that the republic is prepared to back down on its declaration of independence.

2 Eight years ago, my husband abandoned me and our two young children.
....

3 Why don't you visit me? I live right next door.
....

4 He shot at two people who tried to stop him outside a luxury hotel.
....

5 A team of one hundred technicians will arrive at the castle.
....

6 They are on record as saying they won't change their stand on the issue of democracy.
....

7 Suddenly, she felt as if she had interrupted a private conversation.
....

137

Verbs used with *on*: 3

1 Here are some more groups of verbs which are followed by the preposition *on* (or *upon*) and a noun group or an '-ing' clause:

■ **verbs indicating that a person or animal eats something**

| chew | dine | feast | feed | live |

He **chewed on his toast**, taking his time.

The adult flies **feed on nectar**.

■ **verbs used when indicating what resources someone has which enable them to live**

| exist | get by | live | survive |

They may not look for work once they are accustomed to **living on benefit**.

She **is getting by on borrowed money**.

■ **verbs concerned with using less of something or spending less on it**

| cut back | cut down | economize | save |

Pregnant women are still advised to **cut down on coffee**.

■ **other common verbs**

bet	check up	lose out	reflect	start
catch up	fall	miss out	rub off	stock up
check	insist	read up	run	wait

I'll get somebody to **check on the luggage**.

My 31st birthday **fell on a Friday**.

Every new mother **should read up on the food requirements of her children**.

I mean, even your own personal behavior as a teacher, outside of school hours, **reflects on the school itself**.

A car which **runs on natural gas** has been developed by engineers in Milton Keynes.

We're ready to **start on the runways**.

In the case of *insist* and *miss out*, the preposition *on* is sometimes followed by an '-ing' clause.

Reggae band Inner Circle said they were very upset to **have missed out on performing at the Carnival**.

In the case of *bet* and *insist*, the preposition is sometimes followed by a noun group and an '-ing' clause.

They **insist on three conditions being met**.

Different forms of the pattern

What **are** you **working on** at the moment?

You're one of **the few people** I **can rely** on absolutely.

What the play **concentrates on** is Britten's development as a composer.

2 A few verbs are followed by a prepositional phrase beginning with *on* or *upon*, and a to-infinitive clause.

Verbs with this pattern belong to the following meaning groups:

■ **verbs indicating that someone hopes or is certain that someone will do something**

| bank | count | depend | rely |

One lesson they may have learned is that they **cannot rely on anyone else to fight their battles for them**.

■ **verbs indicating that someone asks or persuades someone to do something**

| call | prevail |

So we **call on everyone to seize this opportunity and to look at it positively**.

He **may be prevailed upon to join the Supreme National Council**. (passive)

3 The verb *look* is followed by a prepositional phrase beginning with *on* or *upon* and another prepositional phrase which consists of *as* and a noun group, '-ing' clause, or adjective group. The second prepositional phrase indicates what someone regards someone or something as being.

Look on it as a challenge.

People who put their own pleasure higher up on the list of priorities **are** often **looked on as selfish or immature**. (passive)

Practice

A In the sentences below, put a dotted line under the verb used with a pattern described in this Unit. Then underline each of the other parts of the pattern.

1 I just missed out on getting an Agfa camera.

2 She practically lived on instant breakfasts.

3 They showed they can be relied on to do the job.

4 His team taught residents how to save on their fuel bills by weatherproofing.

5 What I insist on is a totally positive campaign that goes right through the party.

6 For too long the school has had to exist on a limited budget.

7 The main political parties look on these votes as already lost.

8 I always have chocolate and cheese but I also stock up on tons of fruit.

B Rewrite these sentences, starting with the words provided. Use a prepositional phrase beginning with *on*, and a to-infinitive clause.

1 They hoped that the President would deliver the speech of his life.
They were banking *on the President to deliver the speech of his life.*

2 He suggested that richer nations should relieve the suffering of poorer people.
He called ....

3 He thought that Elaine would be sure to act out of love for him.
He thought that he could depend ....

4 Will you do the same?
Can I count ....

5 She persuaded her parents to let her go to London.
She prevailed ....

6 He was confident his influential friends would get him out of trouble.
He relied ....

C Rewrite these sentences using the verb given in brackets with one of the patterns in this Unit.

1 I'm going to come back and bring my paperwork up-to-date in peace. (catch up)
I'm going to come back and catch up on my paperwork in peace.

2 If you're starting to gain a bit of weight, reduce the carbohydrates. (cut back)
....

3 His father has been finding out about the disease. (read up)
....

4 Once he began telling stories of his time here, we heard the lot. (start)
....

5 I consider it to be an adventure, something positive we can experience together. (look)
....

6 The Prime Minister had roast chicken and peas for dinner. (dine)
....

7 She was firm about paying for the coffee. (insist)
....

139

Some verbs are followed by a noun group and a prepositional phrase which consists of *on* and a noun group. For example, in *He played a trick on her*, the verb *play* is followed by the noun group *a trick*, the preposition *on*, and the noun group *her*. This pattern is **V n *on* n**. With some verbs, the preposition is sometimes followed by an '-ing' clause or a wh-clause.

Sometimes *upon* is used instead of *on*. *Upon* is a more formal or literary word.

Active pattern

	Verb group	noun group	*on*	noun group/-ing/wh
They	advise	governments	on	negotiating.
They	questioned	him	on	what he had said.
The army	inflicted	heavy losses	on	the rebel forces.

Passive pattern

	Verb group	*on*	noun group/-ing/wh
They	were not consulted	on	the policy.
They	were congratulated	on	acting quickly.
Much emphasis	is placed	on	how they perform.

(With phrasal verbs, the particle comes either after the noun group or after the verb.)

Verbs with this pattern belong to the following meaning groups:

■ **verbs concerned with speaking or writing to someone about something**

advise	compliment	consult	let in	question
brief	congratulate	fill in	press	update

*This guide **will brief** you on sightseeing and shopping.*

*I **congratulated** Katherine on her decision to advance her education.*

*I'll **let** you **in** on a little secret.*

*She **complimented** them on staying together for such a long time.*

__Consult__ your vet on how to deal with the problem.

■ **verbs concerned with giving something unpleasant to someone, or making them undergo an unpleasant experience**

bring	impose	serve	thrust
dump	inflict	spring	wish
force	play	take out	

*Rob **dumped** his children on the grandparents but my family does not live nearby.*

*Rose grieved privately with her immediate family and **did not impose** her grief on friends.*

*They **brought** this tragedy on themselves.*

*A Home Office spokeswoman said last night: 'We **have served** a writ on Central Television to prevent the programme being screened.'*

*I didn't mean to **take** my anger **out** on him, but I couldn't help myself.*

■ **verbs concerned with giving something to someone**

bestow	confer

*An honorary doctorate in criminology **was conferred** on him by the University of Manila in 1968. (passive)*

*The King and Queen **bestowed** their grateful thanks upon Lancelot.*

■ **verbs concerned with putting something somewhere metaphorically**

cast	lay	place	put	set	throw

*Only three EC countries **set** no limit on the hours worked.*

*The government have agreed to **place** greater emphasis on the rights of individuals.*

*The prosecutors want to **cast** doubt on whether Smith has a good character.*

A In the sentences below, put a dotted line under the verb used with *on* or *upon*. Then underline each of the other parts of the pattern.

1 I'm not mean enough to wish unemployment on anyone.
2 It dismissed all the evidence that threw doubt on the alleged confession.
3 Through an interpreter, we complimented her on doing an excellent job.
4 The purchase of this object conferred a certain status upon the purchaser.
5 If too much strain is put on the back, a slipped disc may result.
6 I will fill you in on the whole story when I see you.
7 A government spokesman said heavy casualties had been inflicted on the rebels.
8 We'd update people on what's happening around the club.

B Rewrite each of the following pairs of sentences as one sentence.

1 They brief interviewers. They tell them about the ground rules.
They brief interviewers on the ground rules.
2 They congratulated her. She looked so well just two months after the birth.
....
3 Mr Stevens was questioned. Where was the money for the project coming from?
....
4 Could you advise me? I'd like to know how to treat this problem.
....
5 We'll update you. We have the day's top news stories.
....
6 He complimented Tania. He admired her cooking.
....
7 Where did it come from? She consulted the shopkeeper.
....
8 When I come back, you can fill me in. You can tell me about his plans.
....

C Fill in the gaps in the sentences below using the verbs in this list. Use each verb once.

bestow   bring   congratulate   consult   impose   place   press   serve

1 He told them that they had .... disgrace on themselves and their families.
2 There is no more precious gift that can be .... upon a child than the gift of education.
3 They are .... on important economic decisions.
4 Before anybody could .... a warrant on him, he had dropped out of sight.
5 The army immediately .... a curfew on the town.
6 I .... him on why he would lend his weight to the board of a tobacco company.
7 He .... the society on having preserved these important relics.
8 He wasn't a man who .... a strong emphasis on personal relationships.

141

Here are some more groups of verbs which are followed by a noun group and a prepositional phrase beginning with *on* (or *upon*):

■ **verbs indicating that someone focuses their attention, feelings, or efforts on someone or something**

be centred	direct	focus	turn
concentrate	fix	pin	

*Scientists now **pin their hopes on treatment with combinations of drugs** – but these hopes are not high.*

*Firefighters **concentrated** their efforts on trying to free people trapped in elevators.*

*The debate **is centred** on whether the country's president should be elected directly by the people or by parliament.* (passive)

In the case of *turn*, the feeling you focus on someone is usually aggressive.

*The crowd then **turned** their anger on the Prime Minister.*

■ **verbs indicating that someone directs a weapon or camera at someone**

pull	train	turn

*A judge **pulled** a gun on an unruly prisoner yesterday and threatened to shoot him dead.*

■ **verbs concerned with striking one thing on another, or catching one thing on another**

bang	catch	drum	strike	wipe

*He shouted out loud in his anger, and **banged** his fists on the steering wheel.*

*He **caught** his shirt on a nail.*

■ **verbs concerned with writing something somewhere**

carve	print	put down	write	write down

*I wish to thank my friend Theresa King, who encouraged me to develop my ideas and **put** them **down** on paper.*

■ **verbs concerned with basing one thing on another**

base	build	model

*They tried to **build** an empire on shaky foundations.*

*As far as their preferences and dislikes are concerned, most children tend to **model** themselves on their parents.*

*Our politics **should be based** upon ethical standards.* (passive)

■ **verbs concerned with gambling**

bet	lay	place	put	stake

*She and a friend both **bet** five pounds on him.*

The preposition *on* is sometimes followed by a noun group and an '-ing' clause.

*You wouldn't want to **stake** your life on the signal being picked up.*

■ **verbs concerned with spending, saving, and wasting time, money, or resources**

blow	save	spend	waste

*'I **do spend** a lot on expensive jewelry and clothing,'* she admits.

*She **blew** part of the cash on furnishing her flat.*

*How much time and how many resources **have been wasted** on the arms race!* (passive)

■ **other common verbs**

blame	feed	pride	urge
(not) commit	judge	take up	

*They made it available to us and we **took** them **up** on the offer.*

*The President **urged** restraint on the security forces.*

*That earlier accident **was blamed** on a faulty signal.* (passive)

In the case of *commit* and *pride*, the noun group following the verb is always a reflexive pronoun.

*John Major failed to **commit** himself on the issue in the Commons.*

Different forms of the pattern

*What **are** you **going to spend** it on?*

*The material **on which** this book **is based** comes from three distinct sources.*

*They **impose** on the media a duty to report fairly.*

*They have **nothing** to **spend** their money on.*

A Rewrite each of the following pairs of sentences as one sentence.

1 Concentrate your attention. Think about your lower back.
Concentrate your attention on your lower back.

2 I wrote his number down. I used that pad of paper by the phone.

3 He had already placed a bet. He had chosen one of the horses.

4 Enough taxpayers' money is wasted already. It goes on propaganda.

5 The Prime Minister failed to commit himself. He avoided the issue.

6 Some nights I would blow £200. I would pay for a meal with it.

7 The man jumped over the counter and pulled out a knife. He threatened the clerk with it.

B Rewrite these sentences using the verb given in brackets and the pattern **V n on n**.

1 They are expected to tell the government that caution is necessary. (urge)
They are expected to urge caution on the government.

2 Politicians here take pride in their accessibility to the public. (pride)

3 He attributed the job losses to rising production costs. (blame)

4 I wish people would look at my contribution when evaluating me. (judge)

5 I accepted her suggestion. (take up)

6 What do they give the rabbits as food? (feed)

C Put the different parts of these sentences in the right order.

1 their cameras / trained / them / on / the foreigners ....

2 on / her name / wrote / the side of the package / she ....

3 his fingers / drummed / the bar / in time to / he / on / the music

4 on / he / getting the treaty through / has staked / his reputation

5 is modelled / much of the clothing / the clothing that will be worn by the European team / on

6 the things / is going to be judged / those are / he / on ....

7 a question / are spending / it's / of / what / on / they / their time

Verbs used with *out of*: 1

Some verbs are followed by a prepositional phrase which consists of *out of* and a noun group. For example, in *He's pulled out of the deal*, the verb *pull* is followed by the preposition *out of* and the noun group *the deal*. This pattern is **V *out of* n**.

	Verb group	*out of*	noun group
Everyone	piled	out of	the car.
He	had changed	out of	his work clothes.

Verbs with this pattern belong to the following meaning groups:

■ **verbs indicating that someone or something comes out of or leaves a place or thing**

break	clear	go	pile
check	get	move	pull

*On the same day a former police chief **broke** out of prison and took over police headquarters.*

*He **checked** out of his hotel room at nine this morning.*

*'If we ever **move** out of this house, we'll sell everything with it,' he resolves.*

■ **verbs concerned with not being involved in something, not doing something, or withdrawing from something**

back	contract	get	pull	walk
break	drop	opt	stay	wriggle

*Actress Julia Roberts **has backed** out of a £1.8 million movie deal.*

*He **dropped** out of school as early as he could.*

The preposition *out of* is sometimes followed by an '-ing' clause.

*I found myself trying to scheme how I **could get** out of taking my kid to the beach.*

*America had decided to **pull out** of financing the proposed construction of the Aswan Dam.*

■ **verbs indicating that someone or something stops being in a particular state**

fall	get	go	pull	snap

*He **fell** out of favour last summer when he supported an anti-government student demonstration.*

*Big computers **are going** out of fashion.*

*Most economists predict that the economy **will pull** out of the recession by mid-year.*

■ **verbs indicating that someone takes off their clothes**

change	slip

*Then she went into the bathroom to get a robe and **change** out of her wet clothes.*

■ **verbs indicating that one thing develops or results from another**

arise	develop	grow

*Depression and anxiety **may arise** out of loneliness and isolation.*

*This book **grew** out of three experiences which happened in 1968.*

■ **verbs indicating that someone uses or sells all they have of something**

run	sell

*After a few months he **ran** out of money and needed his job back.*

*A sign of increased consumer demand is that some retailers **have sold** out of popular items.*

■ *Grow* also has this pattern when it is used to refer to mental or physical development.

*Most girls go through a phase of loving ponies, and most **grow** out of it.*

*I had to have my older sister's clothes when she **grew** out of them.*

Different forms of the pattern

*Scientific theories are shaped by the shared values of the communities **out of which** they **arise**.*

A Fill in the gaps in these sentences using *out of* or *into* (see Unit 61).

1 She slipped .... the jacket and tossed it on the couch.

2 How are we going to get .... this mess?

3 He lived in the farmhouse, which had fallen .... disrepair.

4 They piled .... the car and ordered: 'Drive!'

5 The London Nursery Campaign developed .... these initiatives.

6 We're running .... time.

7 Civilians had broken .... the building, apparently in the belief that it contained food.

8 The Slovene delegation walked .... the debate in protest.

9 Late in the day they checked .... a motel in a small town near the state line.

10 Youngsters who lack affection and stability at home are more likely to get .... trouble.

B Rewrite these sentences using the verb given in brackets, *out of*, and an '-ing' clause.

1 Is he just trying to avoid doing the dishes? (get)
Is he just trying to get out of doing the dishes?

2 Russia decided not to aid China's nuclear programme. (back)
....

3 His job in banking brought about several moves and he stopped cycling for a while. (drop)
....

4 She could then avoid doing all the things she did not want to do. (get)
....

5 The Government has largely stopped providing continual care for the elderly. (opt)
....

6 I didn't go through with applying but if I'd got the grant it would have saved a lot of money. (pull)
....

7 But many who lost their jobs complain that insurance firms are now trying to avoid paying up. (wriggle)
....

C Fill in the gaps in the sentences below using the verbs in this list. Use each verb once.

arise   change   get   move   sell   stay

1 Lesley had .... out of her shirt and jeans into a straight white sleeveless dress.

2 I'm 30 now, so I do not think that I will .... out of Denmark again.

3 It's amazing what people will do to .... out of paying taxes.

4 'Okay,' Nancy murmured, 'I'll try to .... out of trouble, because I love you, too.'

5 My local supermarket .... out of beef last week for the first time ever.

6 The concept of community schools .... out of a push to make education more relevant to community needs.

Verbs used with *out of*: 2

Some verbs are followed by a noun group and a prepositional phrase which consists of *out of* and a noun group. For example, in *I dragged the information out of him*, the verb *drag* is followed by the noun group *the information*, the preposition *out of*, and the noun group *him*. This pattern is **V n *out of* n**.

Active pattern

	Verb group	noun group	*out of*	noun group
They	didn't get	any advantage	out of	this.
They	kicked	him	out of	the country.

Passive pattern

	Verb group	*out of*	noun group
They	were conned	out of	several hundred pounds.
They	have been driven	out of	their homes.

Verbs with this pattern belong to the following meaning groups:

■ **verbs concerned with fraudulently taking something, usually money, away from someone.** The prepositional phrase indicates what is taken away.

cheat	con	do	swindle	trick

*He feels I **did him out of a profit on some shares**.*

■ **verbs concerned with getting something from someone with some difficulty.** The prepositional phrase indicates the person involved.

charm	drag	screw		wring
con	get	squeeze		

*The company has a monopoly position that it uses to **screw more money out of people**.*

■ **verbs concerned with gaining something from an activity or thing**

get	make

*The attempt to **make money out of the historic find** has caused outrage.*

The preposition *out of* is sometimes followed by an '-ing' clause.

*You **might get** a lot of pleasure out of refurnishing and re-equipping a new home.*

■ **verbs indicating that someone or something forces someone to leave a place, position, activity, or state**

chase	kick	put	turn
drive	knock	shake	vote
force	order	throw	

*He said he would oppose moves to **force the president out of office**.*

*Ivan Lendl **has been knocked out of the Wimbledon Tennis Championships**. (passive)*

■ **verbs concerned with excluding someone or something**

block	edge	leave	put	squeeze
cut	freeze	lock	rule	

*She **had locked him out of the apartment**.*

*You know it can happen but you **have to block it out of your mind**.*

*They were concerned that they **were being left out of the decision-making process**. (passive)*

■ **verbs concerned with rescuing someone from a bad situation**

bail	get	pull	talk

*We**'d bail him out of trouble** when he owed money.*

In the case of *talk*, the noun group following the preposition is always a reflexive pronoun. This verb sometimes indicates that someone gets themselves out of a good situation rather than a bad one.

*I always have the sense that I **can talk myself out of trouble**.*

*He **talked himself out of a job**.*

■ **verbs indicating that someone makes something**

carve	create	fashion	manufacture
construct	cut	make	

*She **makes beautiful bowls out of red earthenware clay**.*

■ *Talk* also has this pattern when it is used to indicate that someone persuades someone not to do something. The preposition *out of* is sometimes followed by an '-ing' clause.

*My mother tried to **talk me out of getting a divorce**.*

Different forms of the pattern

*Proteins are the very large and complex molecules **out of which** living things **are made**.*

*He said his priority was to **force out of the country** the remnants of forces loyal to the former president.*

A In the sentences below, put a dotted line under the verb used with *out of* (see this Unit and Unit 72). Then underline each of the other parts of the pattern.

1 Parents often bailed their children out of financial, legal, and emotional difficulties.
2 He had left out of his account something that was crucial.
3 Food markets in the capital were said to have sold out of bread and milk.
4 Soil is the raw material out of which a gardener creates his dreams.
5 If people want to get rid of legislators, then all they have to do is vote them out of office.
6 The thousands of people that she threw out of work are still having a difficult time.
7 The American, Fred Couples, has pulled out of the event with a back injury.
8 They are fighting against the health problems which have arisen out of poor housing.

B Fill in the gaps in these sentences using the noun groups given in brackets.

1 He is good at charming .... out of ....
   (money / companies)
2 Jacob cheated .... out of ....
   (his birthright / his brother Esau)
3 He was jailed for conning .... out of ....
   (their life savings / women)
4 The bank has done .... out of ....
   and I'm absolutely furious. (thousands of dollars / me)
5 I don't think we'd get .... out of ....
   (any useful information / him)
6 She didn't come straight out and tell me, I had to drag .... out of .... (it / her)
7 He had recently discovered that Fisch was a crook who had tricked ....
   out of .... (several thousand dollars / him)
8 They forced him to try to screw .... out of ....
   (some extra concessions / the West)
9 This has become just another way of squeezing .... out of ....
   (cash / the government)

C *Talk* is used with a reflexive pronoun and *out of* with three slightly different meanings. Here are three examples.

a You may realise what is happening but talk yourself out of taking any action.
b He talked himself out of a really good deal.
c If he had done, he might have talked himself out of dismissal that day at Wembley.

In which of the sentences above does *talk* mean:

1 get yourself out of a bad situation? ....
2 get yourself out of a good situation? ....
3 persuade yourself not to do something? ....

147

Verbs used with *over*

1 Some verbs are followed by a prepositional phrase which consists of *over* and a noun group. For example, in *They're arguing over details*, the verb *argue* is followed by the preposition *over* and the noun group *details*. This pattern is **V over n**. With some verbs, the preposition is sometimes followed by a wh-clause.

	Verb group	*over*	noun group/wh-clause
They	argued	over	whether to extend the deadline.
He	ruled	over	a vast kingdom.

Verbs with this pattern belong to the following meaning groups:

■ verbs indicating that two or more people argue or disagree about something

argue	disagree	haggle	squabble
differ	fight	quarrel	

*The candidates **differed** over a number of issues, including government, foreign affairs, and the environment.*

*But yesterday Baker said the two sides still **disagree** over when those meetings should be held.*

*We **argued** over household chores.*

■ verbs indicating that someone changes their plans or their attitude to something

back down	climb down	compromise

*The Prime Minister was forced to **back down** over plans to pardon corrupt businessmen and politicians.*

■ verbs indicating that someone does not discuss or deal with something as thoroughly as they should

gloss	skate	skip

*Official histories tend to **gloss** over this state of affairs.*

These verbs are sometimes used in the passive.

*The stories are too long to **be skated** over here.*

■ verbs concerned with being in a superior or powerful position

preside	prevail	rule	triumph	win out

*Today, Mr. Corry **presides** over a company whose fortunes have changed abruptly.*

*In the end, good **prevailed** over evil.*

*Free-market liberals **have won out** over soft-hearted social democrats.*

■ other common verbs

descend	extend	hang	range	stumble	wash

*As Gascoigne slowly sank to the ground, a deathly hush **descended** over the stadium.*

*A question mark still **hangs** over the future of 3,000 jobs at British Coal.*

*His speech **ranged** over too many issues.*

*She **stumbled** over her words sometimes.*

*A wave of guilt and shame **washed** over me.*

2 Some verbs are followed by a noun group and a prepositional phrase which consists of *over* and a noun group. For example, in *Pour the sauce over the fish*, the verb *pour* is followed by the noun group *the sauce*, the preposition *over*, and the noun group *the fish*. This pattern is **V n over n**.

Active pattern

	Verb group	noun group	*over*	noun group
The youths	poured	kerosene	over	the floor.

Passive pattern

	Verb group	*over*	noun group
Cooling water	was sprayed	over	the engines.

Verbs with this pattern are all concerned with pouring or scattering something over something else.

distribute	pour	scatter	spray	sprinkle

__Scatter__ the basil leaves over the salad.

A In the sentences below, put a dotted line under the verb used with a pattern described in this Unit. Then underline each of the other parts of the pattern.

1 The storm clouds now extend over much of the planet.
2 The Financial Times says, in effect, the party has chosen to compromise over reform.
3 Water is being sprayed over the cargo holds in an attempt to keep them cool.
4 Nicola, a violinist, triumphed over more than 500 entrants in television's most popular music event.
5 The pain and the psychological upheavals were ignored or glossed over.
6 Economists disagree over how to measure real interest rates.
7 Pour the water into the dish, and pour the apple juice over the apple.
8 He also wrote scores of articles on matters ranging over the whole history of Welsh literature.

B Fill in the gaps in these sentences using *over* or *from*.

1 a) A crystal chandelier hung .... the high old-fashioned ceiling.
   b) A surreal calm hung .... the airport.
2 a) Michael could feel their eyes on him as he climbed down .... the bus.
   b) Britain has had to climb down .... the status of Hong Kong's negotiators in the British team.
3 a) Inevitably, liberals and conservatives differ .... the causes of homelessness.
   b) In what respect would your policies differ .... those of the Prime Minister?
4 a) The sun's energy is distributed .... the entire surface of the earth.
   b) Food is being distributed .... a truck at one end of the port.
5 a) A mood of national mourning descended .... Zambia as worldwide condolences poured in.
   b) Drenching rain descended .... grey skies on the opening day of the Festival.

C Fill in the gaps in the sentences below using the verbs in this list. Use each verb once.

back down   fight   preside   rule   skate   sprinkle   wash   win out

1 It's time the general public learnt that mankind does not .... over this natural environment.
2 A mixture of various seeds is .... over the fruits.
3 We would rush to the mailbox and .... over who got to read the magazine first.
4 Relief .... over her beautiful features.
5 Denver hopes to .... over other cities for a $1 billion United Airlines maintenance facility.
6 In March 1976, he .... over a major international conference on terrorism in Washington.
7 The government has .... over plans to change the fire brigades' pay formula.
8 Clever scientists have tended to .... over the difficulties of explaining dreams.

Verbs used with *through*

Some verbs are followed by a prepositional phrase which consists of *through* and a noun group. For example, in *She was looking through a magazine*, the verb *look* is followed by the preposition *through* and the noun group *a magazine*. This pattern is **V through n**.

	Verb group	*through*	noun group
She	sailed	through	her exams.
Lloyd	sorted	through	the entire batch.

Verbs with this pattern belong to the following meaning groups:

■ **verbs concerned with experiencing something or coping with something in a particular way**

battle	go	pull	sit
come	live	sail	sleep
get	pass	scrape	

*'I **wouldn't go** through that again,'* says Gill with feeling.

*Some patients fail to **live** through the surgery.*

*He **slept** through the entire performance.*

■ **verbs concerned with reading or searching**

browse	glance	look	skim	wade
flick	go	read	sort	
flip	leaf	sift	thumb	

*I've **been looking** through this handbook*, but it doesn't mention anything that fits the description.

*Police **have been sifting** through the rubble to find out what kind of device it was.*

*It was evident that someone **had gone** through my possessions.*

■ **verbs concerned with making a hole or breaking a barrier**

bore	break	cut	dig	drill	smash

***Drill** through the joint from below.*

*Demonstrators scrambled over walls or used trucks to **smash** through the embassy gates.*

■ **verbs concerned with moving or travelling through a place, thing, or group of things**

cut	filter	plough	sweep

*The boys **cut** through an alley, crossed a street, and turned at the next corner.*

*Only a little sunlight **filtered** through the single dirty window.*

■ **verbs indicating that someone has a thought or feeling, usually briefly.** The Subject indicates the thought or feeling.

flash	go	race	run	surge

*Several possibilities **flashed** through my mind.*

*A convulsive shudder **ran** through his body.*

Different forms of the pattern

*It will make **everything** I've gone through worthwhile.*

A In the sentences below, put a dotted line under the verb used with *through*. Then underline each of the other parts of the pattern.

1 I sat through a long interview with the minister for tourism.
2 At least three local rescue teams are on the scene digging through a wall of coal and rock.
3 She was flicking through some magazines when Harry Penrose came into the room.
4 He is a strong man, and he will pull through this operation.
5 Do you have any questions about what we've just read through?
6 A fire officer's car was destroyed as a lorry ploughed through a hedge.
7 He listed the wars he's lived through.

B Put the different parts of these sentences in the right order.

1 my father / surgery / through / came / without difficulty
....
2 of / raced / her mind / bits and pieces / the past / through
....
3 our seats / through / glanced / took / and / the menu / we
....
4 of / a fire engine siren / have been known / I / through / to sleep / the wailing
....

C Fill in the gaps in the sentences below using the verbs in this list. Use each verb once.

break   drill   flash   get   sail   scrape   skim   sweep

1 I went back to our room and .... through the newspapers.
2 He helped his son .... through a serious crisis.
3 Democratic fervor was .... through eastern Europe.
4 The crowd moved back and did not try to .... through the police chain.
5 Wilkinson was a gifted psychology student who .... through college exams.
6 Many kitchen and bathroom fittings must be screwed to the wall, and this may mean
   .... through a tile.
7 I flushed bright red as a spurt of anger .... through me.
8 I became one of the worst students ever to .... through the botany school at Oxford.

D Fill in the gaps in these sentences. For each pair, one verb from this Unit goes in both sentences.

1 a) Raiders .... through padlocks and chains to get into the warehouse.
   b) Soon the little sail had caught the breeze, and the boat began to .... through
      the water.
2 a) I thought you'd be tired after .... through so many photos.
   b) All the parties agree the country cannot .... through another gruelling and
      costly election.

Verbs used with *to*: 1

Some verbs are followed by a prepositional phrase which consists of *to* and a noun group. For example, in *I apologized to him*, the verb *apologize* is followed by the preposition *to* and the noun group *him*. This pattern is **V *to* n**. With some verbs, the preposition is sometimes followed by an '-ing' clause.

	Verb group	*to*	noun group/-ing clause
Daniel	had moved	to	Los Angeles.
He	admits	to	having self-doubts.

Verbs with this pattern belong to the following meaning groups:

■ **verbs indicating that someone goes to or reaches a place**

come	escape	go round	return	withdraw
come round	get	move	run away	
cross	go	retire	transfer	

*Our next door neighbour's **moved** to New Zealand.*

*As soon as I heard this I **went round** to his mother's house to give what comfort I could.*

■ **verbs indicating that something comes to someone or that someone gets something**

come	fall	occur	transfer
come back	go	pass	

*The attention they deserve **will come** to them quite naturally.*

*I had rather forgotten what the garden looked like, but as Patty described it, it all **came back** to me.*

■ **verbs used to indicate that something extends to a particular point, lasts until a particular time, or began at a particular time**

date back	go back	reach
extend	live	stretch

*The cornfields **stretch** to the horizon in every direction.*

*I **may live** to a ripe old age, but who knows.*

*Parts of the church **date back** to the seventh century.*

■ **verbs indicating that someone speaks or writes to someone else**

apologize	lie	reply	speak	write
boast	pray	report	talk	write back
complain	propose	report back	talk down	write in
confess	read	sing	whisper	write off

*He needed to **talk** to someone.*

*'Don't **lie** to me,' she shouted.*

*She was certain that in the next few months he **would propose** to her.*

Some of these verbs, particularly *lie*, *speak*, and *talk*, are sometimes used in the passive.

*We**'re being lied** to every day.*

With verbs in this meaning group, a prepositional phrase beginning with *about* is sometimes used after or before the other prepositional phrase to indicate the topic of the speech or writing.

*She says when she **complained** to her supervisor about the behaviour, no action was taken.*

■ **verbs concerned with admitting something**

admit	confess	own up

*Within a week two young men **had confessed** to the crime and been arrested.*

*He **admitted** to liking all the attention.*

■ **verbs concerned with saying or showing that something happened, exists, or is true**

point	swear	testify

*She can't remember committing the murder, although all the evidence **points** to her guilt.*

*It was him, Sergei. I**'d swear** to it.*

*One witness **testified** to hearing the words: 'Don't do it, Peter!'*

■ **verbs indicating that someone communicates by means of a gesture or movement**

bow	nod	signal	wave

*She **nodded** to Jarvis as he came in.*

A In the sentences below, put a dotted line under the verb used with a pattern described in this Unit. Then underline each of the other parts of the pattern. (For different forms of the pattern, see Unit 78.)

1 They just wanted to make a quick fortune so they could retire to the Spanish coast.
2 Many of your best ideas may occur to you at odd moments during the day or night.
3 They realised one day that they had to have a place to escape to.
4 Where are you going to move to?
5 Your child needs to learn that owning up to making a mistake isn't the end of the world.
6 I think you'll find him rather difficult to talk to.
7 Ginny became the friend to whom she could talk about every aspect of her life.
8 I don't know where everyone has gone to.
9 The blown-out church tower testifies to the severity of mortar attacks which have been launched against the small village.
10 Dunne waved to her, indicating there was space beside him on the sofa.

B These sentences show the pattern **V that**. Rewrite them using the verb with *to* and an '-ing' clause.

1 Despite the recession, seven out of ten adults admit that they spend money on activities like horse-racing and lotteries.
....
2 Red also confessed that he had driven the getaway car.
....
3 Why had Martin sworn that he'd seen Grace on the July 3rd?
....
4 Eva testified that she had seen Herndon with his gun on the stairs.
....

C Fill in the gaps in the sentences below using the verbs in this list. Use each verb once.

cross   date back   lie   pass   reach   report back   signal   withdraw

1 I'll appoint somebody to take notes on what you're saying and .... to the class.
2 'Would you please .... to the other side of the street,' he said.
3 When he died in 1971, control of the business .... to his sons.
4 Federal troops have .... to barracks and a ceasefire is in place.
5 Teddy Bears .... to 1902 when Theodore 'Teddy' Roosevelt, the US President, could not bring himself to shoot a cub.
6 Bedspreads that .... to the floor are generally a nuisance.
7 Margaret .... to the waiter, who came at once.
8 It's terrible to know your dad has been .... to you all your life about his past.

Here are some more groups of verbs which are followed by the preposition *to* and a noun group or an '-ing' clause:

- **verbs concerned with doing what someone else wants you to do.** The prepositional phrase indicates that person or their demands.

bend	cave in	give in	submit	surrender
bow	defer	sell out	suck up	yield

The Government **will not bow** to pressure from the Right.

The President is showing no signs that he **will give in** to union demands.

- **verbs concerned with starting to do something different or starting to be in a different situation**

change	get back	move over	shoot
change over	go over	progress	switch
come	move	return	switch over
get	move on	revert	turn

Switch to low-fat, wholemeal foods wherever possible.

In various interviews with the media today, he explained why he agreed to **return** to his old job as foreign minister.

She **shot** to fame as a 16-year-old in the film 'Wish You Were Here'.

At first she used a shopping trolley for support, then she **progressed** to walking with a stick.

- **verbs indicating that someone starts to talk about a different topic**

come	get back	move	switch	turn
come back	go back	return	switch over	

Let us now **turn** to the problem of compensating the population for higher food prices.

Going back to the school, how many members of staff are there?

- **verbs concerned with starting or resuming a task**

get back	get round	return
get down	go back	turn

Right, lads, let's **get down** to work.

If you'll excuse me, I really **have to get back** to work.

She ignored him and **returned** to painting her nails.

- **verbs indicating that someone keeps to a belief, agreement, or course of action**

adhere	cling	hold	keep	stick

As long as you **stick** to your diet you will lose weight.

They still **cling** to their belief in democracy.

- **verbs concerned with responding to an event or situation**

adapt	adjust	react	respond

One of the first world leaders to **react** to the news from Moscow was the British Prime Minister.

At first Maria **could not adjust** to life in London.

- **verbs indicating that someone dies**

bleed	choke	freeze	starve

Reports say he **bled** to death after a bullet severed a main artery in his leg.

Freeze and *starve* may be used with this pattern to indicate that someone is very cold or very hungry.

Please open the door – I'**m freezing** to death out here.

- **verbs indicating that someone goes to sleep**

drift off	drop off	go	nod off

She **drifted off** to sleep before he could reply.

- **verbs concerned with dealing with something or serving someone**

attend	see	tend

He added that the President had left the meeting early to **attend** to other matters.

He told me, 'Well, don't worry about it, I'**ll see** to it.'

These verbs are sometimes used in the passive.

Lamy **was attended** to by medics and then airlifted by helicopter to Northampton General Hospital.

- **verbs concerned with giving, lending, or selling something to someone.** The thing given or sold is not explicitly mentioned.

contribute	give	hand over	lend	pass	sell

The survey shows that Americans **are** still **giving** to charity despite hard economic times.

In this climate, banks were eager to **lend** to anybody with **a good business idea.**

A Fill in the gaps in the sentences below using the verbs in this list. Use each verb once.

adapt   change   contribute   go   keep   return   surrender   tend

1 Her talk kept .... to the subject of the decline of the younger generation.
2 About twenty prisoners are still refusing to .... to the authorities at Strangeways jail in Manchester.
3 When I came home, I .... to sleep because I was so tired.
4 He told me that Communism was not working and they needed to .... to a new economic policy.
5 I'm afraid I didn't .... to our bargain – I'm sorry.
6 You must be flexible, able to .... to any problem or change of circumstance.
7 He won't run in the election because he has to .... to his sick wife.
8 Do you want to .... to the school fund?

B Fill in the gaps in the sentences below using the noun groups in this list. Use each noun group once.

my belief   some business   change   charity   death   pressure   sleep

1 A survey asked 1,245 college professors how much they gave to .... each year.
2 He returned late last week to Italy to attend to ....
3 The company is slow to respond to ....
4 Scientists believe the Iceman froze to .... and was covered by a blanket of snow.
5 The thunder started just as we were nodding off to ....
6 I still hold to .... that people should be allowed to have private lives.
7 The government will not submit to ....

C Match up the two halves of each sentence.

1 We must now move on ...
2 The president will temporarily hand over ...
3 I woke up and couldn't get back ...
4 I am disabled and she sees ...
5 It took him some moments for his eyes to adjust ...

a ... to sleep.
b ... to the darkness of the interior.
c ... to all my needs.
d ... to the next phase of development.
e ... to the vice-president.

D Fill in the gaps in the sentences below with the correct particle.

1 I must have dropped .... to sleep.
2 Alex has fought such a battle to get .... to a normal life.
3 The Government will not cave .... to terrorism.
4 The intelligence people switched .... to more regular duties.
5 As I set off, it occurred to me that I had never got .... to making a will.
6 His former allies in the nationalist movement had, he said, sold .... to the communists.
7 To go .... to what you were saying, there's actually nothing to touch it when it goes well.
8 Handing .... to his co-pilot, Pegg took Davies into one of the cabins.

Verbs used with *to*: 3

1 Here are some more groups of verbs which are followed by the preposition *to* and a noun group or an '-ing' clause:

■ **verbs indicating that one thing is similar to or the same as another, or is related to it in some way**

amount	apply	correspond	measure up	relate

*That number **corresponds** to a telephone number on this list he gave me.*

*The subject of quality and how it **relates** to school work would be discussed with students.*

■ **verbs indicating that something changes to something else**

change	convert	drop	rise	sink	turn

*Stir until the mixture **changes** to a smooth paste.*

*Before long, the crowd's amusement **turned** to anger.*

*Her voice **dropped** to a whisper.*

■ **verbs indicating that a quantity, level, or thing increases or decreases. The prepositional phrase indicates the final quantity or level.**

build	decrease	go down	plunge	slide
build up	dip	go up	rise	slip
climb	dive	increase	shoot up	slump
come down	drop	jump	shrink	soar
decline	fall	plummet	sink	tumble

*The number of people injured **has increased** to almost a thousand.*

*My weight **went down** to seventy pounds.*

■ **verbs used when indicating a total or the result of a calculation**

add up	amount	average out	come

*He said defence spending **amounted** to 17,600 million rupees this year.*

*In 1894 Hamilton scored 196 runs, which **averaged out** to slightly more than 1 per game.*

■ **other common verbs**

add	dance	listen	resort
agree	extend	lose out	sing along
appeal	fall	(not) matter	stand up
belong	get through	object	tune in
come round	happen	rally	turn
contribute	lead	refer	warm

*This is money which **belongs** to me.*

*What **happened** to James?*

*The poorer nations **objected** to this plan.*

Agree, listen, object, refer, and *resort* are sometimes used in the passive.

*Voters rejected the plan even though it **had been agreed** to by all of Canada's political leaders.*

In the case of *object* and *resort,* the preposition *to* is sometimes followed by an '-ing' clause.

*This law was prompted by fears that poor people **might resort** to selling their body parts for hard cash.*

In the case of *lead* and *object,* the preposition *to* is sometimes followed by a noun group and an '-ing' clause.

*The popularity of the fax **has led** to large sums being invested in its development.*

In the case of *refer,* the prepositional phrase is sometimes followed by another prepositional phrase beginning with *as* which indicates what someone or something is called.

*She always **referred** to the murder as 'that business'.*

Different forms of the pattern

*Who **did** you **talk** to when you were there?*

*We have got to try and find out **who** this **belongs to**.*

*Let us consider first the paintings **to which** Foucault **refers**.*

*The music is not quite loud enough to **dance to**.*

*I have some business to **attend to**.*

*He does not call it capitalism, but that is **what** it **amounts to**.*

2 A few verbs are followed by two prepositional phrases, the first beginning with *to* and the second beginning with *for*. This pattern is **V to n for n**.

Most verbs with this pattern are concerned with asking someone for something.

appeal	apply	pray	turn	write

*Detectives **have appealed** to the public for information on the missing girl.*

***Write** to the appropriate tourist office for details.*

Apologize also has this pattern. The prepositional phrase beginning with *for* indicates why someone apologizes.

*She **apologized** to them for the delay.*

A In the sentences below, put a dotted line under the verb used with a pattern described in this Unit. Then underline each of the other parts of the pattern.

1 Something must have happened to him.

2 In response, some people have resorted to carrying guns.

3 But he is prepared to stand up to the critics.

4 They have a right to be listened to by adults.

5 I will not accept the disappearance of the European civilisation to which I belong!

6 There was immediate public concern about what this might lead to.

7 Shortly afterwards he found himself homeless and applied to the council for accommodation.

8 Just knowing that you have someone to turn to can be very helpful.

9 Most people do not object to their records being used for medical research.

10 She steadfastly maintained that her grandsons, whom she always refers to as 'the boys', were innocent.

B Rewrite each of the following pairs of sentences as one sentence.

1 In the same month Canada's jobless rate increased. By the end of the month it was 9.3 per cent.
In the same month Canada's jobless rate increased to 9.3 per cent.

2 His voice rose. It became a scream.
....

3 The average monthly wage has fallen. It's now about £19.
....

4 Her expression changed. It became one of horror.
....

5 The tax on fuel will go up next spring. It will then be 17.5 per cent.
....

6 By the 1970s, the number of political clubs had declined. There were only 300.
....

C Rewrite these sentences using the verb given in brackets with the pattern **V** *to* **n** *for* **n**.

1 He asked the United States for help in stopping the war. (appeal)
....

2 I asked God to give me some guidance. (pray)
....

3 Nicoll was unsure of his ground and sent a letter to Waite asking for advice. (write)
....

4 I told Fraiser I regretted my treatment of him. (apologize)
....

Verbs used with *to*: 4

Some verbs are followed by a noun group and a prepositional phrase which consists of *to* and a noun group. For example, in *I lent some money to my father*, the verb *lend* is followed by the noun group *some money*, the preposition *to*, and the noun group *my father*. This pattern is **V n to n**. (With phrasal verbs, the particle comes either after the noun group or after the verb.)

Active pattern

	Verb group	noun group	*to*	noun group
We	explained	the situation	to	him.
I	showed	the sketches	to	my producer.

Passive pattern

	Verb group	*to*	noun group
The car	must be restored	to	its rightful owner.
Your findings	should be reported	to	the police.

Verbs with this pattern belong to the following meaning groups:

■ **verbs concerned with giving, selling, or transferring something to someone**

accord	distribute	hand back	pass on	supply
assign	donate	hand on	pay	surrender
award	export	hand over	present	transfer
bring	extend	introduce	rent	transmit
commit	feed	lease	restore	turn over
concede	give	leave	sell	
contribute	give back	lend	serve	
dedicate	grant	let	slip	
deliver	hand	pass	submit	

*I **gave the cards to Helen**.*

*The president **assigned** this task to Vice President Al Gore.*

*The building **was leased** to International Creative Management*. (passive)

*The fear is that the disease **could be transmitted** to humans who eat beef*. (passive)

■ **verbs concerned with communicating something to someone**

address	describe	pass on	reveal
admit	dictate	present	say
announce	disclose	put	suggest
bid	explain	read	teach
break	express	recommend	tell
call out	give	relate	wave
communicate	introduce	remember	write
confess	leak	repeat	
deliver	mention	report	

*She turned and **addressed** her next remarks to Mary Ann.*

*Police **were** last night **breaking** the news of the tragedy to Faye's parents*, who were away on holiday.

*Please **don't** ever **mention** this to Frank.*

*She **wrote** a letter to her parents.*

■ **verbs indicating that someone offers or promises something to someone**

offer	pledge	promise

*Travel companies yesterday **offered** cheap deals to holidaymakers who book next year's break early.*

*He **promised** grants to landowners and farmers.*

■ **verbs indicating that someone shows something to someone**

demonstrate	display	show

*He promised me I'd admire this part of the country, wanted to **show** it to me.*

■ **verbs indicating that someone tells people in authority that someone has done something wrong**

betray	denounce	report	turn in

*The few who challenged him disappeared or **were betrayed** to the police*. (passive)

In the case of *turn in*, the noun group following the verb is often a reflexive pronoun.

*The third suspect **turned** himself **in** to the police department later that afternoon.*

Practice

A In the sentences below, put a dotted line under the verb used with *to*. Then underline each of the other parts of the pattern. (For different forms of the pattern, see Unit 81.)

1 We never displayed emotion to each other.
2 The gallery director surrendered his keys to the building manager.
3 The guest house had been recommended to me by a friend.
4 Over the past five years, offices in the city have been rented to the public sector.
5 You've never been able to pledge your loyalty to me.
6 He announced that Egypt had presented proposals to the United Nations.
7 In the end, Newman reports to the police an attack on him and a neighbour by the local gang.
8 It's a tragedy he may not be able to pass the company on to his children.

B Rewrite these sentences using the pattern **V n to n**.

1 She convinced her husband to lend their son $1,200 to start his own business.
   She convinced her husband to lend $1,200 to their son to start his own business.

2 She also taught university students English.
   ....

3 I handed Eleanor the letter.
   ....

4 In 1979, only 8 per cent of British firms awarded managers annual bonuses.
   ....

5 When I told my doctor this, he looked worried.
   ....

6 A widower has left a dogs' home £60,000.
   ....

7 He had sold Paramount the film rights in 1926.
   ....

8 He gave the President a message from his kidnappers.
   ....

C Fill in the gaps in the sentences below using the verbs in this list. Use each verb once.

admit   break   deliver   demonstrate   denounce
describe   dictate   present   promise   suggest

1 I was a little doubtful when this project was .... to me by the Editor.
2 He .... a speech to the Rio summit yesterday.
3 Italy has .... economic aid to Albania to discourage migration.
4 The award was .... to her by the Rt. Honourable Lord Dennis Howell.
5 The bank .... its error to the Clarkes and offered to rectify the situation.
6 If he .... Evans to the police, none of them would ever keep the money.
7 The news was .... to Diana late on Tuesday night.
8 Get a picture in your head and .... that person to me.
9 This technique was .... to me by my friend, Ellen Zariodis.
10 The Story of Art was .... to a typist three mornings a week entirely from memory.

Verbs used with *to*: 5

Here are some more groups of verbs which are followed by a noun group and a prepositional phrase beginning with *to*:

■ **verbs concerned with adding something to something else or connecting one thing to another, either physically or metaphorically**

add	compare	lend	relate
attach	connect	link	stick
bring	join	match	tie

*This herb **adds** a lovely flavour to the food.*

*The optic nerve **connects** the eye to the brain.*

*The government **has attached** conditions to its peace proposals which are unacceptable to the rebels.*

*The President appeared to **link** a solution to the Gulf crisis to talks on other Middle East disputes.*

*George Orwell **compared** writing a book to having an illness.*

■ **verbs concerned with attributing a particular thing, event, or quality to someone or something**

ascribe	attach	attribute	put down

*He said their success **could be put down** to their simplicity and their clean image.* (passive)

The preposition *to* is sometimes followed by an '-ing' clause.

*Kelly **attributes** her coping ability to growing up in a big family.*

The preposition *to* is sometimes followed by a noun group and an '-ing' clause.

*Some officials **attribute** this to people not knowing where to go.*

■ **verbs concerned with sending or taking someone or something to a place, or allowing them into a place or organization**

admit	drive	post	send	transmit
commit	lead	refer	take	
direct	mail	return	transfer	

*He **directed** them to a classroom and dashed off.*

*He borrowed heavily to **send** his three sons to the best schools.*

*I **sent** a letter to the hospital, explaining what an exceptional patient she was.*

■ **verbs concerned with appointing someone to a position, or with moving them from one job or role to another**

appoint	nominate	promote	recruit	transfer

*The Hungarian Prime Minister **has appointed** two new ministers to his government.*

*The women **were transferred** to other jobs that paid less.* (passive)

■ **verbs concerned with changing something to something else**

change	cut down	lower	reduce
convert	drop	promote	shorten
cut	increase	raise	turn

*As part of his conversion he **changed** his name to Muhammad Ali.*

*He had a tendency to **drop** his voice to a whisper.*

*Her mother's pension **has** just **been raised** to 16,000 roubles a month.* (passive)

*Kelly **was promoted** to senior vice-president.* (passive)

Many of these verbs are sometimes followed by a noun group and two prepositional phrases, the first beginning with *from*, and the second beginning with *to*.

*The bank **increased** its interest rate from 8 percent to 8.75 per cent.*

*The period for appeal against death sentences **was reduced** from ten days to three.* (passive)

A Match up the two halves of each sentence.

1 Why do you compare yourself ...
2 The public no longer attaches any stigma ...
3 Try to relate your child's homework ...
4 You may put this down ...
5 We will then post the leaflets ...
6 The Prime Minister promoted her ...
7 The detector converts the light ...
8 He calmly admitted them ...

a ... to everyday life.
b ... to the house.
c ... to divorce.
d ... to an electrical signal.
e ... to them having no sense of humour.
f ... to you free of charge.
g ... to a Cabinet position.
h ... to your sister all the time?

B Put the different parts of these sentences in the right order.

1 to / tie / the ladder / a branch / firmly ....
2 six points / have reduced / Arsenal / to / Liverpool's lead ....
3 he / to / in 1968 / Assistant Director / was promoted ....
4 the hospital / referred / to / her / I / for a scan ....
5 details of the bet / the central computer / were transmitted / to
....
6 have cut / 9 percent / to / Chase Manhattan and Mellon banks / their lending rates
....

C Fill in the gaps in the sentences below using the nouns in this list. Use each noun once.

accidents   applicants   fires   job   painting   profits   visits

1 As many as 70 per cent of .... are attributed to driver error.
2 The captain was informed he had been appointed to another ....
3 .... will be returned to the United States in dollars.
4 She would like to cut the .... down to one a month.
5 They held details of job vacancies and they tried to match .... to jobs.
6 So far only one death is attributed to the ....
7 Rubens brought a new vitality to ....

D Rewrite the sentences below using the words or figures given in brackets and the prepositions *from* and *to*.

1 The government computer changed his birthdate. (1917 / 1971)
   The government computer changed his birthdate from 1917 to 1971.
2 Several of the major banks dropped their interest rates. (7.5 percent / 8 percent)
   ....
3 Soon after I arrived, I raised our advertising budget. ($15 million / $100 million)
   ....
4 They have rejected plans to lower the voting age. (18 / 20)
   ....
5 The Free Democratic Party was able to increase its vote. (9 percent / 11 percent)
   ....

Here are some more groups of verbs which are followed by a noun group and a prepositional phrase beginning with *to*:

■ **verbs concerned with inviting someone to take part in something**

ask	challenge	invite

She **invited** us *to a lavish party* to celebrate her fiftieth birthday.

■ **verbs concerned with putting someone or something in a particular state, or making them behave in a particular way**

drive	move	reduce	restore	put up

Atkins admits that the nightmare **has driven** her *to thoughts of suicide*.

She **was reduced** *to begging on the streets*. (passive)

■ **verbs concerned with making someone experience something unpleasant**

condemn	expose	put	sentence	subject

The main aim must be to find these children families and **not condemn** them *to institutions*.

In the case of *put*, the prepositional phrase is always *to death*.

They **were** declared heretics and **put** *to death*. (passive)

■ **verbs indicating that someone injures, scares, or bores someone.** The prepositional phrase is used to indicate the result or degree of the action or effect.

beat	crush	kick	stab
bore	drink	scare	starve
burn	frighten	shoot	

I wish Alex would take me out, but I'm afraid I **bore** him *to death*.

They were afraid that if they made the slightest mistake they **would be beaten** *to a pulp*. (passive)

In the case of *drink*, the noun group following the verb is always a reflexive pronoun. The verb *starve* often has this pattern as well.

He thought he was a failure and **drank** *himself to death*.

■ **verbs concerned with concentrating on or restricting yourself to one particular thing**

address	confine	give	pay	turn
apply	dedicate	give over	restrict	
commit	devote	limit	switch	

He wants to **devote** more time *to his family*.

Sean then **turned** his attention *to marketing his company's product*.

I no longer **paid** attention *to my lessons*.

With many of these verbs, the noun group following the verb is often a reflexive pronoun. In the case of *address*, it is always a reflexive pronoun.

The Guardian **addresses** itself *to the question of how the Labour opposition should act over the issue*.

We don't want to **commit** ourselves *to doing anything that might require too much strength, endurance, or time*.

You should try to **limit** yourself *to three cups of tea a day*.

■ **other common verbs**

apply	expose	introduce	owe	trace back
attract	give	leave	postpone	treat
do	help	lend	prefer	
draw	hold	mean	trace	

Gently **apply** the cream *to the affected areas*.

I want to **draw** your attention *to some other statistics that were published during the late 1980s*.

He is a fine sportsman who **has given** pleasure *to millions of people*.

I'**m going to hold** you *to your promise*, so don't you forget.

The goalkeeper seemed to **prefer** dribbling the ball up the field *to defending his goal*.

In the case of this sense of *lend*, the noun group following the verb is always a reflexive pronoun. The verb *help* often has this pattern as well.

The system **did not lend** itself *to rapid reform*.

Do help yourself *to another drink*.

In the case of *mean*, the noun group following the verb is always an **amount**.

Our mothers' approval **means** a lot *to us*.

Different forms of the pattern

What **did** he **say** *to you*?

Who **did** you **give** the money *to*?

Do you know what she **said** *to me* today?

He was to have been guest of honour at a banquet *to which* 250 guests **had been invited**.

He said he **would hand over** *to the police* any weapons found in the building that day.

I wanted to punish him for what he **did** *to me*.

A In the sentences below, put a dotted line under the verb used with *to*. Then underline each of the other parts of the pattern.

1 Looking for alternatives, he was attracted to the newspaper business.
2 We have to trace the problem right back to its source.
3 His family will have to take measures to prevent him from drinking himself to death.
4 Why should householders be subjected to the same question year after year?
5 Last week thousands were moved to tears at the sombre memorial service in the town.
6 That was the goal to which she had dedicated herself since Franklin's birth.
7 He told me to just ask you to the dance like a normal person.
8 I split up from a long-term girlfriend and started to apply myself to my work in a really concentrated way.

B Fill in the gaps in the sentences below using the verbs in this list. Use each verb once.

bore   challenge   condemn   devote   limit   postpone   prefer   reduce

1 He overheard two women talking about a new children's book that had .... them to tears.
2 On March 24, he .... Brookes to a fight.
3 He'd really thought he could continue drinking if he .... himself to champagne.
4 The hearing has now been .... to August 3.
5 Many papers continue to .... several pages to the various aspects of events in the Soviet Union.
6 The government .... them to a life of poverty.
7 I think I .... the snow to this dreary rain.
8 He'll probably .... you to death talking about carpentry all day!

C Rewrite these sentences using the verb given in brackets with the pattern **V n *to* n** or its passive.

1 I would like to focus your attention on the article overleaf. (draw)
   I would like to draw your attention to the article overleaf.

2 She could receive the death sentence if she is convicted. (sentence)
   ....

3 Your job is important to you, isn't it? (mean)
   ....

4 Why are we having to suffer all these inconveniences? (expose)
   ....

5 Callwell also dealt with the difficult problem of reprisals. (address)
   ....

6 None of his immediate family were on the guest list for his wedding. (invite)
   ....

7 They would still rather have fish and chips than fruit and fibre. (prefer)
   ....

82 Verbs used with *towards*

1 Some verbs are followed by a prepositional phrase which consists of *towards* or *toward* and a noun group. For example, in *We are heading towards war*, the verb *head* is followed by the preposition *towards* and the noun group *war*. This pattern is **V towards n**. With some verbs, the preposition is sometimes followed by an '-ing' clause.

	Verb group	*towards*	noun group/-ing clause
We	are racing	towards	complete economic collapse.
Bernard	worked	towards	reversing these attitudes.

Verbs with this pattern belong to the following meaning groups:

■ verbs indicating that someone or something is going to be in a particular state or situation, or is going to do a particular thing

drift	head	race	shift
edge	move	rush	turn

*The ruling party seems to **be heading towards a resounding defeat**.*

*The United States **has** apparently **shifted towards neutrality**.*

■ verbs indicating that someone or something is likely to have a particular characteristic or opinion, or to do a particular thing

lean	tend

*They're very anxious, and they **tend towards depression**.*

■ verbs concerned with trying to achieve something

strive	work

*Students participating in the programme are encouraged to **strive towards a high level of achievement**.*

*We need to **work toward giving women and children the power and resources to protect themselves**.*

■ verbs indicating that something or someone is partly responsible for something happening or being achieved

contribute	count	help	lead

*The slowing down of the domestic economy **helped towards the improvement in exports**.*

*People from the neighbourhood **have contributed towards the cost of the shrine**.*

*The document they have drafted **should help towards finding a solution to the crisis**.*

Different forms of the pattern

*This is **something** we **are** continually **working towards**.*

2 Some verbs are followed by a noun group and a prepositional phrase which consists of *towards* or *toward* and a noun group. For example, in *She is now directing her talents towards music*, the verb *direct* is followed by the noun group *her talents*, the preposition *towards*, and the noun group *music*. This pattern is **V n towards n**. With some verbs, the preposition is sometimes followed by an '-ing' clause.

Active pattern

	Verb group	noun group	*towards*	noun group/-ing
They	contributed	$3	towards	costs.
He	directed	his efforts	towards	helping people.

Passive pattern

	Verb group	*towards*	noun group/-ing
We	are drawn	towards	a life of simplicity.
The savings	were put	towards	reducing the deficit.

Verbs with this pattern belong to the following meaning groups:

■ verbs concerned with causing someone to do something or be attracted to something

draw	push

*This, coupled with his wife's death, **pushed** him **towards resignation** in 1983.*

*O'Keeffe **was drawn towards art** from an early age.* (passive)

■ verbs concerned with providing part of a sum of money

contribute	give	put

*The British government **contributed** £50,000 **toward the cost of the relief operation**.*

*Any spare money **is put towards buying a flock of sheep**.* (passive)

■ *Direct* also has this pattern.

*Planning **is** therefore largely **directed towards improving or preserving existing living conditions**.* (passive)

Practice

A In the sentences below, put a dotted line under the verb used with a pattern described in this Unit. Then underline each of the other parts of the pattern.

1 Politically I lean towards the right.

2 Marriage was something I believed every girl strove towards.

3 While offering credit, the course would not count toward graduation requirements.

4 We need to pull the British economy out of the recession it now seems to be heading towards.

5 It's a typical political diversion to direct responsibility towards the family.

B Put the different parts of these sentences in the right order.

1 is working / he / his Air Transport Pilot's Licence / towards

....

2 being organised / firms / towards / on a regional basis / are edging

....

3 inevitably / towards / are pushed / using bank overdraft facilities / they

....

4 moved / the president / decentralizing his country's rigid state-run economy / towards

....

C Fill in the gaps in these sentences using *towards* or *to* (see Units 77 and 78).

1 We're probably heading .... avoiding major choices and major decisions.

2 His debts amounted .... over a thousand million dollars.

3 The American healthcare system is shifting .... preventive care.

4 The Parliament has agreed .... changes in the constitution.

5 The island's banks will not normally lend .... small and medium-sized companies.

6 The sleet changed .... snow and a blanket of white soon obscured the trail.

7 His £1,000 grant will help .... the cost of books, paper and especially postage.

8 Chinese cuisine is 4000 years old and tends .... the exotic and spectacular.

D Rewrite these sentences using the verb given in brackets with *towards*.

1 It's in their interest to promote whatever encourages greater cooperation. (lead)
It's in their interest to promote whatever leads towards greater cooperation.

2 We are now heading for a terrible war that would be fought with highly destructive bombs. (rush)

....

3 Small businesses had each donated $3000 for the event. (contribute)

....

4 It is not surprising that they are trying to have separate identities. (strive)

....

5 Some of the president's advisers are beginning to favour the use of air attacks. (lean)

....

6 On the surface, the country is gradually getting closer to democracy. (move)

....

7 An increasing number of men are interested in facial cosmetic surgery. (turn)

....

Verbs used with *with*: 1

Some verbs are followed by a prepositional phrase which consists of *with* and a noun group. For example, in *I couldn't cope with the pressure*, the verb *cope* is followed by the preposition *with* and the noun group *the pressure*. This pattern is **V *with* n**. With some verbs, the preposition is sometimes followed by an '-ing' clause.

	Verb group	*with*	noun group/-ing clause
I	can't cope	with	relationships.
The volunteers	will help	with	teaching English.

Many verbs with this pattern are **reciprocal verbs**. These verbs are dealt with in Unit 87, and are not included in the lists in this unit.

Verbs with this pattern belong to the following meaning groups:

■ **verbs concerned with coping or dealing with a problem**

battle	deal	grapple	wrestle
cope	fight	struggle	

*She **has had to cope** with losing all her previous status and money*.

Deal is sometimes used in the passive.

*The matter **has been dealt** with by the school to our satisfaction*.

■ **verbs concerned with continuing to do something, or doing something that has been planned**

carry on	go ahead	persevere	proceed
continue	go on	persist	push ahead
get on	go through	press on	stick

*We **must continue** with the campaign*.

*In the New Year, the district board will vote on whether to **go ahead** with the plan*.

*I **couldn't get on** with clearing up in the kitchen because they kept quarrelling*.

■ **verbs indicating that someone gets involved with something or someone, sometimes when this is undesirable**

(not) bother	interfere	play around	work
dabble	mess about	tamper	
experiment	play	toy	

*I **didn't experiment** with drugs until I was in my mid-20s*.

*They say they **will not interfere** with press freedom*.

*I **played around** with the colour until I got the effect I wanted*.

Most of these verbs are sometimes used in the passive.

*The vehicle's brakes **had been tampered** with*.

■ **verbs concerned with helping someone to do something**

assist	help	help out

*She loved **helping out** with amateur dramatic productions*.

*They **can assist** with organising car hire, ferry tickets, and flights to Geneva*.

*They **help** with feeding the cows*.

■ **verbs concerned with associating with someone, or beginning to have an association with them**

associate	get in	go round	keep in	register
carry on	get off	integrate	move in	take up

*The point is, I'm not supposed to **associate** with Westerners, except in the way of business*.

*His wife says she'd have known if he **was carrying on** with any other woman*.

*Before you **register** with a new doctor, ask around to find one who is good with children*.

■ **verbs concerned with speaking to someone**

consult	laugh	plead	reason

*I tried to **reason** with him*.

In the case of *plead*, the prepositional phrase is sometimes followed by a to-infinitive clause.

*I **pleaded** with her to stop but she wouldn't*.

A In the sentences below, put a dotted line under the verb used with a pattern described in this Unit. Then underline each of the other parts of the pattern. (For different forms of the pattern, see Unit 84.)

1 If you are taking tranquillizers and want to stop, consult with your doctor first.
2 I don't know whether I can go through with this.
3 Do you cope well with stress?
4 I found this quite hard to deal with.
5 We are in a country where nature has been interfered with for a very long time.
6 And on the dressing table sits the clutter of make-up that Nikki loved to experiment with.
7 I pleaded with Frances to get a move on as she dawdled to the car.

B Rewrite these sentences using the pattern **V with n.**

1 The President is putting his life at risk by continuing to exercise in a stressful way.
The President is putting his life at risk by continuing with stressful exercise.

2 He simply carried on working. ....
3 They had planned to go on investigating. ....
4 Meanwhile, the House of Lords select committees have been pressing on and doing important work.
....
5 The task of a coalition government would be to push ahead and create a market economy.
....

C Rewrite each of the following pairs of sentences as one sentence, using *with* and a noun group or '-ing' clause.

1 They carve, sell and demonstrate their products. Their children help.
Their children help with carving, selling and demonstrating their products.

2 There may be a major famine in Mozambique. We do not have the resources to cope.
....
3 We are planning the closing ceremonies for October. Volunteers are needed immediately to assist.
....
4 I used to wear expensive jewellery. Now I don't bother.
....
5 Have you considered a softer hair-style? Now is the time to experiment.
....

D Fill in the gaps in the sentences below using the verbs in this list. Use each verb once.

deal   integrate   interfere   reason

1 For immigrants there are difficulties in .... with the local community.
2 I try to .... with him but sometimes he just doesn't listen and I end up shouting at him.
3 He's threatening to use his gun on anyone who tries to .... with him.
4 Special police squads were set up to .... with the problem of football violence.

Verbs used with *with*: 2

Here are some more groups of verbs which are followed by the preposition *with* and a noun group:

■ **verbs indicating that someone does something, or has a particular physical sensation, because of an emotion**

burn	laugh	scream	sigh
cry	roar	shake	tremble

The audience **screamed** *with delight*.

She **was trembling** *with rage*.

Productive use: Any verb which indicates behaviour or a physical feeling can be used with this pattern.

■ **verbs concerned with beginning or ending**

begin	finish	open	start off
end	kick off	start	

The proceedings **began** *with a minute's silence* in memory of those who died in the revolution.

The preposition *with* is sometimes followed by a noun group and an '-ing' clause.

An earlier attempt by police to remove the demonstrators **ended** *with a policeman being shot dead*.

■ **verbs concerned with responding to something that has been done.** The prepositional phrase indicates what someone does in response.

compensate	counter	reply	respond

I said hello. Brent **responded** *with a glare*.

■ **verbs indicating that something has or contains a lot of something else, or that someone is full of a quality or feeling**

abound	bulge	be crawling	fill	swarm
bristle	be bursting	drip	fill up	teem

The town **was crawling** *with visitors today*.

Both horse and rider **were dripping** *with sweat within five minutes*.

Fill and *fill up* indicate that something becomes full of something else.

Catherine's eyes **filled** *with tears*.

■ **verbs indicating that something is compatible with something else, or like something else**

accord	(not) compare	comply	fit in	tie in

Nearly all chores can wait or be organised to **fit in** *with a weekly schedule*.

The emergency lighting system **should comply** *with British Standard 5266*.

■ **verbs indicating that someone agrees or disagrees with something such as a plan**

agree	(not) argue	disagree	fall in	go along

I **do not disagree** *with this viewpoint*.

The three main political parties are likely to **go along with the plan**, *despite some private reservations*.

■ **verbs concerned with reaching or remaining at a particular level or position**

catch up	fall behind	keep up

If children are removed from their poor environments, they **can catch up** *with other children*.

He faces losing his home after **falling behind** *with the payments while in jail*.

■ **other common verbs**

belong	meet	rest	sympathize
check	rank	stock up	

You **should** *always* **check** *with your doctor before starting on regular medication*.

The continuing process of patient negotiation **has met** *with limited success*.

The decision to free him **rests** *with the Belgian Justice Minister*.

Productive uses

1 The prepositional phrase indicates what someone uses to do something. An example is *I* **shave** *with an old-fashioned Gillette razor*.

2 The prepositional phrase indicates what company someone uses, for example when travelling or investing money. Examples are *We* **flew** *with British Airways* and *My husband* **has banked** *with the Co-op since before the war*.

Different forms of the pattern

In the cases **that** *we*'**re dealing** *with, they were not sure what their rights were*.

There are some feelings **which** *are hard to* **cope with**.

Sit him in a highchair with **a toy** *to* **play with**.

What *we* **are dealing** *with here is pure wickedness*.

A Fill in the gaps in the sentences below using the nouns in this list. Use each noun once.

despair   exhaustion   joy   laughter   relief   resentment   terror

1   He had his audience of 500 journalists roaring with .... at his first joke.

2   Forstmann was a deeply angry man, burning with ....

3   She wraps her arms around herself and starts to cry with ....

4   Two minutes later he clambered out and stood, shaking with ...., at the side of the pool.

5   Crews and sponsors sigh with .... when boats reach the finish in one piece.

6   He is so happy that he just laughs with ....

7   He remembers screaming with .... at being taken away by a stranger.

B Match up the two halves of each sentence.

1 The ships bristle ...	a ... with tears.
2 His face was dripping ...	b ... with reporters.
3 Our wallets bulge ...	c ... with confidence.
4 The house was swarming ...	d ... with sweat.
5 The priest's eyes filled ...	e ... with fish.
6 I was bursting ...	f ... with wounded.
7 The rivers and lakes abound ...	g ... with new equipment.
8 Our hospital quickly filled up ...	h ... with credit cards.

C Fill in the gaps in the sentences below using the verbs in this list. Use each verb once.

check   compare   counter   fall in   fit in   keep up   meet   start   stock up   sympathize

1   Alison .... with her employer's wishes.

2   It doesn't .... with the real thing, does it?

3   But this plan has .... with resistance within the SPD.

4   There was trouble last night that .... with a fight in a restaurant.

5   'Where you off to?' he asked Hugh, walking quickly to .... with him.

6   I think those who .... with the group make up a fairly significant percentage of the population.

7   Women do not enjoy equal status with men. My critics will doubtless .... with the argument that men and women cannot be equal because they are different.

8   What the hospitals want .... with some of the president's goals for health care reform.

9   He tells me to .... with him before I buy any new equipment for the business.

10 I put the answering machine on, ... with plenty of food and arrange not to see anyone.

Verbs used with *with*: 3

Some verbs are followed by a noun group and a prepositional phrase which consists of *with* and a noun group. For example, in *I covered my face with my hands*, the verb *cover* is followed by the noun group *my face*, the preposition *with*, and the noun group *my hands*. This pattern is **V n *with* n**.

Active pattern

	Verb group	noun group	*with*	noun group
People	associate Blend	good looks the spinach	with with	good deeds. the egg yolks.

Passive pattern

	Verb group	*with*	noun group
The paper The cake	will be printed was topped	with with	your own name. chocolate icing.

(With phrasal verbs, the particle comes either after the noun group or after the verb.)

Verbs with this pattern belong to the following meaning groups:

■ **verbs concerned with considering two people, things, or groups as being the same or connected**

associate	confuse	identify	match	mix up
compare	connect	link	match up	muddle up

*You have to stop **associating** beauty with gardens or lawns.*

*For most of her long professional life she **was identified** with the theatre.* (passive)

The verb and the preposition *with* are sometimes followed by '-ing' clauses.

*Again and again, we seem to **confuse** talking about an issue with doing something about it.*

■ **verbs concerned with joining or mixing two or more things, physically or metaphorically**

blend	connect	link	mix
combine	integrate	merge	

Mix the egg yolks with the milk.

*Heavy consumption of alcohol **is linked** with cancer of the liver.* (passive)

The verb and the preposition *with* are sometimes followed by '-ing' clauses.

*Laura **combines** bringing up a family with buying and selling young horses.*

■ **verbs concerned with giving something to someone or something**

arm	fit	infect	leave	serve
equip	fix up	inject	present	shower
feed	furnish	issue	provide	supply

*He refused to **provide** them with this information.*

*I'll see if I **can fix** you **up** with a job.*

■ **verbs concerned with changing the appearance of something by adding things to it**

decorate	hang	mark	print	stamp	trim

*The wall facing him **was decorated** with elaborate dark wood carvings.* (passive)

*Each photo is automatically **printed** with the date on which it was taken.* (passive)

■ **verbs concerned with putting something around or on top of something, or with covering the surface of something, physically or metaphorically**

cover	spread	top	wrap up
line	surround	wrap	

Cover the pan with a damp cloth and leave it to cool.

*Her technique was to **surround** herself with strong women and weak men.*

■ **verbs concerned with filling something, physically or metaphorically**

cram	fill up	load	pack	soak
fill	flood	load up	pile	stuff

*Then it was time to pack the bags, **load up** the vehicles with bikes and trophies, and make for the airport.*

*I try to **fill** my mind with other things by getting out and about.*

■ **verbs concerned with scattering objects or a liquid on something**

shower	spray	sprinkle	strew

*Firemen **sprayed** the wreckage with foam to prevent the plane catching fire.*

A Rewrite these sentences using the pattern **V n _with_ n** or its passive.

1 Spread the rest of the butter on the bread.
   Spread the bread with the rest of the butter.

2 Paul and the boys have loaded baskets onto a wagon.

3 Sprinkle chopped chives over the fish.

4 Nicotine should be sprayed on the trees about a week after the petals have fallen.

5 I was cramming sausage into my mouth when I heard the news.

6 Fixed entry times will be printed on the tickets to cut unnecessary queuing.

7 As far as he knew, none of the three had supplied any information to the police prior to the raid.

8 The award was to have been presented to Mr Mandela at the concert in his honour on Monday.

9 The band are so noisy that before taking the stage they stuff little bits of foam in their ears.

B Rewrite these sentences using the verb given in brackets instead of _give_ or _put_.

1 The government has given its troops modern Chinese-made weapons. (equip)
   The government has equipped its troops with modern Chinese-made weapons.

2 We put balloons and streamers round the dining room. (decorate)

3 Staff will be given new grey-and-yellow designer uniforms. (issue)

4 Put a clean handkerchief over your nose and mouth. (cover)

5 This gave Frances a perfect excuse for leaving home. (provide)

6 We put into carts all the blankets, bandages, and medication we could spare. (load up)

C Match up the two halves of each sentence.

1 Certain people are linked in our minds ...   a ... with the painting of Picasso.
2 Envy is often confused ...   b ... with flower petals, spices, or dried leaves.
3 In 1960 the News Chronicle was merged ...   c ... with jealousy.
4 Other teas are blended ...   d ... with existing radiators.
5 The boiler can be connected ...   e ... with certain scents.
6 Her work in dance has been compared ...   f ... with the Daily Mail.

Verbs used with *with*: 4

Here are some more groups of verbs which are followed by a noun group and a prepositional phrase beginning with *with*:

■ **verbs concerned with doing something with another person**

agree	do	negotiate	take up
check	exchange	pick	talk over
conclude	fight	play	talk through
debate	have	share	trade
discuss	hold	strike	
dispute	make	swap	

*The university might acquire some more property if it **can agree** a deal with the city council.*

*Many prefer to **talk** these issues **through** with a careers adviser or close friend.*

*But who would choose to **pick** a fight with this man?*

*Further talks **are being held** with the protest leaders.* (passive)

Many of these verbs are **reciprocal verbs**: see Unit 88.

■ **verbs concerned with speaking to someone about an unwelcome subject**

bore	bother	burden	confront

*I **won't bore** you with private matters.*

*I pulled on a coat and boots and went round right away to **confront** Muriel with her stupidity and cowardice.*

■ **verbs indicating that someone has problems**

be beset	be confronted	be faced	be weighed down

*The oil and gas industries **are beset** with labour production problems.* (passive)

*As the fire burned, Stackpole and his wife **were faced** with making decisions on what they would save.* (passive)

■ **verbs concerned with thinking about or reacting towards something or someone in a particular way**

acknowledge	greet	meet	regard	treat	view

*I asked them to **treat** me with respect.*

*Any newcomers **are** always **viewed** with suspicion.* (passive)

■ **verbs concerned with spending your time doing or dealing with something**

busy	concern	occupy	trouble

The noun group following the verb is always a reflexive pronoun.

*The other women **occupied** themselves with their perpetual sewing.*

*She snapped on the lights and **busied** herself with preparing a quick dinner.*

■ **verbs concerned with beginning or ending a period of time or an event in a particular way**

begin	close	end	finish	open	start

*He **began** the day with a seven o'clock breakfast.*

*You may want to **end** the session with a hug.*

■ **verbs concerned with helping someone**

assist	help	help off	help on

*You **might be able to help** us with a problem.*

*I was then asked to **assist** them with raising the profile of the club.*

*He **helped** her **on** with her coat.*

■ **other common verbs**

charge	do	replace	threaten	trust

*They now seem to be setting out to **replace** the people with robots.*

*1,000 of the world's 9,700 bird species **are threatened** with extinction.* (passive)

In the case of *do*, the noun group following the verb is always an **amount**.

*You **can do** quite a lot with quite a little money if you channel it in the right direction.*

Productive use: A prepositional phrase beginning with *with* is often used to indicate what someone uses to do something. An example is *An ordinary wooden door **has been reinforced** with steel plates*, which means that the steel plates have been used to reinforce the door.

Different forms of the pattern

*What **were** you **charged** with?*

*The other animal we **associate** with Spain is the hard-working, long-suffering mule.*

*Sceptics are right to **treat** with caution the results produced using this method.*

*Each person will be given a box and **some photographs** to **decorate** it with.*

A In the sentences below, put a dotted line under the verb used with *with*. Then underline each of the other parts of the pattern.

1 I just wanted to check one thing with you.
2 We are confronted with the fact that we are aging.
3 Talk all this over with your husband.
4 His victory has been met with enthusiasm from all sides of the party.
5 And what do you suggest we replace it with?
6 It is an episode which few in Hollywood regard with any pride.
7 All the student need concern himself with is reality.
8 There are a lot of players I like to play golf with for a variety of reasons
9 He views with horror the relentless deterioration in Britain's trade balance over the past four decades.
10 Police have so far given no details of the offences with which those arrested will be charged.

B Fill in the gaps in the sentences below using the verbs in this list. Use each verb once.

begin   bore   conclude   confront   discuss   meet   replace   trust

1 I need to .... some matters with you.
2 When most companies are .... with problems, they try simply to fix them.
3 The floor boards had completely rotted and we had to .... them with special fast-drying concrete.
4 I won't .... you with all my personal and professional problems.
5 The President .... his day with a jog in suburban Louisville.
6 It may well be that if we .... a deal with Reed, other shareholders may decide to follow suit.
7 There is no way we're going to .... him with another large job.
8 The announcement was .... with dismay from trade unions.

C Put the different parts of these sentences in the right order.

1 her / with / he / a quick smile / exchanged ....
2 with / they / each other / hatred / view ....
3 he / talks / with / the other leaders / will be holding ....
4 scepticism / has greeted / the Government / with / such reports
    ....
5 the day / start / with / some / meditation or exercise ....
6 I'm / sorry / my troubles / to bother / with / you ....
7 nothing / has / to replace / he / with / them ....

Reciprocal verbs: 1

Reciprocal verbs are used to refer to actions or relationships in which two or more people, groups, or things may be equally involved. Each of them has a particular combination of patterns.

Pattern combination 1

• The verb is used with a plural Subject. This pattern is **pl-n V**.

plural noun group	Verb group
They	were talking.
Those values	don't conflict.

• The verb is also used with a Subject referring to one participant and followed by a prepositional phrase indicating the other. In most cases, the preposition is *with*. This pattern is **V with n**.

	Verb group	with	noun group
We	've been talking	with	our suppliers.
Their views	conflicted	with	those of the President.

Verbs with this combination of patterns belong to the following meaning groups:

■ **verbs concerned with speaking and communicating**

agree	communicate	meet	speak
argue	differ	negotiate	talk
chat	disagree	quarrel	

Her parents never *argued*.
He *was arguing* with *his girlfriend* and she hit him with a frying pan.

Chat, speak, and *talk* are sometimes followed by *to*.

I've been talking to Jim Hoffman.

■ **verbs concerned with fighting, either physically or metaphorically, or competing**

battle	compete	fight	tie
clash	draw	struggle	

Did he say why they were fighting?
About a thousand students fought with riot police in the capital.

Battle, compete, draw, and *fight* are sometimes followed by *against*.

Increasingly, local government is competing against the private sector.

■ **verbs concerned with relationships**

break up	get along	get on	meet up	separate
co-operate	get divorced	go out	pair up	split up
fall out	get married	link up	part	team up

We'd only been going out for about six months at the time.
He used to go out with Kylie Minogue.

His demands increased until we finally broke up.
Just before Penny's marriage I broke up with a man I'd been seeing for over a year.

Part and *separate* are followed by *from*, not *with*.

I have parted from my wife by mutual agreement.

The passive verb *get married* has a plural Subject or is followed by *to*.

She gave a little party for me and Alexander after we got married.
He got married to Sue when he was very young.

The passive verb *get divorced* has a plural Subject or is followed by *from*.

We got divorced a few months ago.
He is getting divorced from his wife of 11 years.

■ **verbs indicating that two or more things are similar or compatible, or are not similar or compatible**

agree	coincide	contrast	differ	match up
clash	conflict	correspond	match	

Do your needs clash?
Don't make any policy decisions which clash with official company thinking.

Correspond is sometimes followed by *to*.

The French grading system does not correspond to the English.

Differ is followed by *from*, not *with*.

How does your work differ from theirs?

■ **verbs indicating that two or more things occur together, are in contact, or come into contact**

coexist	collide	intersect	overlap
coincide	combine	merge	

The two Skyhawk jets apparently collided in mid-air as they were practising takeoffs.
A car collided with a motorcycle at a junction.

A Rewrite these sentences using the pattern **pl-n V**.

1 He was arguing with my mum every night, hour after hour.
He and my mum were arguing every night, hour after hour.

2 I disagree with Stephen about lots of stuff.
....

3 Warwickshire drew with Northamptonshire at Edgbaston.
....

4 I've just split up with my girlfriend.
....

5 We get on very well with them.
....

Now rewrite the following sentences using the pattern **V *with* n.**

6 When my husband and I broke up five years ago it was amicable.
....

7 Why don't Johnson and Kravis team up?
....

8 High-spending countries and low-spending countries can coexist.
....

9 The interests of the governors and the governed should coincide.
....

10 The Haywards Heath Building Society and the Yorkshire Building Society are to merge.
....

B Fill in the gaps in these sentences using *against*, *to*, or *from*.

1 He chatted .... me at the bar for a while.
2 The French fought .... the Communists for eight years.
3 Charlotte Pilcher is getting married .... James Studholme in July.
4 She also thinks that women's taste in music differs .... men's.
5 Kristina will be competing .... her sister Nicola for a place in the team.
6 In the previous year I had separated .... my husband after nineteen years of marriage.

C Divide the list of verbs concerned with relationships into three smaller groups:

1 five verbs indicating that people begin a relationship
....

2 six verbs indicating that a relationship ends
....

3 four verbs indicating that people have a relationship, or have a good relationship
....

Pattern combination 2

- The verb is used with a plural Subject and is followed by a noun group. This pattern is **pl-n V n**.

plural noun group	Verb group	noun group
MPs They	have been debating swapped	the issue. gossip.

- The verb is also used with a Subject referring to one participant and is followed by a noun group and a prepositional phrase indicating the other participant. The preposition is *with*. This pattern is **V n with n**:

	Verb group	noun group	*with*	noun group
I	am not going to debate	the issue	with	you.
I	could swap	data	with	them.

Verbs with this combination of patterns belong to the following meaning groups:

■ **verbs indicating that people discuss something**

debate	discuss	dispute	talk over	talk through

We discussed her options.
She'd never discussed it with her children.
The results of the test are discussed with a doctor.
(passive)

■ **verbs indicating that two people or groups agree on future arrangements, or are trying to agree on them**

agree	do	negotiate	sign
conclude	make	reach	strike

The US and Canada then negotiated an agreement that was completed in 1987.
The city's Peace Officers Association is currently negotiating a new contract with the city.
'I came in here thinking we were going to do a deal,' Roberts said.
European airlines are not ready to do a deal with him.

■ **verbs used with noun groups such as *talks* and *a conversation* to indicate that two or more people talk to each other**

have	hold

Northern Ireland's Catholics and Protestants are holding talks today in Belfast.
He's also scheduled to hold talks with Jordanian officials before returning to Washington.

Talks are being held between the unions and the government at the moment but no agreement looks likely. (passive)

■ **verbs concerned with relationships**

break off	form	make	patch up	resolve
establish	have	make up	renew	settle

The two West African states had broken off relations two years ago after bloody clashes erupted in the frontier area.
The Soviet Union broke off relations with Israel in 1967 at the time of the Six Day War.

Unless France and Britain can resolve their differences there will be no treaty on political union.
The former captain has now resolved his differences with team officials.

In the case of *break off* and *make up*, when the noun group comes directly after the verb, it is always *it*.

Then did she come here to make it up with him?

■ **verbs indicating that people give, say, or do things of the same kind to each other**

exchange	swap	trade

They took photographs of each other and exchanged addresses.
The separatists exchanged fire with security forces at two places in the old city area.

■ **verbs concerned with fighting or competing**

fight	fight out	have	play

We had a fight yesterday, and he walked out.
I had a fight with my husband.

In the case of *fight out*, the noun group following the verb is usually *it*.

Let the two of them fight it out.

■ *Share* also has this combination of patterns.

My sister and I shared a bedroom until I was seven.
Livy wished she wasn't sharing a room with Caroline.

Practice

A In the sentences below, put a dotted line under the verb used with the pattern **pl-n V n** or **V n** *with* **n**, or its passive. Then underline each of the other parts of the pattern.

1 For over two hours the police fought a pitched battle with the marchers.
2 They had clearly been having this conversation for some time.
3 When did you renew contact with your sister?
4 I've been having a chat with that son of yours.
5 And if you have any questions, you can talk them over with Mr. Bacon himself.
6 Why don't we talk it through tomorrow night?
7 Japan and South Korea have reached an agreement on the legal status of Koreans living in Japan.
8 It was reported that contact had been made with nationalist ex-soldiers fighting on the borders.
9 Britain and China have settled their differences over the plan for a new airport in Hong Kong.
10 The two have been trading insults and accusations since well before the start of the campaign.

B Rewrite these sentences using the pattern **pl-n V n**.

1 So I struck a deal with them.
  So we struck a deal.

2 Above her head, he exchanged glances with Lloyd.

3 Mr. Bush discussed the proposed arms reductions with Mr. Gorbachev.

4 The only time I really had a conversation with him was at luncheon in the Elysee.

5 My husband was playing golf with the children on the green outside our house.

Now rewrite the following sentences using the pattern **V n** *with* **n**.

6 Nigeria and Cameroon share a common border.

7 My boyfriend and I discussed it. We just don't think it's necessary.

8 He and Grandpa were supposed to play chess today.

9 Patrick and I were having a discussion about games.

10 Israel and Bulgaria have re-established diplomatic relations after a break of twenty-three years.

177

Reciprocal verbs: 3

Pattern combination 3

- The verb is used with a plural Subject. This pattern is **pl-n V**.

plural noun group	Verb group
They Their eyes	embraced. met.

- The verb is also used with a Subject referring to one participant and followed by a noun group referring to the other. This pattern is **V n**.

	Verb group	noun group
She Her eyes	embraced met	Jack. Harry's.

Verbs with this combination of patterns belong to the following meaning groups:

- **verbs concerned with affectionate contact**

embrace	hug	kiss

They kissed. She drove away.
She **kissed me** and turned out the light.

- **verbs concerned with relationships**

date	divorce	marry

They divorced in 1976.
She **divorced her Army husband** at 23.
Norman **was divorced** by his wife Jo eight years ago. (passive)

- **verbs concerned with fighting or competing**

fight	meet

In the park, **three boys were fighting** and I said 'You can stop that immediately!'
I **had to fight him** even though I hate violence.

Sudan and Uganda will meet in the final of the East and Central African Challenge Cup on Thursday.
Manchester City **meet Leeds** at home tomorrow.

- **verbs indicating that two or more things are in contact, physically or metaphorically**

cross	intersect	join	meet	overlap	touch

Her apartment was three miles out of Georgetown, at the junction where **two highways meet**.
Dentists may detect bone loss at the part of the jaw where the teeth **meet the bone**.

- *Meet* also has this combination of patterns when it is used to talk about one person meeting another person.

John and I met in high school.
I **met her** about a month ago.

- *Match* also has this combination of patterns.

The signatures matched.
They told him he couldn't board the plane unless the name on his ticket **matched the one** on his passport.

Emphasizing reciprocity

With most reciprocal verbs, a **reciprocal pronoun** (*each other* or *one another*) can be used after the appropriate preposition or after the verb to emphasize that an action involves both or all the people mentioned as Subject.

All across the world today **people are fighting with each other** and killing each other because of their racial and religious differences.

The fans **would exchange** *information with one another*.

They **hugged** *each other*.

Each other and *one another* are also used to give ordinary verbs a reciprocal meaning.

They **hate** *each other*.

We **gave** *each other support*.

Sara and I **looked** *at each other*.

Practice

A Rewrite these sentences using the pattern **pl-n V**.

1 She married him in 1981. *They married in 1981*

2 His militant views matched hers.

3 The experiences of women are beginning to overlap those of men.

4 Despite a declaration of cease-fire in Yugoslavia, Serbians were fighting Croats this morning in Osijek.

5 His fingers touched mine as I gave him the glass.

Now rewrite the following sentences using the pattern V n.

6 He and his first wife divorced in 1939.

7 Richard watched as Henry and Joanna embraced.

8 Catherine and John have been dating for five months.

9 His ashes will be immersed at the place where the Rivers Ganges and Jamuna meet.

10 She and her husband met ten years ago when he came to Moscow on a business trip.

B Rewrite these sentences using *each other* or *with each other*.

1 Police and demonstrators fought for four hours.
Police and demonstrators fought each other for four hours.

2 We embraced, laughing.

3 His guests seemed to agree about everything.

4 Counseling can help two people to learn to get along.

5 Is it true that women are more able to discuss personal things?

6 Lines of longitude all cross at the poles.

7 The Association says schools should not compete.

8 Increasingly, people needed better ways to communicate.

9 These orbiting particles collided, and ended up forming a flat disc.

Ergative verbs: 1

Ergative verbs are verbs with a particular combination of patterns. The commonest type of ergative verb has the following patterns:

● The verb is used on its own. This pattern is **V**.

	Verb group
Her life	had changed.
My spirits	lifted.

● The verb is followed by a noun group. This pattern is **V n**.

	Verb group	noun group
The war	had changed	her life.
Sunlight	can lift	the spirits.

As you can see, the sort of person or thing indicated by the Subject of the pattern **V** may also be indicated by the noun group in the pattern **V n**.

Verbs with this combination of patterns belong to the following meaning groups:

■ **verbs concerned generally with change**

alter	change	vary

Society has changed.
He thought his book would change society.

■ **verbs concerned with physical or chemical change.**
  Many of these verbs relate to cooking.

bake	cool	dry	fill up	melt
boil	cool down	dry out	flood	soften
burn	dissolve	fade	freeze	spoil
cook	drain	fill	heal	warm up

While the water boiled, I picked up the shopping and put it away.
Milwaukee residents have been advised to boil their tap water or drink bottled water.

Stir the mixture with a metal spoon until the sugar has dissolved.
Dissolve the sugar in the warm water and add the dried yeast.

It is a good idea to brush the fish with oil while it is cooking.
Cook the fish for 3-4 minutes on each side.

■ **verbs concerned with something breaking or with something or someone being damaged or destroyed**

blow up	burst	hang	snap
break	crack	mark	split
burn	crash	rip	tear
burn down	drown	shatter	wear away

With most of these verbs, the Subject of the pattern **V n** refers to the person or thing causing the damage. With a few verbs, the Subject may refer to the person or thing that suffers damage or loss, as in *I broke my arm.*

*When he is captured, he **will hang**.*
*The convicted men were due to **be hanged** this week, having lost their appeal recently.* (passive)

*He slammed the door with such force that a window **broke**.*
*They threw stones and **broke the windows of buses**.*

■ **verbs concerned with the size, degree, or shape of something changing**

bend	diminish	expand	shrink	tighten
contract	drop	grow	straighten out	widen
decrease	double	increase	stretch	

*The cables are designed not to **stretch**.*
*Ease the pastry gently into the corners of the tin, making sure you **don't stretch** it.*

*With the use of random drug testing, the chance of being caught **has increased**.*
*Just one severe sunburn in childhood **can increase the chances of developing skin cancer**.*

■ **verbs concerned with change of an abstract kind**

clear up	ease off	lift	strengthen	weaken
develop	improve	revive	turn around	wind down

*In the course of the 1950s the situation **improved**.*
*We are convinced that he **could improve the political situation**.*

*Unemployment has soared as state industries **wind down**.*
*The recession went on and on, and I slowly **wound down the business**.*

A These sentences are about damage and show the pattern V n. Rewrite them using the pattern V.

1 He snapped the stem of his wine glass.
The stem of his wine glass snapped.

2 They burned down one of the city's main hotels.

3 Eddie cracked the ice on the pond.

4 She had torn her new dress.

Now rewrite these passive sentences using the pattern V.

5 A warship was blown up in the harbour.

6 The gold on the rim of the glass has been worn away.

7 The rear window of her patrol car was shattered.

8 Apparently, the Titanic's hull had been broken twice on or near the surface.

B Fill in the gaps in the pairs of sentences below using the verbs in this list.

bake   change   clear up   cool   fade   improve   melt

1 a) I could smell loaves of bread .... *baking* .... in the oven.

   b) Most British housewives rarely .... *bake* .... their own bread.

2 a) The material had .... with wear.

   b) Light will .... the colours in organic materials.

3 a) In many cases this condition will .... of its own accord.

   b) Moisturizing cream will often .... the irritating rash.

4 a) Stir over low heat until the jelly has ....

   b) .... the butter over a gentle heat.

5 a) The sooner the law ...., the better for us all

   b) We've waited a long time for them to .... the law.

6 a) The flavour will .... if the vinegar is kept for a long time.

   b) Processing can .... the appearance and flavour of some foods.

7 a) Let the oil .... completely and then strain it.

   b) .... the rhubarb mixture until it is half-set.

Ergative verbs: 2

Here are some more groups of ergative verbs with the patterns **V** and **V n**:

■ **verbs concerned with a change in the pace of something**

accelerate	quicken	slow	slow down	speed up

The pace of the negotiations **has quickened** in recent months.
The crisis has at least indirectly forced the President to **quicken the pace of change**.

The car never **slowed down**.
Narrowing the road **would slow down** traffic.

■ **verbs concerned with a thing, organization, or group of people dividing into two or more parts**

break down	break up	divide	split	split up

When the Soviet Union **split up**, Sahlins lost touch with the theater completely.
One of the largest commuter airlines in the country **may be split up**. (passive)

■ **verbs concerned with someone starting to have a feeling or emotion, or to be in a particular state**

calm down	panic	revive	wake	worry
cheer up	relax	tire	wake up	

Just **calm down** and tell me what's happened.
Frannie spent two hours on the phone with Dede, trying to **calm her down**.

He **woke** some hours later, completely refreshed.
She **woke** Betsy and they called the police.

■ **verbs concerned with something moving or being moved**

bounce	move	settle	spin	turn over
break off	open	shake	tip up	
close	pile up	shift	turn	
get away	rock	shut	turn around	

Her arms **were moving** like a ballerina's.
He was paralysed from the waist down and **could** only **move his left arm**.

The ground **shook** beneath his feet.
The shock waves **shook the ground** throughout most of Wales.

The door **opened** and Mrs MacMahon, carrying a tray, entered.
He **opened the door** and hurried out.

He found a part of the arrow that **had broken off**.
Edgar **broke off** another chunk of chocolate.

■ **verbs concerned with the driving or operation of a vehicle**

back	land	sail	start	stop
halt	reverse	stall	start up	

The van came to a halt, **reversed**, halted again.
A gunman opened fire as PC White **reversed the car** in a desperate attempt to escape.

Then my engine **stalled**, and had to be restarted.
She **stalled the engine**, and restarted it.

Most of these verbs have another **V** pattern in which the Subject indicates the person driving, operating, or travelling in the vehicle.

When she got out, the driver **reversed**, crushing her against the patrol car.

Verbs in this group which refer to movement also have the patterns **V prep/adv** and **V n prep/adv**: see Unit 93.

■ **verbs concerned with a place opening or closing**

close	close up	open up	shut down
close down	open	shut	

Rumbelows said 200 of its 500 shops **may close** within two years.
The company **is closing** its copper cable factory at Bishopstoke, Hampshire.

His new shop **opens** today at 659 Fulham Road.
I want to **open a dress shop**.

A Say whether the sentences below show the pattern **V**, or the pattern **V n** or its passive.

1 Nine nuclear power stations had been closed down. ....*V n (passive)*........

2 Stop the car! ....

3 We can speed up the process. ....

4 Southern Illinois was shaken by an earthquake this morning. ....

5 She shut the door slowly. ....

6 Suddenly their seat tipped up. ....

7 The truck was accelerating. ....

8 I turned the key in the lock. ....

9 Has the engine stopped? ....

10 Whole families have been split up by the fighting. ....

11 Turn the fish pieces over carefully. ....

12 The left rear tyre spun helplessly. ....

B In each of the pairs of sentences below, one of the verbs from this list is missing. Mark where it goes and say what it is.

cheer up   panic   relax   revive   tire   wake up   worry

1 a) When she / she felt completely refreshed. ....*woke up*................
   b) I had to / her / every four hours to give her her medicine. ....*wake up*................

2 a) People were beginning to in the midday heat. ....
   b) Anyone with this condition should avoid exercise which them. ....

3 a) When one side of the boat began taking in water, people and rushed to the other side, causing the boat to sink. ....
   b) Her screams the men and they fled. ....

4 a) I was feeling a bit down, and she told me to. ....
   b) Ethel suggested Paul should her daughter by visiting her while she recovered from a skiing accident. ....

5 a) Seeing how free and easy he was, everyone and started talking freely too. ....
   b) A high-carbohydrate dinner will you for sleep during the flight. ....

6 a) In a few minutes the girls had enough to be able to tell their story. ....
   b) Horrified staff tried to him but he was dead by the time he reached hospital. ....

7 a) Don't, John, I'm not going to let you down. ....
   b) What me is that we might get an increase in inflation. ....

1 Here are some more groups of ergative verbs with the patterns **V** and **V n**:

■ **verbs concerned with an activity or situation starting, stopping, or continuing**

begin	continue	halt	start
break up	end	resume	stop

The blaze **started** in the kitchens of the thirty-six floor hotel.
The following year she **started** a blaze at her husband's parents' home.

For now, the fighting **has stopped**, but the guns haven't.
Today's agreement has done nothing to **stop** the fighting.

■ **verbs concerned with something coming into existence or becoming noticeable**

develop	form	show up	turn up
evolve	show	spread	

Some rare early photographs of the city of Jerusalem **have turned up** in Minnesota.
A search of the woods around the murder scene also **turned up** a knife.

A queue **forms** outside Peter's study.
Form a queue at the nearest doorway.

■ **verbs concerned with a machine or device working**

blow	light	play	run	work
explode	operate	ring	sound	

A taped message from his mother **plays** in the background.
I think I'**ll play a record**.

When the final whistle **blew**, a lot of fans came onto the pitch.
We were waiting for the referee to **blow his whistle**.

2 Another type of ergative verb has the following patterns:

● The verb is followed by an adjective group. This pattern is **V adj**.

	Verb group	adjective group
The doors	slid	open.
The lock	snapped	shut.

● The verb is followed by a noun group and an adjective group. This pattern is **V n adj**.

	Verb group	noun group	adjective group
She	slid	the door	open.
The Major	snapped	his box	shut.

Verbs with this combination of patterns belong to the following meaning groups:

■ **verbs concerned with something opening or closing, usually noisily or violently**

blow	slam	slide	snap	swing

In a second someone was inside, and the door **slammed shut**.
He managed to drag her back inside the vehicle and **slam the door shut**.

A second later the door **swung open**.
Walking to the gate, I **swung it open**, crossed to the front door and rang the bell.

■ **verbs concerned with someone or something becoming detached from something**

pull	shake	work

The adjective is usually free or loose.

He shook his head back and forth, and tried to **pull free**.
With a sob, she **pulled herself free**.

One of the pins **had worked loose** from the outer plate.
While we were still trying to **work it loose** we saw two more wild cats creeping towards us.

Practice

A These sentences are about things starting, stopping, or continuing, and show the pattern **V**. Rewrite them using the pattern **V n** and the Subject given in brackets.

1 The countdown for the launch has begun. (they)
   They have begun the countdown for the launch.

2 Our meetings rarely started on time. (we) ....

3 This idiocy must stop. (you) ....

4 His marriage broke up. (his affair) ....

5 The talks are continuing during the afternoon. (the two sides)

   ....

6 Production of chemical weapons has already halted in both countries. (both countries)

   ....

7 Play will resume on Wednesday. (the remaining teams)

   ....

8 He said that decisive action would be taken unless the protest ended. (the students)

   ....

B Fill in the gaps in these pairs of sentences using the nouns in this list.

bell   bomb   heating system   horn   matches

1 The .... wouldn't light.
  He'd burnt himself trying to light ....

2 A .... exploded in the capital last night, injuring two children.
  The separatists also exploded a .... in a stationary bus.

3 He walked around to the front and rang the ....
  The .... rang, signalling the start of classes.

4 An oncoming truck sounded its ....
  The .... sounded as Lauren was pushed against the wheel.

5 The .... doesn't work.
  We need to know if she understood how to work the ....

C Rewrite the sentences below, using the verb and adjective given in brackets. The pattern may be **V adj** or **V n adj**.

1 The top drawer of his desk opened easily. (slide / open)
   The top drawer of his desk slid open easily.

2 She shut the door. (slam / shut)

   ....

3 They could be injured if the window shuts. (blow / shut)

   ....

4 He opened his briefcase. (snap / open)

   ....

5 He paused before letting the gate shut behind him. (swing / shut)

   ....

185

Another type of ergative verb has the following patterns:

● The verb is followed by a prepositional phrase or, in some cases, an adverb. This pattern is **V prep/adv**.

	Verb group	prep. phrase/adverb
The smile	turned	into a grin.
The troops	had marched	away.

● The verb is followed by a noun group and a prepositional phrase or, in some cases, an adverb. This pattern is **V n prep/adv**.

	Verb group	noun group	prep. phrase/adverb
Parents	can't turn	their house	into a fortress.
They	marched	the men	out.

Note that the noun group may come after an adverb, as in *He slid back the door*.

Verbs with this combination of patterns belong to the following meaning groups:

■ **verbs concerned with change**

change	convert	form	turn

He **changed** *into a fish*.
I always try to **change** *a dissatisfied customer into a happy one*.

■ **verbs concerned with something breaking or dividing**

break	divide	shatter	snap	tear
break up	separate	smash	split	

It **shattered** *into tiny pieces*.
The steam **shatters** *the rock into tiny fragments*.

Let's **separate** *into smaller groups*.
The police wanted to **separate** *them into smaller groups*, but they insisted on staying together.

■ **verbs concerned with something moving somewhere**

blow	move	slide	spread	transfer
bounce	pass	smash	squeeze	
dig	roll	spill	stick	
drop	rub	spin	swing	
float	shift	splash	tip	

The red soil **blew** *away in the wind*.
A storm **blew** *away the sand dunes*.

It developed into a huge game, with water **splashing** *everywhere*.
Leaning over the fountain, Joanna **splashed** *water upon her face*.

Make sure that the person **can transfer** *from wheelchair to seat* with relative ease.
They learn a few technical skills, such as how to lift a frail old person and **transfer** *that person from a chair or bed*.

■ **verbs concerned with vehicles going somewhere**

back	fly	land	reverse	sail	swing

The traffic jam was caused by a caravan **backing** *out of a driveway*.
He **backed** *his car out of the drive*.

Most of these verbs have another **V prep/adv** pattern in which the Subject indicates the person driving, operating, or travelling in the vehicle.

They **reversed** *out of the field* the way they had come.

■ **verbs concerned with a person, group of people, or animal going somewhere**

crowd	gather	pull	walk
gallop	march	transfer	withdraw

The horse started **walking** *away*.
They **walked** *their horses up the road*.

We **gathered** *in my office* at 7:30 a.m. every day.
Now, in the greatest secrecy, he **had gathered** *them all together*.

■ **verbs indicating that something begins or ends in a particular way**

begin	end	finish	open	start

The meeting **opened** *with a speech by the prime minister*.
The local chairman **opened** *the meeting with the usual pleasantries*.

A In the sentences below, put a dotted line under the ergative verb used with the pattern **V prep/adv**, or the pattern **V n prep/adv** or its passive. Then underline each of the other parts of the pattern and say which pattern it is.

1 The war has turned into a nightmare for them. ....*V prep*.................

2 The house had been converted into a wooden fortress. ....

3 Alan began to tear the portrait in half. ....

4 The car reversed out. ....

5 He backed the car down the driveway. ....

6 He restarted the engine, swung the car around and drove back to Hillsden's apartment.

   ....

7 When the plane landed at Stockholm's Arlanda airport, the hijacker gave himself up to police.

   ....

8 Teddy galloped around the course at terrific speed. ....

9 A large number of weapons, explosives and vehicles went missing when British troops were pulled out of Germany. ....

10 Sharpe toyed with the idea of marching his own men into that open space, but he knew he was too late. ....

B The following sentences are about something moving, and show the pattern **V n prep/adv**. Rewrite them using the pattern **V prep/adv**.

1 She dug her fingers into his arm.
   Her fingers dug into his arm.......................................

2 He spilled coffee onto the carpet.

   ....

3 They rolled the drum down the hill.

   ....

4 He swung his legs backwards and forwards.

   ....

5 He smashed his fist into her cheek.

   ....

Now rewrite these passive sentences using the pattern **V**.

6 My hat was blown off.
   My hat blew off.......................................

7 The central hatch cover was slid back.

   ....

8 The bottle was passed from hand to hand around the circle.

   ....

9 The drum is spun around, creating an unsettling illusion of movement.

   ....

10 The film is moved through the projector on a series of toothed wheels turned by a motor.

   ....

Verbs used with introductory *it*: 1

Sometimes the pronoun *it* does not refer back to something that has been mentioned, but points forward to a clause later in the sentence. We call this **introductory *it*.**

In the following patterns (Units 94–96), introductory *it* is the subject.

Verbs followed by a clause

it	Verb group	clause
It	seemed	that he would keep his word.
It	may help	to talk about it.
It	looks	as if there will be a rebellion.

1 The verb is followed by a that-clause. This pattern is *it* **V that.**

Verbs with this pattern belong to the following meaning groups:

■ **verbs indicating that something happens or becomes known, or that something is logically the case.** With *turn out*, the word *that* is sometimes omitted, as in *It turned out she was married.*

come about	emerge	follow	happen	turn out
come out	figure	get round	leak out	

It *happened* that Christopher Keene was available and interested.

It *emerged* that they shared a passion for sailing.

All eyes turned towards him, but it *turned out* he had nothing to say.

■ **verbs used when indicating what a situation is, or seems to be.** With *appear* and *seem*, the word *that* is often omitted, as in *It seems I'm wrong.*

appear	be	seem

It *appears* that the protest has thrown the government into a major political crisis.

Be usually occurs in a negative clause, or is used with a modal or an adverb such as *just* or *simply.*

It's *not* that I don't want a relationship, it's *just that* it would be really inconvenient.

It *may be* that another great change is on the way.

Seem is sometimes followed by a prepositional phrase beginning with *to* which indicates whose opinion you are giving.

It *seemed* to her that there was something odd about it.

■ **verbs indicating how someone feels about a situation or event**

help	hurt	matter

It *helps* that we work in the same business.

It *hurts* that people have such short memories.

Does it *matter* that you don't understand it?

Matter is also often followed by a wh-clause, or a prepositional phrase beginning with *to* and a wh-clause.

It *doesn't matter* how old you are.

It *doesn't matter* to them whether or not they sell your product.

2 The verb is followed by a to-infinitive clause. This pattern is *it* **V to-inf.**

Three of the verbs with this pattern indicate that something is helpful to someone, or is a good thing.

(not) do	help	pay

I explained that sometimes it *pays* to know the regulations.

It *doesn't do* to exaggerate.

The verb *hurt* also has this pattern.

It *hurt* to breathe.

3 The verb is followed by a clause beginning with *as if, as though,* or, in informal English, *like.* This pattern is *it* **V as if.**

Verbs with this pattern are used when indicating what a situation seems or feels like.

appear	be	feel	look	seem	sound

It *is* as if nothing at all has happened.

It *felt* as though a house had fallen on his leg.

These verbs are sometimes followed by a prepositional phrase beginning with *to.*

It *sounds* to me as though you've tried your best.

A In the sentences below, put a dotted line under the verb used with a pattern described in this Unit. Then underline each of the other parts of the pattern.

1 It helps to talk.
2 If more families will now settle in the area, it follows that there will be more children in school.
3 It looked to me as if this gun had been used recently.
4 The break-down of the talks came as it emerged that two protesters died in a demonstration outside the capital.
5 It is simply that owning one's own home is regarded as important to people.
6 In terms of both attainment and behaviour it matters which school a child attends.
7 It doesn't do to grab more than one's fair share.
8 It feels as if spring is in the air.

B Fill in the gaps in the sentences below using the verbs in this list. Use each verb once.

be   come about   hurt   matter   pay   turn out

1 I do not know how it .... that he saw them.
2 I had bet everything on the race, but it .... that I lost.
3 He wasn't a bad man. It .... just that he believed in discipline.
4 I'm disappointed. It .... to lose.
5 Please help. It doesn't .... whether your contribution is large or small.
6 Whether you plan to stay in Britain or go abroad, it .... to read the holiday brochure very carefully before you book.

C Rewrite these sentences using the verb given in brackets with introductory *it*.

1 Everybody found out that the accusation had been made. (leak out)
   It leaked out that the accusation had been made.
2 I thought that I was an important part of their lives. (seem)
   ....
3 Who won the game is not important. (matter)
   ....
4 I think you'll have to move house. (look)
   ....
5 I'm better off because I've got a tremendous family. (help)
   ....
6 I don't think they're going to pay any attention. (sound)
   ....
7 They don't mind whether or not they sell your product. (matter)
   ....

Verbs used with introductory *it*: 2

Passive verbs followed by a clause

it	Verb group	clause
It	is estimated	that a hundred people have now died.
It	was not disclosed	how much the sale will raise.

1 The verb is followed by a that-clause. This pattern is *it be V-ed that*. With some verbs, the word *that* is often omitted.

Verbs with this pattern belong to the following meaning groups:

■ **verbs indicating that something is said or shown**

be acknowledged	be confirmed	be reported
be agreed	be demonstrated	be revealed
be alleged	be disclosed	be rumoured
be announced	be emphasized	be said
be argued	be pointed out	be shown
be claimed	be proposed	be suggested

*Eventually it **was agreed** that the present laws would continue to apply in the same areas for two years.*

*Last week it **was reported** that the new coach had asked Martyn to stand down as captain.*

*It **was pointed out** that several different solutions fitted the known data.*

■ **verbs indicating that something is thought or discovered**

be accepted	be envisaged	be known
be anticipated	be established	be learned
be assumed	be estimated	be noticed
be believed	be expected	be presumed
be calculated	be feared	be reckoned
be considered	be felt	be seen
be decided	be found	be suspected
be determined	be hoped	be thought
be discovered	be intended	be understood

*They became concerned when it **was discovered** that more than nine thousand ballot papers had been forged.*

*It **is expected** that agreement will be reached by that date.*

2 The verb is followed by a wh-clause. This pattern is *it be V-ed wh*.

Verbs with this pattern indicate that something is known or becomes known.

be decided	be established	be revealed
be determined	be explained	be seen
be disclosed	be known	be shown
be discovered	be learned	be understood

*It **has** never **been established** whether either of the men survived.*

*It **is not known** who was behind the attack.*

Verbs followed by an adjective group and a clause

it	Verb group	adjective group	clause
It	is	important	that you are honest.
It	would look	pretty silly	to turn the proposal down.

1 The verb is followed by an adjective group and a that-clause. This pattern is *it V adj that*.

Verbs with this pattern are used when indicating what a situation is, seems, or becomes. The word *that* is often omitted, as in *It **is** certain he will be there.*

appear	become	look	remain
be	feel	prove	seem

*I think it**'s** important that you get to know them beforehand.*

*It quickly **becomes** apparent that he is not mad at all.*

*It **looks** likely that David has played his last game for the club.*

With *appear, be, become, remain,* and *seem,* the adjective group is sometimes followed by a wh-clause instead of a that-clause, depending on the adjective used.

*It **is not** clear why he is being held.*

2 The verb is followed by an adjective group and a to-infinitive clause. This pattern is *it V adj to-inf*.

Verbs with this pattern are used when indicating what an action is, seems, or becomes.

appear	become	look	remain
be	feel	prove	seem

*It **is** important to use lawyers who are experienced in these matters.*

*It **seemed** reasonable to hope that the war would soon be over.*

The adjective group is often followed by a prepositional phrase beginning with *for.*

*It **is becoming** difficult for our club to cope.*

With *be, feel, look,* and *seem,* the adjective group is sometimes followed by an '-ing' clause.

*It **was** nice talking to you.*

A In the sentences below, put a dotted line under the verb used with a pattern described in this Unit. Then underline each of the other parts of the pattern.

1 It was clear that he had lost a great deal of weight.
2 It seems doubtful whether any foreign government would support the plan.
3 It was reported a few minutes ago that oil has come ashore on a headland in South Devon.
4 By the year 2050 it is expected that one out of four persons will be over 65.
5 If it was ever discovered how Beryl had died, they would both be in serious trouble.
6 I mean, it does feel important to have children because it's always been something I've wanted.
7 The 11-plus exam is being brought back, it was announced yesterday.
8 It is understood the airline will begin two weekly services to Cairns in September.
9 It is not known who was responsible for the bomb, which was hidden in a crate in a busy market place in the old city.
10 In ancient Greece, students wore sprays of rosemary in their hair because it was believed that it improved the memory!

B Make these statements less direct or definite by rewriting them using the verb given in brackets with the pattern **it be** V-ed **that**.

1 The drug can be used to prevent a heart attack. (think)
   It is thought that the drug can be used to prevent a heart attack.
2 He only had a few weeks until he planned to retire after 41 years. (reveal)
   ....
3 A new town square with surrounding shopping should be developed on the site. (propose)
   ....
4 About three million dollars' worth of property has been destroyed. (say)
   ....
5 The vaccine will be successful. (hope)
   ....

C Match up the two halves of each sentence.

1 It appears increasingly likely ...   a ... to get doctors to work in country hospitals.
2 It became clear   ...   b ... that a United Nations force will be sent there.
3 It is difficult ...   c ... meeting you.
4 It was lovely ...   d ... seeing him suffer like this.
5 It was kind of you ...   e ... to take the trouble to write.
6 It is terrible ...   f ... that the plane had crashed.

Verbs used with introductory *it*: 3

Verbs followed by a noun group and a clause

it	Verb group	noun group	clause
It	bothered	her	that he hadn't asked for her.
It	seemed	a pity	to break up the peaceful scene.

1 The verb is followed by a noun group and a that-clause. This pattern is **it V n that**.

Verbs with this pattern belong to the following meaning groups:

■ **verbs used when indicating what a situation is, seems, or becomes.** The word *that* is often omitted, as in *It's a pity you weren't there.*

be	become	remain	seem

It's a shame that you live so far away.

Of course it remains a possibility that Mr Meier was the intended victim.

■ **verbs indicating how a situation makes someone feel**

amaze	disappoint	frighten	sadden	worry
bother	disturb	hurt	shock	
concern	embarrass	please	surprise	

It frightens me that kids are now walking around with guns.

Does it worry you that you don't eat properly?

Many of these verbs are sometimes followed by a wh-clause or a when/if-clause instead of a that-clause.

It amazes me how many plastic shopping bags are given out by cashiers in large supermarkets.

It always pleases me when guests compliment me on the look of my food.

■ **verbs indicating that an idea occurs to someone**

dawn on	hit	occur to	strike

Suddenly it hit me that this was not how I wanted to live my life.

It didn't occur to me that he didn't know me.

The noun group is sometimes followed by a wh-clause instead of a that-clause.

Even in that first moment it struck me how utterly dependent he was.

2 The verb is followed by a noun group and a to-infinitive clause. This pattern is **it V n to-inf**.

Verbs with this pattern belong to the following meaning groups:

■ **verbs indicating what an action or situation is, seems, or becomes**

be	become	remain	seem

It used to be a crime to help a slave escape.

The noun group is sometimes followed by a prepositional phrase beginning with *for*.

Death by poisoning would be simple to conceal here, because it was the custom for bodies to be burned.

■ **verbs indicating how a situation makes someone feel**

alarm	disturb	interest	scare	touch
bother	frighten	pain	shock	upset
delight	hurt	please	surprise	worry

You are always in my thoughts and it pains me to think of you struggling all alone.

It pleased him to see that he'd delighted her with his choice.

■ *Cost* and *take* also have this pattern. *Cost* is followed by an **amount**.

It takes courage to face the unknown.

It costs a fortune to fly these people in from all over the country.

Cost and one sense of *take* are sometimes followed by a noun group, an amount, and a to-infinitive clause.

It cost him a lot to admit he needed help.

It took them a long time to reach the other shore.

Take is sometimes followed by an amount, a prepositional phrase beginning with *for*, and a to-infinitive clause.

It took seven years for a settlement to be reached.

A In the sentences below, put a dotted line under the verb used with a pattern described in this Unit. Then underline each of the other parts of the pattern.

1 It seems a shame that it's taken him 32 years to change his image.
2 I couldn't face going to the hospital to visit my brother. It hurt me to see him so sick.
3 It shocked him to think he was capable of murder.
4 It took us at least two weeks to complete the assignment.
5 Didn't it strike you that he was awfully uptight and tense?
6 I could live for a week on what it cost to buy this shirt.
7 It struck her how self-centred she'd been, considering only her sorrow, not his.
8 It surprised him that so many had come to listen to him during lunchtime, but it saddened him that he did not see his brother in that audience.
9 It embarrassed her when friends insisted she was beautiful.
10 It was a pleasure to see my brother and his family.

B Rewrite each of the following pairs of sentences as one sentence.

1 Many of these people are regarded as frauds. This concerns me.
It concerns me that many of these people are regarded as frauds.

2 I wasn't as pleased to see John as I used to be. This bothered me.
....

3 The country is now in a position to mobilize its forces. This worries me.
....

4 She had not received either a note or a phone call from him. This disturbed her.
....

5 The Government never has enough cash for the public's needs but never fails to provide for MPs' salary increases. This amazes me.
....

6 He might have been on the wrong train. This hadn't occurred to me.
....

C Match up the two halves of each sentence.

1 It is my duty ...
2 It takes experience ...
3 It seemed a shame ...
4 It costs a lot of money ...
5 It surprised her ...
6 It frightened her ...

a ... to let her down.
b ... to find a building here in the wilderness.
c ... to print thick, full-colour catalogues.
d ... to contemplate the operation and its risks.
e ... to know how to get through the process.
f ... to support my husband.

Verbs used with introductory *it*: 4

In the following patterns (Units 97 and 98), introductory *it* is the Object.

Verbs followed by *it* and a clause

1 The verb is followed by *it* and a that-clause. This pattern is **V *it* that**.

Most of the verbs with this pattern indicate how a situation makes someone feel. These verbs have no equivalent passive pattern.

appreciate	hate	love
(cannot) bear	like	(cannot) stand

I really **appreciate** *it that you raised me in such a warm and happy family.*

I **hate** *it that you can paint contentedly while I'm feeling restless and bored.*

The verbs *arrange, have,* and *take* also have this pattern or its passive.

Rumour **has** *it that he is still alive.*

I **take** *it you haven't read the papers today.*

So it **was arranged** *that we should spend a week with Sally in London.* (passive)

2 The verb is followed by *it* and a clause beginning with *when* or *if*. This pattern is **V *it* when/if**.

Most of the verbs with this pattern indicate how a situation or possible situation makes someone feel or react.

accept	(cannot) handle	regret
appreciate	hate	(cannot) stand
(cannot) bear	like	(cannot) take
(cannot) believe	love	(cannot) understand
(cannot) endure	(not) mind	welcome
enjoy	prefer	

'I really **hate** *it when you cry like that,'* Oliver said.

I **can't stand** *it when you expect me to give up my friends for you.*

I **love** *it when music does something to my emotions.*

Frankly, we' **d prefer** *it if you could find an adequate excuse to leave the country for the time being.*

The verb *help* also has this pattern, when used with *cannot.*

I **can't help** *it if you think I'm odd.*

Verbs followed by *it*, a prepositional phrase beginning with *to*, and a clause

In the case of *put*, the clause is a that-clause. This pattern is **V *it* to n that**.

I **put** *it to him again that the money has got to come from somewhere.*

In the case of *leave* and *owe*, the clause is a to-infinitive clause. This pattern is **V *it* to n to-inf**.

You just shut your eyes, and **left** *it to the other people to clear up the mess!*

I **owe** *it to my country to fight for what's right.*

Verbs followed by *it*, a prepositional phrase beginning with *as*, and a clause

Verbs with this pattern are used when indicating how someone sees or interprets a situation or action. The clause may be a that-clause, a to-infinitive clause, or a when/if-clause.

accept	regard	see	take	view

They **will see** *it as a major coup that they managed to blow up one of their top priority targets.*

The Romans **regarded** *it as undignified to compete naked in front of spectators.*

I **take** *it as a compliment when people call me aggressive.*

A Match up the two halves of each sentence.

1 I know you'd prefer it ...
2 I loved it ...
3 We couldn't believe it ...
4 I can't stand it ...
5 I'd love it ...
6 She couldn't handle it ...
7 He hated it ...
8 I would appreciate it ...

a ... when I told her the truth.
b ... when one of my horses takes a knock.
c ... if you would locate the file for me.
d ... that he cared enough to ask.
e ... when we were told we were only half-way.
f ... when she spoke so crudely.
g ... if I weren't around here any more.
h ... if you could come.

B Think of two kinds of event or situation you like, and two you hate.

I like it when ....

I like it when ....

I hate it when ....

I hate it when ....

Now think of two things you would love to happen, and two you would hate to happen.

I'd love it if ....

I'd love it if ....

I'd hate it if ....

I'd hate it if ....

C Rewrite these sentences using *it*, *as*, and the verb given in brackets.

1 I believe it is my responsibility to identify the problems. (see)
I see it as my responsibility to identify the problems.

2 Most analysts think it almost inevitable that the alliance will be scrapped. (see)

....

3 Baron von Malchin wrote that he thought it was an honour to have known my father personally. (regard)

....

4 They thought it was a positive sign that the university agreed to the contract extension. (see)

....

5 The Dutch Presidency thought it was unhelpful to talk of independence for Slovenia and Croatia at that stage. (regard)

....

6 The public now expect us to have three finalists in every championship by right and think it is abnormal when we don't. (view)

....

Verbs used with introductory *it*: 5

Verbs followed by *it*, an adjective group, and a clause

1 The verb is followed by *it*, an adjective group, and a that-clause. This pattern is **V *it* adj that**.

Most verbs with this pattern are concerned with how someone evaluates or judges a situation.

believe	consider	feel	find	think

I __consider__ it essential that the photographer should do his own printing.

I __find__ it remarkable that my lad seems unaffected by the insecurity he's lived with for most of his life.

It is thought unlikely that there will be compulsory redundancies. (passive)

With *consider*, *find*, and *think*, the adjective group is sometimes followed by a when/if-clause.

I __found__ it disheartening when the horses were sold.

I __think__ it best if you leave at once.

The verb *make* also frequently has this pattern. The adjective that usually occurs with this verb is *clear*.

From the very beginning he __had made__ it clear that he did not have marriage in mind.

The adjective is sometimes followed by a wh-clause instead of a that-clause.

On the very first day, the United Nations __made__ it absolutely clear what he should do.

2 The verb is followed by *it*, an adjective group, and a to-infinitive clause. This pattern is **V *it* adj to-inf**.

Most verbs with this pattern are concerned with how someone evaluates or judges an action or state.

believe	consider	feel	find	judge	think

Most people __find__ it hard to understand how living with one's own children could be lonely.

He suspected that Samantha had attended such parties previously and __had not felt__ it necessary to tell him.

She dodged into the nearest toilet and remained there until she __judged__ it safe to emerge.

The verb *make* also frequently has this pattern.

The reflection of the sun on the surface of the water __made__ it impossible to see the bottom.

Verbs followed by *it*, a noun group, and a clause

Verbs with this pattern are used when indicating how someone evaluates or judges a situation or action. The clause may be a that-clause, a to-infinitive clause, or a when/if-clause.

believe	consider	feel	reckon
call	count	find	think

I sometimes __find__ it a strain to be responsible for the mortgage and household bills each month.

I __would consider__ it a favour if you would ask me home again next weekend.

The pilot __called__ it a miracle that no one was killed.

A Rewrite these sentences to form sentences showing whose opinion or viewpoint is being expressed, starting with the words provided. Then say what kind of clause follows the adjective group or noun group.

1 It is extraordinary that they should use a hospital as a fortress.
   We consider *it extraordinary that they should use a hospital as a fortress. (that clause)*

2 It is admirable that she wants to be independent.
   I think ....

3 It is unwise to spend large amounts of money on a few players.
   He believed ....

4 At first it was difficult to relax.
   At first I found ....

5 It is my duty to make sure they are given the proper atmosphere to succeed.
   I consider ....

6 It seemed very strange when she said, 'I don't have to answer your question.'
   We thought ....

7 It is a scandal that, in most states, fewer than 60 percent of children are immunized.
   Mrs Edelman called ....

8 It is likely that the tax officers' visits caught everyone by surprise.
   The spokesman thought ....

9 It is not necessary to hold direct talks with the NLD.
   The government does not believe ....

10 It was important that every room had an individual feel and flavour.
   They felt ....

B Use *find* with *it* and a variety of adjectives from this list to express your feelings on each of the matters mentioned below.

amazing   amusing   appalling   extraordinary   interesting   sad

1 People's breakfast habits are changing.
   I find it interesting that people's breakfast habits are changing. ....

2 There is little that can be done about this disease.
   ....

3 The press are prepared to publish unsubstantiated stories.
   ....

4 Alcohol is served in large quantities to young people.
   ....

5 People on the dole receive quite a good deal more money than students get, for doing nothing.
   ....

6 A 113-year-old Welsh church is being shipped to Japan to be made into a golf clubhouse.
   ....

197

Verbs used with general *it*

Sometimes the pronoun *it* does not refer to anything at all, or refers very vaguely to the general situation. We call this **general *it***.

Patterns with general *it* as the Subject

1 The verb can be used on its own, without anything following it. This pattern is *it* **V**.

Verbs with this pattern are all concerned with the weather.

brighten up	freeze	pour	snow	thunder
drizzle	hail	rain	be spitting	

She glanced out the window and saw that *it* **was raining** again.

It **will brighten up** in the next few days.

2 The verb is followed by an adjective group. This pattern is *it* **V adj**.

The verbs *be* and *get* are used when describing the weather, the temperature, or the light.

It **was chilly**, and he was glad of his coat and scarf.

We arrived just as *it* **was getting dark**.

One sense of *get* is used with the adjective *late*.

Well, *it's* **getting late**. I guess your wife will be wondering where you are.

3 The verb is followed by an adjective group and a prepositional phrase or adverb group. This pattern is *it* **V adj prep/adv**.

There is only one verb with this pattern, *be*. It is used to indicate your opinion of being in a place.

It's **nice here**.

It **was awful in hospital**.

4 The verb is followed by a noun group. This pattern is *it* **V n**.

There is only one verb with this pattern, *be*. It is used when indicating the time or the date.

It **was four o'clock in the morning**.

Patterns with general *it* as the Object

Many of these combinations of a verb and *it* are sometimes considered to be phrases. Most of them are informal English. With phrasal verbs, the particle comes after the word *it*.

1 The verb is followed by *it*. This pattern is **V** *it*.

Verbs with this pattern belong to the following meaning groups:

■ **verbs concerned with stopping doing something**

cool	cut out	hold	knock off	stop

These verbs are always or usually used in the imperative.

'**Hold it**, Mom. Better not call the cops,' Frank said quickly.

■ **verbs concerned with failure, success, and risk-taking**

blow	(cannot) hack	lose	overdo
chance	have had	make	push

'I **blew it**,' admitted Cook.

You'**ll make it**, don't worry.

Too much work can lead to exhaustion, so **don't overdo it**!

■ **verbs indicating how comfortable or well-off someone is**

be coining	be coining in	live up	rough	slum

He's had too comfortable a life, our friend. He **can rough** it for once.

He left Washington and he's now in Hawaii, **living it up** on his share of the money.

■ **other verbs**

clinch	settle	sweat out	watch
keep up	stick out	try on	

They'**re** just **trying it on** – I don't believe they'll go that far.

Watch it, Sam. You're going to spill that if you're not careful.

2 The verb is followed by *it* and a prepositional phrase or adverb group. This pattern is **V** *it* **prep/adv**.

Verbs with this pattern are used to indicate someone's opinion of being in a place.

enjoy	hate	like	love	prefer	(cannot) stand

My family **hated it in Southampton**.

I **love it here**. Everybody is so polite.

Practice

A Fill in the gaps in the sentences below using the words in this list, and say whether the pattern is *it* **V** or *it* **V adj.**

cold   hot   raining   snowing   sunny   windy

1 Wear a sweater – it's ....*cold*................   ....*it V adj*................

2 Sure you don't want a lift home? It's .... pretty hard. ....

3 It's .... now. The roads between Larwick and here are starting to get blocked.

   ....

4 It's ...., but not very warm. ....

5 If it's .... we could take the kite and see if we could fly it. ....

6 If it's .... and people have been walking, they are given a large glass of fruit juice clinking with ice. ....

B Use *it* to make statements which are true when you are reading this. Say something about:

1 the date: ....

2 the time: ....

3 the weather: ....

4 the weather yesterday: ....

5 the place you are in: ....

C In the lists of verbs with the pattern **V** *it*, find:

1 four verbs which indicate that someone is not successful

   ....

2 one verb which indicates that someone is successful ....

3 three verbs which indicate that someone is well-off or living comfortably

   ....

4 two verbs which indicate that someone is not living comfortably ....

D The sentences below show the pattern *it* **V adj prep/adv.** Rewrite them using a verb with the pattern **V** *it* **prep/adv,** with *I* as the Subject. Use a different verb each time.

1 It's nice at work. ....*I like it at work*.... or ....

2 It's really nice there. ....

3 It's better here. ....

4 It was horrible at school.

   .... or ....

199

Verbs used with *there*

There are two patterns beginning with the word *there*, as described below. The verb *be* has these patterns much more frequently than any other verb.

There are two ways of forming a negative in patterns with *there*. The verb may be made negative, for example with *not* or *–n't*, or the noun group may be made negative, for example with *no*. You can say *There wasn't any evidence* or *There was no evidence*.

1 Some verbs follow the word *there* and are followed by a noun group. This pattern is **there V n**.

there	Verb group	noun group
There	was	a loud bang.
There	seems	little hope of success.

The noun group is the Subject. It agrees in number with the verb group: if the noun group is singular, the verb group is singular, and if the noun group is plural, the verb group is plural.

The noun group is usually indefinite: it begins with a word such as *a, some, any*, or *a few*. If the noun group is plural, there is often no determiner at all.

Verbs with this pattern belong to the following meaning groups:

■ **verbs indicating that something exists or happens**

appear	exist	occur	seem
be	follow	remain	

Was there any genuine prejudice?

There was bound to be an increase in job losses.

There remain very serious problems.

There followed months of research.

Seem and *appear* are usually followed by a noun group beginning with *little* or *no*, or with the pronoun *nothing*.

There seems little chance of this happening.

■ **verbs indicating that something comes into existence or starts to be seen**

appear	come	emerge	grow up
arise	develop	grow	

There arises no question of loyalty to one's employers.

There emerges a picture of a woman who cares deeply for her man.

Then there appear a number of teachers with circles of devotees and students.

2 Some verbs follow *there* and are followed by a noun group and a prepositional phrase or adverb group. This pattern is **there V n prep/adv**. Most of these verbs also have the pattern **there V n**.

there	Verb group	noun group	prep. phrase/adverb group
There	was	no one	in the room.
There	remained	a risk	in such a situation.

As with the previous pattern, the noun group is the Subject and is usually indefinite.

Sometimes the prepositional phrase or adverb group comes before *there*, as in *For every action there is an equal and opposite reaction*, or after the verb, as in *There was in the flat an ancient wood-burning stove*.

Verbs with this pattern belong to the following meaning groups:

■ **verbs indicating that something exists or happens**

be	lie	remain	stand
exist	occur	seem	

There were no other wounds on the body.

There seems little wisdom in his proposals.

In the case of *lie* and *stand*, the prepositional phrase or adverb group usually comes immediately after the verb or before *there*, rather than after the noun group.

There lay between them something unspoken.

At one end of the room there stood a grand piano.

Productive use: Any verb which indicates where someone or something is, or how they move, can be used with this pattern, for example *Near our camp there flowed a beautiful stream*.

■ **verbs indicating that something comes into existence or starts to be seen**

appear	come	emerge	grow up
arise	develop	grow	

There appeared another little girl in her fantasy.

Out of all this there emerged many things that were positive, if also uncomfortable.

A Rewrite these sentences using *there*.

1 A memorial service will be held at 2 p.m. on April 13.
   There will be a memorial service at 2 p.m. on April 13.

2 At first the authorities denied that a hijack had taken place.

3 Remarkably, no weather-related deaths or serious accidents have occurred.

4 We haven't had any decent rain for four years.

5 Do not stop if a passing motorist tells you that something is wrong with your vehicle.

6 Some friction is inevitable during this ambitious phase.

7 A series of explosions followed.

8 One question remains: who should be tested?

B Rewrite these sentences using the pattern *there* V prep.

1 Each gram of fat contains nine calories.
   There are nine calories in each gram of fat.

2 The Museum contains many interesting objects and artifacts.

3 That camp currently has about thirteen thousand people in it.

4 This book contains over 100 mindbending puzzles to suit all ages and levels of ability.

5 The waiting list has at least 100 names on it.

6 The new Breeders LP actually has no songs on it.

7 More than two hundred thousand people attended the rally.

C Rewrite these sentences, forming the negative in a different way.

1 There were no marks on the body. *There weren't any marks on the body.*
2 There weren't any tables available.
3 There was no other traffic.
4 There isn't any alternative.
5 There were no fresh car tracks in the snow.

Extra Practice

A For each verb in italics in the text below, underline each of the other parts of the pattern it is being used with, and say which pattern it is.

In the middle of the morning Mrs Pearson *walked* (1) into the Incident Room and *asked* (2) to speak to the officer in charge. Her white hair was uncombed and her cheeks were puffy with crying. 'You've got to stop it!' she *said* (3) when she was ushered in to Millson. 'They*'re saying* (4) terrible things in the village about my Lennie. It ain't right. It ain't right at all. And him only dead three days.' Millson put on a sympathetic face. 'What *are* they *saying* (5), Mrs Pearson?' 'They're saying Lennie was meeting the Book Lady on the sly and he *killed* (6) himself 'cos the police *were going to arrest* (7) him for murdering her. He *didn't* even *know* (8) her.'

1 .... 2 .... 3 .... 4 ....
5 .... 6 .... 7 .... 8 ....

B Now do the same with this text.

Stepping (1) from the car, Wade *called* (2), 'Hello, Alma! It's me. I'm just turning around.' She *nodded* (3) somberly, a tall woman in green trousers and plaid flannel shirt, mannish and abrupt, a woman who *kept* (4) herself aloof from the town but *seemed* (5) to love it nevertheless. She *drew* (6) the glass storm door closed and *started* (7) to shut the inner door, when Wade, instead of *getting* (8) back in the car, abruptly strode across the driveway and up the narrow freshly shoveled pathway to the door. Alma *swung* (9) the door open again, and Wade *entered* (10) the house. She *offered* (11) him a cup of tea, and he *accepted* (12) and *followed* (13) her into the kitchen.

1 .... 2 .... 3 .... 4 ....
5 .... 6 .... 7 .... 8 ....
9 .... 10 .... 11 .... 12 ....
13 ....

C Fill in the gaps in these sentences with *allow* or *let*. In one case, either is possible.

1 They would never .... her to stay now.
2 As a senior council officer, there is no way I can .... overspending.
3 Don't .... them wear you down.
4 My wife was .... to sit and sketch in one area.
5 I found the hidden key and .... myself into the house.
6 Is there any way that we can force them to .... us access to their garden?
7 The BBC should have instructed their staff not to .... him near a microphone, whatever his current claim to fame.

202

D The sentences below all contain the verb *talk*. Mark where a preposition should go, if appropriate, and say what it is.

1 I think you're talking rubbish there. ....

2 What are you talking? ....

3 It was nice to have someone like that to talk. ....

4 A passer-by talked a gunman laying down his weapon moments after he shot a policeman in the leg yesterday. ....

5 We talk all the time when we're on the pitch. ....

6 He still talks Wolverhampton as his home. ....

7 Some people tried to talk me joining the force, saying it'd be very tough. ....

8 Armed with a sheaf of sketches and photographs, he talked his way the post of chief costume designer. ....

E Here are some lines of text, as they appear in the Bank of English corpus. The same verb is missing from all of them. What is it?

```
           They were going to put him down but it ...... a shame.' I froze. Two lame lovers is
  his own, Madonna too risque. But Jackson ...... determined continually to raise the
         Perkins shook his head, amused. He ...... essentially a good-humoured man. 'Well,
    not have been with Lady Godetia. There ...... little point in sitting down with her
   carry Taro over in a cardboard box. This ...... peculiar to Bob and Pete, but Mr. and
      is thought to be the slowest ever. It ...... silly to rush back,' said Clive, 43, of
      both inside and outside Pakistan ...... surprised by the result. Was she?
           support (1092). Ten days ago it ...... that the rich world wanted to know
the gross domestic product numbers, there ...... to have been a loss of momentum within
      General Philip Freeman actually ...... to have a handle on the opinionated,
```

F Here are some more lines of text. Which verb is missing this time?

```
     has discussed your symptoms with you and ..... a number of other questions about your
           on borders on the Gholan Heights. He was ..... about the boycott and the settlements and
             When they started up again Richard ....., 'And what about you, my dear ardent
      hardly knew what to reply. But she finally ..... him what he meant. As if you did not
    danced with the president's son -- King was ..... if his appearance amounted to an
          to do this. I had to help him. If he had ..... me to jump off the Brooklyn Bridge, I
            Justice has been done.' Ardiles had ..... the FA to reconsider the sending-off of
       be secured with Hooker assets. Hooker ..... the banks for an immediate injection of
             November 1992. Imagine you were ..... to design the perfect island. You might
    in the lucid way some alcoholics have, he ..... whether I was prepared to drink to anyone
```

G Which verb is missing from these lines?

```
        tentions. 'It's just not going to happen,' ..... a source close to Quayle about his dumping. If
                 with assets of 161 billion.' Both ..... customer services had improved and pledged there
        by soldiers and police the Prime Minister ..... her visit was to see old friends in the
  ng to use the detainees or 'guests', as it ..... on calling them, as either bargaining-chips or
  ircumstances. Despite this, the Commission ..... on going ahead. Bryan told its members that it
             King of Corinth in Euripedes, he ..... on Jason marrying his daughter.
       Tannisho. Although Shinran always ..... on his fidelity to his teacher Honen, there wer
       influence -- in Lebanon. Yet it was he who ..... on this election. It has blown up in his face.
          today. At first, the Camelot spokeswoman ..... that the system was running yesterday. Then she
           's main rival for the party leadership, ..... that a Labour government must set itself an
```

Extra Practice

H Fill in the gaps in these sentences with *look* or *see*, and say what the pattern is.

1 She's been *seeing* a lot of him. *V n of n*

2 She .... like a witch. ....

3 He .... her stop and turn back to face the ocean. ....

4 There he paused, turned and .... very steadily at John, meeting his eyes.

5 He opened the door of a small room which .... over the harbour.

6 You must let him .... through Dad's papers if that's what he wants.

7 I can't think what she ever .... in him.

8 It .... as if it might rain again.

9 She heard him before she .... him.

10 She has .... a winner from the start.

11 I .... George riding his bicycle at the other end of the street.

12 'I .... why you called it a delicate matter,' Simon said.

13 They .... it as an infringement on their own freedom of action.

14 She said he'd been out .... for work earlier in the day.

15 Liz .... her to the door, and returned frowning, shaking her head.

16 In the meantime, I'd told Mr Loveday to .... to the guests and gone upstairs.

17 I didn't think he .... very well when I met him downstairs last night.

18 I just want to ask you a few questions. I'm .... into the murder of Alan Mackenzie.

I The sentences below all contain a phrasal verb beginning with *go*. Each phrasal verb should be followed by a preposition. Fill in the gaps with the correct prepositions.

1 Many things are going up .... price.

2 'You can't go back .... your promise,' she said.

3 She went back .... telling me how bad she felt.

4 With great reluctance I went along .... this idea.

5 Smith keeps trying to get me to go out .... his sister-in-law.

6 He was very popular and didn't go on .... having a famous father.

7 It may well go down .... the biggest rescue operation in recent maritime history.

8 Generally, if a farmer goes over .... a completely organic system, there is a tendency for yields to fall.

9 I told my husband I was going to divorce him, and he threatened to kill me if I went through .... it.

10 Since 1986, when British Gas was privatised, the price they pay for bulk supplies of gas has gone down .... 8 per cent.

J For each sentence, say what comes after *me*: a noun group, an adjective group, or a bare infinitive clause. Then say whether the sentences are about *me* becoming, getting, or doing something.

1 She had made me a birthday cake. ......*noun group, getting something*..........................

2 It made me cry. ....

3 They made me a professor. ....

4 He's always made me laugh. ....

5 It made me very angry. ....

6 He made me a much better player. ....

7 You made me feel special. ....

8 My mother had made me a new white dress. ....

9 She has made me a very happy man. ....

10 It made me a little nervous. . ...

11 Rovers have made me a very good offer. ....

12 He made me look a fool. ....

K Fill in the gaps in these sentences with *say*, *speak*, or *tell*, and say what the pattern is.

1 She didn't ....*say*............... anything. ....*V n*...............

2 She shook her head, still unable to ....

3 He .... them to be nice to me. ....

4 Many people that we met .... English. ....

5 They .... me I had to help them. ....

6 I'll .... you everything about it. ....

7 She .... as if Julie is still here. ....

8 Could you just .... us why you made that decision? ....

9 Did they .... when they'd be back? ....

10 A neighbour ....: 'We never let them go into the park on their own anyway.'
....

11 There are things going on right now that I cannot .... about. ....

12 I have to .... someone. I can't keep it to myself. ....

13 My father hasn't .... to Uncle Claude since then. ....

14 She .... something to the man, and looked at me again, laughing still.
....

15 The government has .... it wants to build a nuclear research centre.
....

16 The first thing we were .... was, 'If you want to watch the games, you're in the wrong place.' ....

Verb Index

The numbers refer to Units, not pages.

Answer Key

Unit 1

A 1 happening/happened
2 jump
3 arrived
4 explain
5 laughing
6 gone up
7 paid off
8 died
9 smoke
10 began, continuing

B 1 emerge, go, go out, leave, set off
2 remain, stay, stop, wait
3 fall, fly, jump
4 swim

C 1 cry
2 sneeze
3 faint, pass out
4 shiver
5 cough
6 wake up
7 frowns
8 smile

Unit 2

A 1 ring
2 use
3 fired
4 played...back
5 set off
6 operate
7 set

B 1 Trim and peel the carrots. Cut them crosswise into 2-inch lengths. Coarsely chop the red bell pepper, discarding the seeds. Peel and chop the garlic. In an electric blender combine the red bell pepper, garlic, lime juice, sugar, and salt. Taste the dressing; you may wish to add a little more salt.

2 We poison our hearts and lungs, we give ourselves bronchitis, we alter the enzymes in our blood and make our children hyperactive. And we give ourselves cancer. We do these things by burning coal, making and driving motorcars, mining and quarrying, by growing crops and spraying them against infection, and then spraying them again to keep the weeds down.

C 2 carry, active
3 affect, passive
4 build, passive
5 attack, active
6 destroy, active
7 pull down, passive
8 reduce, active
9 found, passive
10 create, active

Unit 3

A 1 expect
2 want
3 fear
4 know
5 remember/recall
6 understand
7 look up to
8 miss

B 2 She took a sip of her drink.
3 I generally have a sleep in the afternoon.
4 They have fought a long campaign for full compensation.
5 I was asked to give lectures on political economics in the mathematics department.
6 I don't think your father committed murder.
7 I've been doing some thinking about the plan, and there's a question I forgot to ask you.

C 2 Meryl was able to finish college and begin a successful career.
3 I had no experience running anything, but I did demonstrate a good knowledge of the industry.
4 Since the era of the Babylonians it's been possible to predict an eclipse years in advance.
5 Sugary desserts such as pie, cookies and cake often contain more carbohydrates than do chocolate-flavored foods.
6 They won't have much trouble finding the evidence to prove his guilt.
7 He did another ten thousand words in America and finished the book in November.
8 I shall quote one example that I happen to know from first-hand experience.

Unit 4

A 1 He threatened them with a knife and stole money and jewellery.
2 They decided they should give away all their money. or They decided they should give all their money away.

215

3 Four million people might lose their jobs as a result of market reform. or As a result of market reform four million people might lose their jobs.

4 Simon chose the bedroom with the best view.

5 The group ate crisps and drank white wine. or The group drank white wine and ate crisps.

B The track passes a small lodge. On meeting a main road turn left up the approach to Abbey Lodge, which guards a fine avenue of trees. Cross the bridge and bear right to an iron gate. Walk along the weir and over the lock gates. To reach Henley turn right and follow the river for 2 miles.

C 2 this
3 What
4 the best golfer
5 a horrible thing
6 the radar
7 what
8 This
9 The fish here
10 that

D 2 'What have you forgotten?'
3 'What shall we play?'
4 'What do we need?'
5 'What did you hear?'
6 'What shall we buy?'
7 'What programme were you watching?'
8 'Who would you prefer?'

Unit 5

A 1 boy
2 girl
3 place
4 arrangement
5 thing
6 people
7 business
8 experience

B 2 a) no   b) yes
3 a) yes   b) no
4 a) no   b) yes
5 a) yes   b) no
6 a) yes   b) no

C 2 The bridge was/measured 130 metres long and 30 metres high. or The bridge was/measured 130 metres in length and 30 metres in height.

3 The insect was/measured 2 inches long and 1 inch in diameter. or The insect was/measured 2 inches in length...

4 The oil slick was/measured 10 miles long and 2 miles wide. or The oil slick was/measured 10 miles in length and 2 miles in width.

5 He was/measured 5 feet 8 inches tall and weighed 11 stone.

Unit 6

A 2 a) entered, V
   b) entered, V n
3 a) noticed, V n
   b) notice, V
4 a) attacked, V
   b) attacked, V n (passive)
5 a) help, V n
   b) help, V
6 a) attend, V
   b) attended, V n
7 a) followed, V n (passive)
   b) followed, V
8 a) pushed, V
   b) pushed, V n

B 2 no   5 no   7 yes
3 yes   6 no   8 yes
4 yes

Unit 7

A 1 herself
2 themselves
3 myself
4 yourself
5 myself
6 ourselves
7 itself
8 yourself
9 himself
10 yourself/yourselves
11 herself
12 himself

B 2 You must organize yourself.
3 He refused to explain himself.
4 Enjoy yourself/yourselves!
5 He was finding it difficult to express himself.
6 It is only with friends that most people feel they can relax and be themselves.
7 She took an unnecessarily long time to bath and dress herself.
8 He applied himself and got into Magdalene, his father's college.
9 They appear to be rewriting the rules to suit themselves.
10 He was poor at maths and English but distinguished himself in French.

Unit 8

A 2 On the way out of town, he stopped by the florist and bought her a bouquet of white flowers.

3 Children between 1 and 5 are charged <u>a small flat daily rate</u>.

4 Dr Brock was extremely helpful and promised <u>me a written report</u> in a week's time.

5 Dad handed <u>me a big box</u> wrapped in gold foil and tied with a red ribbon.

6 <u>The message you send your adolescent about drug and alcohol use</u> is important. (One of the noun groups is 'the message about drug and alcohol use')

7 I would do a 12-hour shift, come home and spring-clean the flat and then cook <u>my flatmates a wonderful meal</u>.

8 That will set <u>you back a few pounds</u>.

9 Elizabeth Dekker was refused <u>employment as a teacher</u> at a training centre on the grounds that she was three months pregnant.

10 What were you <u>offered</u>, George?

B 1 c, 2 e, 3 b, 4 a, 5 f, 6 d

C 2 Tod threw them an angry look.
3 He shot me a grateful smile.
4 There had been barely time for Rose to bid Philip good-bye.
5 From time to time a passer-by would cast him a suspicious glance.
6 I thought you might be able to give me some advice.

Unit 9

A 2 In 594 he proclaimed Buddhism the official state religion.

3 September 9 has been declared a day of action for press freedom.

4 We haven't got what you might term a school policy on assessment.

5 He consistently underestimated the Englishman, whom he considered an idiot.

6 It's not surprising, then, that fans throughout the United States have now voted him Entertainer of the Decade.

7 It was among the oldest of the Academy's buildings and was nicknamed 'Perilous Hall', with good reason.

8 I had been driving at about 35mph, which I considered a safe speed for the narrow, wet and winding road.

B 2 He was dubbed 'The King of Wessex'.
3 He was ordained a priest.
4 US officials are hailing the mission a military success.
5 Always sun-tanned, he fancied himself an athlete.
6 Some people find relaxation a useful way of calming down.
7 He claimed he had been branded a liar and a hypocrite.
8 General Powell could be elected the country's first black President.

C 2 no   5 yes
3 yes   6 no
4 no

Unit 10

A 1 feel   4 looking
2 get   5 fell
3 seems   6 passed

B 1 silver   4 bright
2 free   5 loose
3 shut   6 open

C 1 What does your brother look like?
2 How was the party?
3 What did it feel like?
4 How do I look?
5 What was the food like?

D 2 I had forgotten how flat and empty Middle America is/was.
3 I thought how fresh and pretty she looked.
4 He told them how important his family are/were to him.
5 I was struck by how modest she seemed.
6 I was uncomfortably aware how suspicious this must have sounded.

Unit 11

A 2 The troops were marching barefoot to maintain silence.
3 His opponent was playing blindfold.
4 I was hoping to work uninterrupted.
5 There was barely time for the two boys to escape unseen.
6 Her home was broken into by robbers, who miraculously left empty-handed.

B 1 uninjured
2 uninvited
3 unheard
4 unpunished
5 alive

C 2 Grace lifted the child into a corner of a deep chair. 'You have to <u>sit</u> quiet while Mommy makes a little music.'

3 When the newly-weds emerged from the church, a gleaming horse-drawn carriage <u>stood</u> ready to transport them to their reception.

4 Fiona fell to the ground and <u>lay</u> motionless for a few seconds.

5 Her fair hair <u>hung</u> loose on her shoulders.

D 1 dead   4 straight
    2 thin   5 young
    3 innocent

Unit 12

A 2 Surveys suggest that people like <u>their</u> <u>councils</u> <u>small</u> and <u>local</u>.

3 It was six months before Joanna was <u>diagnosed</u> <u>pregnant</u>.

4 <u>Courts</u> should be given the power to <u>declare</u> invalid contracts written in <u>complex</u> or obscure <u>language</u>.

5 Mr. Schorr showed that the news media consider <u>financial</u> <u>gains</u> more <u>important</u> than ethics.

6 According to his mother he was a sober character, but I found <u>him</u> <u>capable</u> of profound emotion.

7 All the crew members of the oil tanker are <u>reported</u> <u>safe</u>, but a huge oil slick is <u>reported</u> to be spreading around the two vessels.

8 He presented himself at the library at a little after ten-thirty – <u>an</u> <u>hour</u> he <u>judged</u> appropriate for <u>cornering</u> an <u>American</u> scholar.

9 The lighting crew avoided directing very bright lights at him, <u>which</u> he <u>found</u> uncomfortable.

10 Whatever your reasons for pursuing a language course, you will soon find <u>yourself</u> able to speak and write <u>with</u> much <u>greater</u> confidence and clarity.

B 2 She confesses herself unable to give a definite view of the situation.

3 Her doctor ruled her unfit to travel.

4 We count ourselves lucky to have such a skilled worker around.

5 Patterson's wife thought him intelligent and well educated.

6 The owner cannot be held responsible for injury or damage.

7 Everyone knows the railway line should be built, but no one wants it close to their own village.

8 The jury found him guilty.

9 In this instance a fine was deemed appropriate.

10 Sammy was not a nice man. Many people wished him dead.

Unit 13

A 1 He removed his glasses in order to wipe them dry.

2 John kicked the door shut after him.

3 He eased open the unlocked door of a wall cupboard.

4 Serve the pudding well chilled with a few pistachio nuts.

5 I think maybe I was born unlucky.

B 1 brown   6 steady
    2 alight   7 alive
    3 mad   8 unconscious
    4 shut   9 loose
    5 white   10 exhausted

C 1 forcing   5 keep
    2 is born   6 tore
    3 make   7 squashed
    4 captured   8 send

Unit 14

A 2 I carried on living with my mum right up until we moved into this house.

3 The team has not finished analysing that data yet.

4 I went around asking people how they felt about America.

5 I couldn't sleep and kept thinking of the wonderful dancing I'd seen.

6 Dunne looked up at the ceiling and then resumed staring at the fire.

7 He took to walking long distances in an attempt to physically exhaust himself.

B 2 When I was young, people didn't bother locking their doors.

3 The dustmen made so much noise that I gave up trying to sleep.

4 'Quit reading those books,' he said. 'They put ideas into your head.'

5 Hughes resisted using a wheelchair for almost two years.

6 His old comrades have stopped writing to him.

C 2 They are counting on getting money from the government.
3 I had been self-employed for so long that I couldn't imagine working for someone else.
4 He intended continuing work on his writing.
5 You should reckon on paying around £25,000 for a one-bedroomed flat.
6 I shall go and consult my lawyer. Then I must see about selling the house.

Unit 15

A 2 He admitted making the telephone calls.
3 I can't help feeling resentful.
4 She put off telling Ida until the last minute.
5 He believed he might be able to get away with cheating.
6 I don't know how they can justify charging £22.50 for a fishing licence.
7 The law forbids people campaigning in the final two days before voting.

B 2 future   6 past
3 past   7 past
4 future   8 future
5 past

C 1 e,   2 f,   3 d,   4 b,   5 c,   6 a

Unit 16

A 2 Remember to keep the list in a safe place.
3 He managed to escape during the night.
4 I'd forgotten to bring a towel.
5 The man was nervous and refused to give his name.
6 The number of people who bother to vote in these elections is small.
7 And did you get to meet Warhol?
8 Mr. King, the contractor, has declined to answer our numerous phone calls.
9 This is the first time in nine years that the Lakers have failed to reach the finals.

B 2 He decided to ask Claire to marry him.
3 I promised to have a word with Nick when he returned.
4 We have agreed to follow up this incident.
5 She swore not to tell anyone.
6 He had already resolved to agree to nothing at this first meeting.
7 He kept threatening to push the button on this remote control bomb device.

C 1 struggle   4 intend
2 began   5 cease
3 seem

Unit 17

A 1 to hear
2 carrying out
3 to hire
4 to be taken
5 making
6 shooting
7 to be
8 to leave
9 consulting
10 to walk
11 commuting
12 to study

B 2 'I'd love to.'
3 'No, I don't want to.'
4 'I'm trying to.'
5 'I'm planning to.'
6 'Well, not as much as I'd like to.'
7 'I meant to but I didn't get the chance.'
8 'Well, this is always hard to say, but he appears to.'

C 1 They all long to be the most popular girl in the school.
2 They would love to see more women in the competition.
3 I expect to be in hospital for about five days.
4 Everyone dropped everything and rushed to help.
5 Most mothers with young children would prefer to be at home.

Unit 18

A 1 James started to talk about the quiz show.
2 The sport continued to grow through the Seventies.
3 She said that she wouldn't bother to come to the meeting.
4 I tried to remember what I like to eat.
5 I can't bear not to see him.

B 1 The team will begin building the observatory later this year.
2 The firm ceased operating three weeks ago.
3 He'd omitted telling the police about the missing cash.
4 First of all, he loves making movies, he loves the process.
5 You prefer being taught by somebody who has actually done the job rather than somebody who's studied the job.

C 1 to see   6 to say
2 tumbling   7 looking/to be looked
3 shopping   8 to win
4 to post   9 to speak
5 beating   10 feeling

Unit 19

A 2 When I was in my twenties, she put up with me drifting in and out of her life.
3 Despite Robin's importance he was kept waiting a long time.
4 I was amazed that I could watch Nicholas being delivered without feeling funny.
5 She wrote in her diary of two small boys she had seen begging in the street.
6 All the unaccompanied children had been taken away, except for the boys whom she had heard being rejected.

B 2 He pulled in three or four huge lungfuls of smoke that set him coughing.
3 He began his career playing in dance bands.
4 Every day I occupy myself doing chores about the house.
5 When she came back with the vase, she found him staring at the picture of himself.
6 The process of digestion involves the animal using energy.

C 2 I'll never forget him saying, 'You don't have to say anything, just be here.'
3 You have to put up with the room being hot.
4 Don't waste time chasing around the streets.
5 Erin didn't want to risk her father seeing them together.
6 The rifle's smoke prevented him seeing whether he had done any damage.

Unit 20

A 2 I would like you to see the house.
3 They would prefer the talks to be held in a neutral country.
4 His wife would love him to give up his job.
5 I want them to leave me alone.

B 2 I begged her not to go.
3 I asked him to tell me everything he could about the product.
4 He forbade me to leave the room.
5 I urged Jennifer to take responsibility for herself.
6 His lawyer advised him not to talk to the press.
7 Police warned the public to be on the look-out for other bombs.

C 1 to return   5 to play
2 to see   6 to kill
3 wearing   7 cooking
4 to wear   8 using

Unit 21

A 2 The two officers are believed to have been poisoned 25 days ago.
3 The accused is alleged to be a member of an extreme right-wing gang.
4 The round shape is said to represent the sun.
5 The President is known to favour more negotiations on environmental protection.
6 This is said to be one of the most powerful radar systems of its kind in the world.
7 Madonna is rumoured to be planning tours of the Far East and South America later this year.
8 The German foreign minister is understood to be very annoyed that he was not consulted about the visit in advance.

B 1 b,   2 c,   3 a,   4 e,   5 d

C 2 She was seen to weep during the Hungarian anthem.
3 Cats have been observed to show strong maternal instincts.
4 In one outburst, he was heard to yell: 'You're so bloody wrong!'
5 Two other men were seen to shoot at him.
6 When he attended the summit earlier this week, he was observed to be suffering from a heavy cold.

Unit 22

A 2 Let me say a few more words about economic affairs.
3 We had assembled a team of people to help advise us how to deal with the French government.
4 The first requirement for the undergraduate college is to help students achieve proficiency in written and oral language.
5 They whisper to me that James Hopper likes me, but I don't dare believe them.
6 But you do so much already and, really, you needn't do anything at all.

B 1 didn't dare
2 needn't
3 did not help
4 needn't
5 did not help
6 didn't dare

C 2 Only one man noticed a woman pick something up and hand it to another woman.
 3 The university supervisor observed the students teach and conduct conferences.
 4 I saw him dive into the deep end.
 5 From her bedroom window, Jessica watched the police car leave the village.

D 2 She made me promise that I would not tell the others anything about it.
 3 Don't let yourself be overcharged.
 4 Most women say that face masks make their skin feel very smooth.

Unit 23

A 2 Does the boss like to hear three possible courses of action discussed before a recommendation gets offered?
 3 A search is going on after a yacht was found abandoned about eighty miles off Shetland.
 4 The group would like EC laws changed to allow motorists to 'shop around' for cheaper deals abroad.
 5 The door is kept locked at night, and they didn't come into the building.
 6 To get you started, we've provided some favorite recipes.

B 2 Alison says she wants to have/get her ears pierced.
 3 He made a mental note to have/get the car serviced.
 4 I asked him if he would have/get my jewellery valued for insurance purposes.
 5 Henry eventually married Anne Boleyn and later had her beheaded.
 6 Kevin was unfairly dismissed for refusing to have/get his hair cut.
 7 Six months after the baby was born in 1964, Pauline had her adopted.
 8 Have you had your child vaccinated against whooping cough?

C 2 They should have their salaries increased.
 3 For the third time in three weeks I've had my car vandalized.
 4 I had my first novel accepted for publication that year.
 5 The driver has had his/her sentence reduced by the court of appeal.
 6 Then I rang Doc and had my suspicions confirmed.
 7 This is the second time Ms McInnes has had her work screened at Cannes.

8 He ought to have his teaching certificate taken away from him.
 9 Under the scheme, teachers will have their work reviewed by a senior colleague every two years.

Unit 24

A 1 forecasts/forecasted
 2 dreamt/dreamed
 3 forgotten
 4 boast
 5 advise
 6 repeated
 7 pray
 8 complained

B 2 I shouted that I was going to call the police
 3 She replied that she'd like an ice-cream.
 4 The officer insisted that he had had no knowledge of the espionage operation. or The officer insisted that he had no knowledge of the espionage operation.
 5 The President announced that the government will/would be lifting controls on the prices of luxury goods.
 6 He added that he was sorry he cannot/could not reveal the decision yet.

Unit 25

A 2 Mind you don't let the cat out.
 3 I'd be surprised to find out that Spitt ever stole a penny from anybody.
 4 As this example illustrates, people enjoy the sense of exercising control in difficult situations.
 5 She also regrets the fact that modern children lack freedom.
 6 He didn't think much of Goldstone's argument and said so.
 7 As I walked back to the car, I decided I would say nothing to Bertie Owen and Charlie Hughes.
 8 The papers confirm the fact that the murdered man was also a serving police officer.
 9 The regulations will require that labels show the nutritional contents of every food product sold.
 10 The audience, I noted, found it hilarious.

B 2 You may have guessed that she was suffering from back pain.

3 She said that this would allow more effective planning in the Royal Household.

4 The survey discovered that children who take part in competitive sports are more likely to become winners in life.

5 Yul Brynner demonstrated in numerous films that he was an excellent horseman.

6 I had arranged that the intermission for each story would occur at different times.

7 We revealed in February that the famous Kent complex was sold by Ready Mixed Concrete.

8 They acknowledged that no rail service would mean no future for the village.

C 2 'I hope not.'

3 'I believe so.'

4 'I suspect not.'

5 'I think not/I don't think so.'

6 'I presume so.'

Unit 26

A 2 She promised herself that she would pay Granny back someday.

3 He persuaded the court that his basement was used exclusively as an office.

4 She'd been taught that when you said a word often enough, you understood its true meaning.

5 I could still convince myself that I was the victim of a subversive organisation.

6 I had to point out to him that gasoline was cascading down the side of the car.

7 A couple of editors mentioned to Kate that a research job was coming up.

8 Later that evening, I was informed that my father wished me to come to his study.

9 Sometimes I think he just needs to reassure himself that the place hasn't burnt down while he looked the other way.

10 She started hinting to him that he should take a course in business management.

B 1 I confessed to Stanley that the entire incident depressed me horribly.

2 I reminded him that we have/had a wedding to go to on Saturday.

3 He said to me at lunch that his doctors have/had warned him to take care.

4 The President promises the people that the worst is over.

5 She told herself that it was really not her business.

6 Mary Sweeney whispered to me that he was Amanda's editor.

C 1 The directors were warned that funds for new equipment were limited.

2 I was told (by the beautician) that my skin lacked moisture.

3 We were promised (by our bosses) that there would be enough work for everyone.

4 However, when he arrived at the airport, he was informed (by a colleague) that the meeting was off.

5 The Japanese government has been assured (by the US navy) that there is no risk of further accidents.

Unit 27

A 2 You can easily guess what to expect from him.

3 Conservative MPs have until next Tuesday to decide who to vote for.

4 Bank customers found out why there were no staff when they heard cries coming from an office.

5 Most voters do not mind whether their representative is a man or a woman.

6 I won't ask why you've suddenly got an urge to write a book about him.

B 1 how   6 why
2 what   7 whether
3 when   8 why
4 who   9 whether
5 how

C 2 Scientists have discovered why some men are aggressive.

3 He could see how the room would have looked to Jill.

4 Mr Young has refused to reveal where he found the ornament.

5 They wondered who the fans were shouting for.

6 I've guessed why you sometimes come to see us here.

7 The committee recommended how children should be tested.

8 We investigated what the proposed changes will mean.

Unit 28

A 2 The video will show you what to eat on a food-combining diet.
  3 Riddick Bowe has already warned Bruno what to expect.
  4 Jurors are told who the key participants are.
  5 Nancy was tempted to reveal to Mrs Struthers what she had learned.
  6 They did not want to be advised what to do.
  7 There are many other factors which influence what we choose to eat.
  8 The producer mentioned to her who he was having dinner with.
  9 Please indicate whether you require CD or vinyl.
  10 Several times a day she would remind herself how lucky she was.

B 2 This incident reminded me why I never abandon my patients.
  3 I told her how my attitude has changed over the years.
  4 It's difficult for him to admit to anyone what has happened.
  5 The police hope the security system video recording will show (them) who planted the bomb.
  6 Shelley asked John why he had taken his shoes off.
  7 On a boat, the weather determines where meals are served.
  8 Our staff will advise you what steps you should take next.

C 1 dictates
  2 inform
  3 disclose
  4 demonstrated/demonstrates
  5 suggest

Unit 29

A 1 boasted
  2 ordered
  3 prayed
  4 asked, replied
  5 admitted
  6 suggested
  7 insisted
  8 interrupted
  9 predicted
  10 exclaimed, echoed

B You may have the Subject, verb, and quote in a different order.
  2 John announced: 'I've come to a decision.'
  3 'The company will start making a profit next year,' he predicted.
  4 'I'll wait for you,' she promised.

  5 'I've never seen anything like it before,' said Steve.
  6 'I've been out all night,' the cab-driver complained.
  7 'Kathryn is acting strangely,' murmured Agnes.
  8 'It's good to breathe fresh air again,' remarked Alice.

C 1 breathe, mumble, murmur, mutter, whisper
  2 call, call out, cry, cry out, scream, shout, shout out

Unit 30

A 2 'I'm a very selfish person on some levels,' he confesses to me.
  3 'He's got a knife!' Jacky screamed at me, terror contorting her face.
  4 'My dog eats anything that doesn't eat him first,' she remarked to John, who smiled.
  5 'I feel sick!' Chet groaned, supporting himself against the cupboard.
  6 'Relax, will you,' he snapped at her.
  7 'We are eating vegetarian,' Mrs McCartney announced to the waiter in an officious manner.
  8 'I wonder where the gang found that wreck?' Joe mused.
  9 'I think I'd better go now,' she whispered to her table companions.
  10 I said to myself, 'Settle down. Try to enjoy this.'

B 1 goes
  2 yelled
  3 fumed/fumes
  4 admitted
  5 thought
  6 read/reads
  7 wonder
  8 muttered
  9 wrote
  10 nodded/nods
  11 explained
  12 sobbed/sobs

C 1 groan, sob
  2 jeer, sneer, sniff
  3 explode, fume, rage, snap

Unit 31

A 2 'You'll need proof,' Frank reminded her. 'Then I'll get proof!' Miss Hardy declared.
  3 One energetic 90-year-old was told by her doctor, 'You have the heart of a 20-year-old.'

4 'Come, eat!' the old woman urged.

5 'Bob and I were sitting around at Headquarters discussing the case and...' 'Headquarters?' the director interrupted him sharply.

6 I used to pronounce your name 'Bo-shomp' instead of 'Beechum'.

7 Even foods that are labelled 'additive-free' may have hidden preservatives.

8 'Get a doctor!' Eva begged. 'Somebody do something, quick!'

9 'But I know...' She corrected herself: 'We know that you've seen Lily.'

10 'Look in that room,' the major ordered Hubert.

B 1 assured
2 corrected
3 was entitled
4 asked
5 begged
6 told

C You may have the quote in a different place in the sentence.
2 'Everything will look different tomorrow,' he told himself.
3 'We'll be late if you don't hurry up,' she warned him.
4 'Go and get some sleep,' Joe advised her.
5 'Mr Watson is on the line,' her secretary informed her.
6 Jay promised her: 'I'll take care of everything.'
7 'Smile for the camera!' he urged her.

Unit 32

A 2 Where are you going?
3 She tried to read his face, but he turned away and busied himself with the dishes.
4 Inside were half a dozen pill bottles she'd never seen before.
5 He put down the phone and sat there thinking for a bit.
6 She left the house and followed the moonlit path that led to the clearing beside the river.

B 1 'Well, I should probably go inside,' Erin said. 'Uh, sure. Well, see you at school tomorrow.' Zack turned and started to walk down the path. Erin went back into the house. She was shocked to find her whole family waiting for her. Her father was standing near the couch with his arms crossed. Her mother was sitting on the couch.

2 The sheriff turned right at the only traffic light, led him through the business district, turned left and headed up a low hill. On the left was an area of trees that might have been a park. A white church stood at the top of the hill.

3 I was walking down the hill near Crinan Bottom when a man with a parachute on his back suddenly dropped out of the skies and landed at our feet, having jumped off the summit a few moments earlier. 'Far more exciting than walking down,' he told us.

C 1 When you come out of the post office, turn left up Bread Street. When you get to the traffic lights, turn right and go along the High Street. Continue down the High Street, passing under the railway bridge, until you arrive at the police station.

2 Possible answer: Go down the High Street, passing under the railway bridge. Continue down the High Street, until you get to the traffic lights, then turn left into Bread Street. The post office is on the right, opposite the turning into Parrot Street.

Unit 33

A 2 Why are you acting like this?
3 Cosmetics will last longer if stored in a cool, dark place.
4 Despite Mr Neil's nerves, the actual launch went off perfectly.
5 The cover is easy to remove and washes well.
6 An oak tree may live for hundreds of years.
7 Des and Raquel have moved in together.
8 She always dresses in black and I've started to copy her because it makes life so easy.
9 Flat owners now club together to hire security guards to police their blocks.
10 The other republics, increasingly pre-occupied with their own economic and political problems, have so far reacted cautiously.

B 1 by   2 with   3 with   4 in   5 on   6 by

C 1 b,   2 d,   3 e,   4 g,   5 f,   6 a,   7 c

D 1 The interview lasted for about an hour.
2 The arrangements were coming along nicely.
3 Why do women behave in this way?
4 The company reacted with predictable outrage.
5 His books never sold well.
6 The tour started badly and got worse.

Unit 34

A 2 The authorities might kick her out of Barbados.
3 Davenport removed his coat and brushed off the snow.
4 Let me show you to your rooms.
5 We know many more people have died but the army has taken the bodies away.
6 The cage was knocked over and the bird escaped.
7 On Mondays, Rachel often brought to school things she had made at the weekend.
8 Then you have to remember where you buried it.
9 There is no jail to put him in.
10 Within hours of the accident, Mr Graff had been flown to Brisbane for specialist treatment.

B 1 in a semi-circle
2 over the meat
3 to the wall
4 from the town
5 across the Atlantic
6 at the dining table
7 behind the shop
8 under Carl's nose

C 1 He stuffed the banknotes into his wallet.
2 She spread peanut butter on a slice of wholemeal bread.
3 The furniture was shipped over in three huge containers.
4 Wren dropped her lipstick into her purse.
5 They sent the UN trucks away.
6 I nailed sheets of wood over the windows.
7 She put the tray on the table.
8 Christopher offered to drive her home.

Unit 35

A 1 She stamped her feet on the pavement to keep out the cold.
2 He threw his arms around his wife and told her not to worry.
3 She tossed her hair back with a jerk of her head.
4 Larry rubbed his hands together with satisfaction.
5 She turned her face away from him.
6 Very slowly he pulled himself to his feet using the table as an aid.

B 1 got   4 bring
2 kept   5 thrown
3 pushed   6 placed

C 2 V adv, go   5 V prep, flow
3 V n adv, take   6 V adv, race
4 V n prep, pass

D 1 tee-shirts   4 cooker
2 switch   5 coat
3 dressing-gown   6 light

Unit 36

A 1 e,   2 f,   3 h,   4 g,   5 a,   6 b,   7 d,
8 c

B 2 She pushed her way to the front of the queue.
3 They zigzagged their way across the snow.
4 We edged our way past the soldiers.
5 Jack was working his way through a mountain of paperwork.
6 When the larvae hatch, they bore their way into the beans.
7 William made his way to the door.
8 Somehow the news found its way into the Italian newspapers.

C Here are some possible answers:
1 They shouldered their way through the crowd.
2 She inched her way along the narrow ledge.
3 He whistled his way through the National Anthem.
4 We're hitchhiking our way round Europe.
5 She bluffed her way into the job.
6 She was eating her way through a bag of crisps.
7 We can't borrow our way out of the recession.
8 He stammered his way through the poem.
9 He murdered his way to the throne.
10 They hacked their way through the undergrowth.

Unit 37

A 1 The girls were chatting about fashion.
2 My father worries about her being so tired.
3 I asked about the woman and her daughter.
4 How do you know about the kidnapping?
5 She was always going on about how ugly she was.
6 Write about something you know about.

B 1 phoning
2 read
3 disagreed
4 worry
5 wrote in
6 forgotten
7 heard

C 2 He seemed not to understand what I was talking about.
3 What have we got to worry about?
4 He shouldn't be a doctor if all he thinks about is money.
5 They are useful earplugs, and reasonably comfortable and easy to forget about.
6 Antonio's favourite dishes include mushrooms, about which he has written extensively.

D 2 Despite her enormous wealth, she was always complaining about one thing or another.
3 My sister is the only one who knows about my eating problem.
4 How did the press find out about it?
5 I know several players got really upset when they read about him criticising the team.
6 My mother and I joke about the fact that whatever she loves I'll hate, and vice versa.
7 He was living the life that others only dared to dream about.

Unit 38

A 2 Dr. Miller has been advising the government about milk production.
3 What do people think about your policy?
4 I didn't know what to do about it.
5 A senior lawyer said that several people had been contacted about taking part in the trial.
6 But what did he say about us?
7 Harry was questioned about where his father got the money.
8 As usual, they told me nothing about the case.

9 I reminded him about changing the name on the box.
10 Artie was probably one of the rogues Molly had warned her about.

B 1 d, 2 e, 3 a, 4 f, 5 b, 6 c

C 2 What I like about my job is the day-to-day contact with clients.
3 What I like about him is his evident determination to think things out for himself.
4 What I hate about my car is the uncomfortable seats.
5 What I love about these shops is that you never know what you'll find.
6 What I love about Australia is that the people really love sport.
7 What I dislike about the fashion world is that it takes itself so seriously.

Unit 39

A 2 He was the strongest man I have ever played against.
3 The victim refused to testify against him.
4 He was offered a place at The Royal College, but he'd already decided against becoming a classical musician.
5 There are a lot of young, fit guys out there to compete against.

B 1 f, 2 a, 3 g, 4 b, 5 d, 6 e, 7 c

C 1 advised
2 won
3 raced
4 react
5 appeal
6 protest

D 1 The rain beat against the windows.
2 A glass ornament smashed against a wall.
3 What are you rebelling against?
4 He stood against the president in the 1990 election.
5 More than forty Conservatives voted against the government.
6 This is something worth fighting against.
7 A cat came into the room and rubbed against its mistress's legs.

Unit 40

A 2 leaned, V n *against* n
3 campaigned, V *against* n
4 protect, V n *against* n
5 pressed, V n *against* n
6 played, V *against* n
7 insulated, V n *against* n (passive)

8 turn, V n *against* n
9 brushed, V *against* n
10 warn, V n *against* n
11 vaccinated, V n *against* n (passive)
12 spray, V n *against* n

B 2 Regular physical exercise also protects you against heart disease.
3 You have to weigh the advantages against the disadvantages before you begin.
4 Her father's wealth cushioned her against several disasters.
5 Before I set off, Mother would warn me against going anywhere dangerous.
6 He banged his hand against the edge of the desk.
7 The same criticism can hardly be levelled against James Baker, the former Secretary of State.

Unit 41

A 2 She had to dress up as a man.
3 She qualified as a chemical engineer.
4 She trained as a commercial artist.
5 He served as Minister of Agriculture for four years.
6 In the early 1960s he stood as a Labour candidate in local elections.
7 Henry will continue as chairman and chief executive officer.
8 He was conscripted into the German army and ended up as a prisoner of war.

B 1 a lawyer   5 females
2 a lorry driver   6 a world power
3 women   7 an office
4 a single person   8 a great cricketer

C 2 These works emerge as more complex and interesting than you might expect.
3 A train has to be one hour behind schedule to count as late compared with five minutes in 1986.
4 13 percent of American households qualify as poor.
5 They come over as nice but characterless.

Unit 42

A 2 When he reached the back porch, he met an officer, whom he addressed as captain.
3 His views have been widely denounced as being racist.

4 We should not dismiss as lies the incredible stories that children may tell us about themselves.
5 In 1960, John Fitzgerald Kennedy was elected as the 37th US President.
6 He had been cast as the king in Shaw's 'The Apple Cart'.
7 Manchester United are the team that have the best chance of finishing the season as Premier League champions.
8 He regarded Harry as being still solidly part of the family.
9 It was a long time before anyone recognised him as the great driver he is.
10 Top executives around the country have rated Atlanta as the nation's best city for business.

B 2 Joe perceived his stress as an inevitable part of his job.
3 His peers acknowledged him as the best rider Australia had produced.
4 The refugees were labelled as 'vagabonds and escaped prisoners'.
5 His irreverence for authority marks him out as a troublemaker.
6 Tilefish is a beautifully colored fish which is often marketed as golden bass.
7 The market became flooded with fake watches. People passed them off as originals.
8 I often wondered why this band chose me as their singer.
9 He denounced the tape as a fake.
10 The documentary portrays Los Angeles as a city about to explode.

Unit 43

A 2 The doctors wrote him off as incurable eight years ago, but he is still alive.
3 The separation and eventual divorce were presented as amicable.
4 Adorno set out to expose as false all claims that the 'good' or 'just' society had been achieved.
5 The demonstrators were trying to draw attention to the export of live sheep to France, which they denounced as cruel.
6 With healthy self-esteem we perceive ourselves as lovable and capable.

7 In the UK all babies who weigh less than 5lb 8oz (2.5kg) at birth are labelled as premature.
8 It's a suggestion that officials dismiss as misleading.
9 The company admitted to re-finishing surplus airplane parts and then passing them off as new.

B 2 The book was condemned as blasphemous by many people.
3 The atmosphere inside the House of Commons was described as absolutely chaotic.
4 Her story was beginning to be widely accepted as true.
5 He denied that he was trying to portray himself as mad.

C 1 satisfactory
2 too violent
3 unfair
4 more important
5 timid and tearful
6 dead

Unit 44

A 2 It's hoped that the game will sell at less than a pound.
3 People complained they'd been sworn at for failing to park according to the rules.
4 Then he gave a cry and the two officers turned to see what he was staring at.
5 They sped off, firing at random at people in the streets.
6 If you can't laugh at yourself, who can you laugh at?
7 Skylark is a temperamental horse and doesn't like being shouted at.
8 Provide interesting pictures, books and mobiles to look at.

B 2 Arnold sipped at his beer.
3 She turned to Frank and grinned at him triumphantly.
4 The police can only guess at the scale of the problem.
5 I waved casually at Sandy.

C 2 a) What are you looking at?
   b) I asked him what he was looking at.
3 a) Who are you waving at?
   b) I asked her who she was waving at.
4 a) Who are they shooting at?
   b) I asked him who they were shooting at.
6 a) What are you hinting at?
   b) I asked her what she was hinting at.
7 a) Who was he shouting at?
   b) I asked someone who he was shouting at.

Unit 45

A 2 After a few moments I realised that her question was directed at me.
3 Angrily, the woman shook her fist at Bragg's departing back.
4 Michael shot a quick glance at him, then turned back to Miss Treves.
5 He flashed a handsome smile at the television cameras.
6 In early trading in Hong Kong, gold was quoted at $366.50 an ounce.
7 Casualties were estimated at over 1,000.
8 Groups of people threw stones at us throughout the journey.
9 In the end I couldn't take the violence and the insults she would hurl at us.
10 The bombs hit the targets they were aimed at about 25 percent of the time.

B 1 hurled
2 directed
3 aimed
4 threw

C 2 The number of people out of work was put at more than thirty-eight thousand.
3 The cost of repairs was estimated at £1 million.
4 The turnout in the election was put at sixty percent.
5 The number of victims was reckoned at around three percent of the population.
6 The dividend was maintained at 9.2 pence.
7 The exchange rate was set at 39 pesos to the US dollar.

Unit 46

A 2 Always try and alternate between two or three tasks.
3 The sheep farmers have 120 million dollars of government handouts to share out between them.
4 For general daylight use, these two cameras are difficult to choose between. (*Choose* is occasionally used with this form of the pattern.)
5 With album releases of this quality he'll soon be rated among the top reggae producers.
6 The group numbers among its members some of the most influential women in Sweden.

7 Last year they raised £22,000, which was split between several charities.

8 The money will be split up between the three of them.

B 1 between   4 between
   2 between   5 between
   3 among   6 among

C 1 football   4 women
   2 family   5 doubt
   3 death

D 2 The President distinguishes between economic and political refugees.
   3 He was willing to arbitrate between the government and the workers.
   4 He distributed pennies among all the neighbourhood children.
   5 I rate him among the fastest bowlers in the world.

Unit 47

A 2 She started off by accusing him of blackmail but he just ignored her.
   3 I'd like to begin by asking about the system of management in the school and how you fit into that.
   4 They finished the day by reaching the final of the Queen Mother Challenge Cup.
   5 Bake the pudding in the oven for
   7 minutes. Finish by browning it under a grill.
   6 He opened the meeting by quoting lyrics from Bob Dylan's 'The Times They Are A-Changin'.'

B 2 The cat reacted by scratching his leg.
   3 The fans retaliated by pelting them with plastic chairs.
   4 Her father responded by throwing her toys on the fire.
   5 They replied by reducing the demand to £730.

C 2 He grabbed me by the hair and pushed me roughly up the trailer steps.
   3 Then she stepped toward the door, but George caught her by the wrist.
   4 He took her by the hand and led her into the next room.
   5 I was holding him by the ears and I was beating his head against the pavement.
   6 She stood there, holding Sofia by the hand but not looking her in the face.

Unit 48

A 2 Its shares slumped by a third after the crash of BCCI.
   3 Economists have forecast that employment will fall by between 10,000 and 30,000.
   4 Sterling has been devalued by some 17 per cent and interest rates have been cut by four points.
   5 The World Health Organisation says the number of cases of cholera reported worldwide has increased by ten per cent.
   6 This historic treaty will reduce by two-thirds current nuclear arsenals.
   7 The Argentine Agriculture Minister rejected EC proposals to cut farm subsidies by thirty percent as totally unacceptable.
   8 The average family spent a third of its budget on food back then, so the cost of the diet was multiplied by three to determine the poverty line.

B 1 climb, go up, increase, jump, rise, shoot up, soar
   2 come down, decline, decrease, dip, dive, drop, fall, go down, plummet, plunge, shrink, sink, slide, slip, slump, tumble

C 2 France won by 25 points to nine.
       or France won by 16 points.
   3 England are winning by 17 points to 13.
       or England are winning by four points.
   4 Edberg is leading by two sets to love.
       or Edberg is leading by two sets.
   5 He lost by 34 votes to 46.
       or He lost by 12 votes.
   6 Manchester are losing by three goals to one.
       or Manchester are losing by two goals.

Unit 49

A 2 What level of responsibility are you aiming for?
   3 Ingrid tried to file for a Swedish divorce, but the technical difficulties made it impossible.
   4 He persuaded the Duchess to hold out for the best deal possible.
   5 She doubted he really checked the instruments or even really knew what to check for.
   6 These are all good points to look for.

7 You can send off for the competition details by cutting the coupon.

B 1 ran 6 listen
2 prayed 7 scream
3 fight 8 aimed
4 searched 9 pleading
5 feeling 10 shop

C 2 Most university students opt for the straight three-year course.
3 The officials said two of them have asked for political asylum.
4 His father, Tony, told him not to settle for second best.
5 I'm not sure that the people pushing for this change have thought through its implications.
6 First, the police must be sent for.

Unit 50

A 1 i, 2 f, 3 b, 4 g, 5 j, 6 e, 7 h, 8 a, 9 d, 10 c

B 2 Teresa has been training for the 2.7km walk by walking the 1.5km to her local shop.
3 The rainy season has just begun and will last for several more months.
4 She has been working for the company for 16 years and says that she is still learning.
5 Can we afford the luxury of what you propose? Who will pay for it?
6 The baby is cared for from 9.30 to 6.30 by an extremely capable 27-year-old trained nanny.
7 He lived for his work and he would have gone on for ever if he could.
8 I have done nothing for which I should apologize.
9 His big break come when he stood in for another dentist who had been taken ill.
10 He went on to say he was proud that he had fought for his country.

C The second part of each answer is a suggested way of filling in the second gap.

2 pleaded, come back
3 wait, come out
4 praying, ring
5 pressing, be taken
6 shouting, stop

Unit 51

A 2 He listened for sounds inside as he climbed the stairs.

3 He studied engineering and went to work for the telephone company.
4 I ordered a birthday gift for my mother last month.
5 We'll trade in the Buick for another car.
6 They made a home for him in the nursery.
7 Was he covering up for Grace? Or was he telling the truth?
8 Some day I'll pay you back for this!
9 He was warmly congratulated by his five colleagues for hosting the first meeting.

B 2 I've begged Gil again and again for money.
3 A crew member reported him for being drunk on duty.
4 I picked up a bucket to fetch some hot water for him.
5 Both leaders were wanted in France for questioning in connection with an alleged plot.

C 2 She forgave Lisette for her deception because she knew what a desperate position she was in.
3 not possible
4 not possible
5 Shirley had bought a double espresso for him to thank him for taking her to Baton Rouge.
6 not possible
7 Devlin got his coat for him and took him out to the car.

Unit 52

A 1 scanned 5 select
2 tested 6 charge
3 prepare 7 interviewed
4 says

B 2 The course did not equip her for a new career.
3 Ashton chose Diana Adams for the ballerina role.
4 All of our local cinemas charge $4 for a child's admission and $7 for an adult admission.
5 I think we should search the house for clues.
6 The magazine held no interest for her.
7 The next meeting is scheduled for Monday.

C 1 She waited 53 minutes for an ambulance.
2 I scour second-hand shops for interesting pieces of clothing.
3 Ingrid was nominated for an Academy Award as best actress.
4 I don't recommend this product for long hair.

5 My doctor wants me to be tested for diabetes.

6 This is not what the grant was intended for.

Unit 53

A 1 f, 2 g, 3 e, 4 c, 5 d, 6 a, 7 h, 8 b

B 1 stand out   6 keep
2 vanished   7 refrained
3 recover   8 come
4 import   9 flow
5 retire   10 benefit

C 2 Our hero sustained wounds in battle from which he later died.
3 They are in the grip of a dreadful power from which they cannot escape.
4 Richard has recently had a bad bout of flu from which he needs to recover.
5 Education is an investment from which everyone benefits.
6 She has been staying with her husband, from whom she separated five months ago.

Unit 54

A 1 d, 2 a, 3 c, 4 e, 5 b

B 2 What were the most difficult things about changing over from the one school to the other?
3 Now the labs are attempting to turn from weapons of mass destruction to more peaceful industries.
4 The Multi-Cultural Programmes Department makes a wide range of programmes varying from topical current affairs to popular entertainment.
5 The 93-day event will last from August 7 to November 7.

C Here are suggested ways of completing the sentences.
1 full-time work
2 less well-known ones
3 dawn
4 something close to heaven
5 chicken and fish

D 2 Next year, Elland Road Stadium's capacity will temporarily fall from 32,728 to 30,000.
3 With imports continuing to rise, the trade deficit has widened from $5 billion to $9.3 billion.

4 For the past 25 years, the business has seen its workforce shrink from 16 people to nine.
5 Truck production is likely to decline from 276,000 to 260,000.
6 Weekly production of Range Rovers went up from 350 to 370.
7 Pre-tax profits are expected to climb from £98 million to £105 million.
8 Unemployment has soared from near zero to over 300,000.

Unit 55

A 2 Who did you learn your chess from?
3 Mark has separated from Annette, so he and I will be sharing a place in Studio City.
4 I must watch carefully, and learn from my father's example.
5 The shock was so profound that it seemed to drain all strength from her.
6 You have to choose your basic design from a few previously drawn by the computer.
7 Think about the word RELAX and let the tension drain from your stomach.
8 With the commander's help we separated the police from the journalists.
9 Apart from her professor's salary, she had money that she had inherited from her father.
10 Fired by this motivation, we are likely to eliminate from our behaviour all that is socially unacceptable.

B 1 exclude   5 divided
2 pulled   6 borrowed
3 collect   7 taken away
4 save   8 got

C 2 They need to think of ways in which they can separate the good guys from the bad guys.
3 He was freed from prison this afternoon after £19,000 bail was paid over.
4 He was charged with using his influence to acquire loans from two government-owned banks.
5 He took the recorder from his shirt and adjusted it.

Unit 56

A 2 People are prohibited from asking for money on the city streets at night.
3 His good manners kept him from telling her what he really thought.

4 The tax and social security laws discourage some couples from marrying.

5 The conservative environment did not stop Renaissance artists from being highly original.

6 Shell Australia's customers are banned from using mobile phones at its service stations.

B 2 The administration plan would raise the grant from $2,400 to $3,700.

3 The Conservatives increased their majority from one to thirty-five.

4 Wine merchants have lowered the price from $115 to $90.

C 1 She tried to hide her despondency from Joey.

2 Parents are supposed to protect their children from harm.

3 Plants are able to manufacture their own food from water.

4 Delegates were barred from entering the hall.

5 Stone Age settlers fashioned necklaces from sheep's teeth.

6 Twenty-six small satellites will pass simple digital messages from place to place.

7 The president is prepared to increase the highest tax rate from 28 per cent to 31 per cent.

8 Rachid Boudjedra translated his novels from Arabic into French. or Rachid Boudjedra translated his novels from French into Arabic.

Unit 57

A 2 The negotiators say environmental protection does not belong in a trade agreement.

3 In my feverish state, one image stuck in my mind.

4 Sainsbury's, Tesco and Safeway have between them £1.4 billion of equity capital to assist in their development programmes.

5 He had been warned in writing not to deal in shares between January and March.

6 Okay, so you know what you want out of a fund and what type of fund you want to invest in.

7 The author suggests that this is the area in which future development lies.

B 1 with
2 in/with
3 in
4 in/with
5 in
6 in

C 2 Fred Astaire and Jack Buchanan star in this tale of a song-and-dance man.

3 He trades in vintage posters, brochures, and other memorabilia.

4 He did not succeed in publishing his book.

5 Yoga can aid in the prevention, cure and management of many diseases.

6 Marriage doesn't figure in their plans.

7 That incident has stuck in my mind all these years, and now I know why.

Unit 58

A 1 go up
2 ended
3 result
4 believe
5 consists
6 double
7 dress up
8 rejoice

B 1 in
2 in
3 from
4 in
5 from
6 in
7 from
8 from

C 2 These changes will eventually result in people having several occupations during their lifetimes.

3 Her policies led to a growing anger against her, which ended in her being removed from power.

4 He went through a rebellious phase which culminated in him taking an overdose of sleeping tablets.

5 His fearless campaigning for racial justice resulted in him being sued for libel.

6 He persuaded her to take the trip to Egypt which ended in her being attacked by robbers.

Unit 59

A 1 d, 2 f, 3 e, 4 a, 5 b, 6 g, 7 c

B 2 Since her divorce last year, she has buried herself in charity work.

3 The children will be caught up in the excitement.

4 Tommy began carefully folding up the brown paper in which the painting had been wrapped.

5 Maybe she could just shut him in his room while Robert was visiting.

6 Similar devices had been placed in several hotels in the area.

7 The 50,000 brochures we inserted in Cycling Weekly in February were well received.

8 I assisted Phil in getting control of his own life situation.

9 Some recipes tell you to coat the meat in flour first.

10 I would include in this category organising social events such as the Christmas party.

C 2 I'm burying myself in writing music.
3 She admits assisting her boss in shredding important documents.
4 He joined Franklin in issuing radio messages.
5 Some 500 people are currently employed in building the dam.
6 Irving Berlin led the audience in singing 'God Bless America'.

Unit 60

A 1 take
2 was ranked
3 shoot
4 stir
5 drill
6 saw
7 hold/held
8 divide

B 2 So I took my lunch box and tried to hit Rab in the face with it.
3 Get off my property before I come out there and punch you in the nose.
4 Nicky, the singer, tried to kick him in the face.
5 A consultant yesterday admitted he had struck his fiancée in the face with a bunch of flowers.
6 Dewey was bitten twice in the chest by two rattlesnakes.

C 2 We may hold him in contempt, but he might be the only viable president.
3 From the outset he had put his trust in me, the son of his old friend.
4 The public tend to hold architects in low esteem.
5 I find comfort in the fact that earnings are up this year.
6 I always take delight in giving photographers my most radiant smile.

Unit 61

A Here are some possible answers:

1 b) She became a snake.
2 a) He started to sing.
   b) Someone had forced their way into my house.

3 a) Her fingers gripped/squeezed his arm.
   b) I've been investigating/exploring Laura's past.
4 a) He put his bathrobe on.
   b) He began to doze fitfully.
5 a) The plate broke.
   b) His car hit a garden fence at 75 mph. or His car collided with a garden fence at 75 mph.
6 a) How did our schools become like this?
   b) The Malloy twins entered the business at age 17.

B 1 get
2 bit
3 piled
4 dissolved
5 melt
6 turn
7 ran
8 looking
9 flew

C 1 d, 2 a, 3 f, 4 b, 5 e, 6 c

Unit 62

A 2 What they did not realise was that they were being lured into a trap.
3 You're not going to trick me into saying things I don't want to.
4 He was so shaken by the heavy lorries roaring past his home he was stirred into action to stop them.
5 For a start, people want to be lulled into a sense of security, false or not.
6 They scramble aboard with knives between their teeth and terrify the crew into surrender.

B 2 Parents should not force kids into taking sides.
3 I've just got to persuade my dad into letting me have a season ticket now.
4 He pressured my parents into getting him a watch when he was seven.
5 The government was trying to coerce him into testifying against my father.
6 We pressured him into telling us everything he knew about the robbery.
7 He sees it as a way to tempt children into taking up the guitar.
8 They found out about the magistrate's own wrongdoings and blackmailed him into stepping down.

C 2 He was talked into renouncing his throne after Franco chose Juan Carlos to be his successor.
3 The Government has been embarrassed into trying to do something about the problem.

4 Chinese tourists have been scared into staying home.
5 So how were you conned into getting involved?
6 Don't rush into buying stuff just for the sake of it.

Unit 63

A 2 That area has been converted into a public parking lot.
3 Everything is capable of being transformed into something else.
4 A minus can be changed into a plus.
5 Our country's been turned into a battlefield.
6 Its fibres can be woven into rope, fabrics and fine paper.
7 Plums and cherries are made into liqueurs.
8 There may be potential for the material to be processed into compost.

B 1 inject   5 thrown
  2 stuck   6 inserted
  3 Stir   7 pump
  4 loaded   8 feed

C 1 b, 2 a, 3 d, 4 g, 5 c, 6 e, 7 f

Unit 64

A 1 It looks like a desert.
2 The roar of the battle sounded like thunder.
3 The young leaves are edible: they taste like spinach.
4 She looked like a film star.
5 Your cotton sheets will feel like silk.
6 This sounds like Russian music.
7 The grass beneath your feet feels like a cushion.
8 This coffee tastes like washing-up water!

B 2 want   5 want
  3 want   6 seem
  4 seem

C 1 living   3 acting
  2 dressed   4 thinking

D 1 g, 2 c, 3 d, 4 a, 5 h, 6 b, 7 e,
  8 f

Unit 65

A 1 b, 2 e, 3 a, 4 h, 5 d, 6 g, 7 f,
  8 c

B 2 The country talked of nothing else and seemed to watch nothing else.

3 They simply cannot conceive of anyone objecting to the way they work.
4 Analysts warn of the risk in releasing a low-budget film during an economic recession.
5 Do you approve of Britain following this path?
6 Glenn's friends speak of him as a man who always wanted to help other people.
7 90 percent of all the poisonous garbage generated in this country is disposed of on site.
8 Do you have to go out and buy a type of saucepan you've never even heard of?

C 2 Neighbours complained of her son causing noise.
3 It was the first I knew of anything being wrong at the football match.
4 He spoke of children growing up with breathing difficulties.
5 At one point she talked of love being her religion.
6 She knew others would soon hear of her coming home.
7 I often dream of him finding me.
8 I have heard of people charging absolutely exorbitant prices.

Unit 66

A 2 It would be too simple to say I was cured of all my symptoms.
3 Manufacturers failed to warn doctors and consumers of the possible side effects.
4 This is a lot to ask of a partner.
5 Three city employees were accused of playing golf while on duty.
6 I assured the president of our intention to maintain only a minimum nuclear strategic force.
7 The government decided to strip the province of its autonomy.
8 What do you make of our neighbours?
9 That means he was not guilty of the crime of which he was accused.
10 Tell me, David, what does the smell remind you of?

B 1 of   5 from
  2 from   6 of
  3 of   7 from
  4 from   8 of

C 2 I soon convinced him of my innocence.
3 Customs officers are obliged to advise passengers of these rights.
4 That story reminded me of one I heard a while ago at college.
5 We had been warned of the danger of pickpockets.
6 The authorities have assured us of their willingness to cooperate.

Unit 67

A 2 She needed to write on what was nearest and most relevant to her life.
3 The accommodation I think could be improved on in many ways.
4 Airlines depend on business travelers for both volume and profit.
5 Computer learning centers focus on teaching children to use computer technology.
6 Many of the papers' lead stories report on the police appeal for help.
7 Even before the agency's first transaction was announced, its every move was speculated on.
8 You're the only person I can count on, Sheppy.
9 Now Paramount is banking on the sequel being another box-office hit.
10 That's what Congress will be voting on.

B 1 that   5 on
2 on   6 on
3 on   7 that
4 that   8 on

C 2 He spoke on a variety of social and economic topics.
3 It's fascinating to reflect on how fashions in the home have changed in the last 15 years.
4 They cash in on the generosity of visitors.
5 Prosecutors in that case didn't touch on his fund-raising efforts.
6 The legal dispute is likely to centre on whether or not commitments were made.
7 The task is not to break new ground, but to build on what has already been accomplished.

Unit 68

A 1 c,   2 a,   3 g,   4 f,   5 d,   6 h,   7 b,
8 e

B 1 go back   5 settled
2 informed   6 look in
3 intrude   7 weighed
4 tapped   8 sneak up

C 2 Eight years ago, my husband walked out on me and our two young children.
3 Why don't you drop in on me? I live right next door.
4 He fired on two people who tried to stop him outside a luxury hotel.
5 A team of one hundred technicians will descend on the castle.
6 They are on record as saying they won't compromise on the issue of democracy.
7 Suddenly, she felt as if she had walked in on a private conversation.

Unit 69

A 2 She practically lived on instant breakfasts.
3 They showed they can be relied on to do the job.
4 His team taught residents how to save on their fuel bills by weatherproofing.
5 What I insist on is a totally positive campaign that goes right through the party.
6 For too long the school has had to exist on a limited budget.
7 The main political parties look on these votes as already lost.
8 I always have chocolate and cheese but I also stock up on tons of fruit.

B 2 He called on richer nations to relieve the suffering of poorer people.
3 He thought that he could depend on Elaine to act out of love for him.
4 Can I count on you to do the same?
5 She prevailed on her parents to let her go to London.
6 He relied on his influential friends to get him out of trouble.

C 2 If you're starting to gain a bit of weight, cut back on the carbohydrates.
3 His father has been reading up on the disease.
4 Once he started on stories of his time here, we heard the lot.
5 I look on it as an adventure, something positive we can experience together.

6 The Prime Minister dined on roast chicken and peas.

7 She insisted on paying for the coffee.

Unit 70

A 2 It dismissed all the evidence that threw doubt on the alleged confession.

3 Through an interpreter, we complimented her on doing an excellent job.

4 The purchase of this object conferred a certain status upon the purchaser.

5 If too much strain is put on the back, a slipped disc may result.

6 I will fill you in on the whole story when I see you.

7 A government spokesman said heavy casualties had been inflicted on the rebels.

8 We'd update people on what's happening around the club.

B 2 They congratulated her on looking so well just two months after the birth.

3 Mr Stevens was questioned on where the money for the project was coming from.

4 Could you advise me on how to treat this problem?

5 We'll update you on the day's top news stories.

6 He complimented Tania on her cooking.

7 She consulted the shopkeeper on where it came from.

8 When I come back, you can fill me in on his plans.

C 1 brought   5 imposed
2 bestowed   6 pressed
3 consulted   7 congratulated
4 serve   8 placed

Unit 71

A 2 I wrote his number (down) on that pad of paper by the phone.

3 He had already placed a bet on one of the horses.

4 Enough taxpayers' money is wasted already on propaganda.

5 The Prime Minister failed to commit himself on the issue.

6 Some nights I would blow £200 on a meal.

7 The man jumped over the counter and pulled a knife on the clerk.

B 2 Politicians here pride themselves on their accessibility to the public.

3 He blamed the job losses on rising production costs.

4 I wish people would judge me on my contribution.

5 I took her up on her suggestion.

6 What do they feed rabbits on?

C 1 The foreigners trained their cameras on them.

2 She wrote her name on the side of the package.

3 He drummed his fingers on the bar in time to the music.

4 He has staked his reputation on getting the treaty through.

5 Much of the clothing is modelled on the clothing that will be worn by the European team.

6 Those are the things he is going to be judged on.

7 It's a question of what they are spending their time on.

Unit 72

A 1 out of   6 out of
2 out of   7 into
3 into   8 out of
4 into   9 into
5 out of   10 into

B 2 Russia decided to back out of aiding China's nuclear programme.

3 His job in banking brought about several moves and he dropped out of cycling for a while.

4 She could then get out of doing all the things she did not want to do.

5 The Government has largely opted out of providing continual care for the elderly.

6 I pulled out of applying but if I'd got the grant it would have saved a lot of money.

7 But many who lost their jobs complain that insurance firms are now trying to wriggle out of paying up.

C 1 changed
2 move
3 get
4 stay
5 sold
6 arose

Unit 73

A 2 He had left out of his account something that was crucial.

3 Food markets in the capital were said to have sold out of bread and milk.

4 Soil is the raw material out of which a gardener creates his dreams.

5 If people want to get rid of legislators, then all they have to do is vote them out of office.

6 The thousands of people that she threw out of work are still having a difficult time.

7 The American, Fred Couples, has pulled out of the event with a back injury.

8 They are fighting against the health problems which have arisen out of poor housing.

B 1 He is good at charming money out of companies.

2 Jacob cheated his brother Esau out of his birthright.

3 He was jailed for conning women out of their life savings.

4 The bank has done me out of thousands of dollars and I'm absolutely furious.

5 I don't think we'd get any useful information out of him.

6 She didn't come straight out and tell me, I had to drag it out of her.

7 He had recently discovered that Fisch was a crook who had tricked him out of several thousand dollars.

8 They forced him to try to screw some extra concessions out of the West.

9 This has become just another way of squeezing cash out of the government.

C 1 c   2 b   3 a

Unit 74

A 2 The Financial Times says, in effect, the party has chosen to compromise over reform.

3 Water is being sprayed over the cargo holds in an attempt to keep them cool.

4 Nicola, a violinist, triumphed over more than 500 entrants in television's most popular music event.

5 The pain and the psychological upheavals were ignored or glossed over.

6 Economists disagree over how to measure real interest rates.

7 Pour the water into the dish, and pour the apple juice over the apple.

8 He also wrote scores of articles on matters ranging over the whole history of Welsh literature.

B 1 a) from   b) over
2 a) from   b) over
3 a) over   b) from
4 a) over   b) from
5 a) over   b) from

C 1 rule   5 win out
2 sprinkled   6 presided
3 fight   7 backed down
4 washed   8 skate

Unit 75

A 2 At least three local rescue teams are on the scene digging through a wall of coal and rock.

3 She was flicking through some magazines when Harry Penrose came into the room.

4 He is a strong man, and he will pull through this operation.

5 Do you have any questions about what we've just read through?

6 A fire officer's car was destroyed as a lorry ploughed through a hedge.

7 He listed the wars he's lived through.

B 1 My father came through surgery without difficulty.

2 Bits and pieces of the past raced through her mind.

3 We took our seats and glanced through the menu.

4 I have been known to sleep through the wailing of a fire engine siren.

C 1 skimmed   5 sailed
2 get   6 drilling
3 sweeping   7 flashed
4 break   8 scrape

D 1 a) cut   b) cut
2 a) going   b) go

Unit 76

A 2 Many of your best ideas may occur to you at odd moments during the day or night.

3 They realised one day that they had to have a place to escape to.

237

4 Where are you going to move to?

5 Your child needs to learn that owning up to making a mistake isn't the end of the world.

6 I think you'll find him rather difficult to talk to.

7 Ginny became the friend to whom she could talk about every aspect of her life.

8 I don't know where everyone has gone to.

9 The blown-out church tower testifies to the severity of mortar attacks which have been launched against the small village.

10 Dunne waved to her, indicating there was space beside him on the sofa.

B 1 Despite the recession, seven out of ten adults admit to spending money on activities like horse-racing and lotteries.

2 Red also confessed to having driven the getaway car.

3 Why had Martin sworn to having seen Grace on the July 3rd?

4 Eva testified to having seen Herndon with his gun on the stairs.

C 1 report back   5 date back
   2 cross   6 reach
   3 passed   7 signalled
   4 withdrawn   8 lying

Unit 77

A 1 returning   5 keep
   2 surrender   6 adapt
   3 went   7 tend
   4 change   8 contribute

B 1 charity   5 sleep
   2 some business   6 my belief
   3 change   7 pressure
   4 death

C 1 d,   2 e,   3 a,   4 c,   5 b

D 1 off   5 round
   2 back   6 out
   3 in   7 back
   4 over   8 over

Unit 78

A 2 In response, some people have resorted to carrying guns.

3 But he is prepared to stand up to the critics.

4 They have a right to be listened to by adults.

5 I will not accept the disappearance of the European civilisation to which I belong!

6 There was immediate public concern about what this might lead to.

7 Shortly afterwards he found himself homeless and applied to the council for accommodation.

8 Just knowing that you have someone to turn to can be very helpful.

9 Most people do not object to their records being used for medical research.

10 She steadfastly maintained that her grandsons, whom she always refers to as 'the boys', were innocent.

B 2 His voice rose to a scream.

3 The average monthly wage has fallen to about £19.

4 Her expression changed to one of horror.

5 The tax on fuel will go up next spring to 17.5 per cent.

6 By the 1970s, the number of political clubs had declined to only 300.

C 1 He appealed to the United States for help in stopping the war.

2 I prayed to God for some guidance.

3 Nicoll was unsure of his ground and wrote to Waite for advice.

4 I apologized to Fraiser for my treatment of him.

Unit 79

A 2 The gallery director surrendered his keys to the building manager.

3 The guest house had been recommended to me by a friend.

4 Over the past five years, offices in the city have been rented to the public sector.

5 You've never been able to pledge your loyalty to me.

6 He announced that Egypt had presented proposals to the United Nations.

7 In the end, Newman reports to the police an attack on him and a neighbour by the local gang.

8 It's a tragedy he may not be able to pass the company on to his children.

B 2 She also taught English to university students.
3 I handed the letter to Eleanor.
4 In 1979, only 8 per cent of British firms awarded annual bonuses to managers.
5 When I told this to my doctor, he looked worried.
6 A widower has left £60,000 to a dogs' home.
7 He had sold the film rights to Paramount in 1926.
8 He gave a message to the President from his kidnappers. or He gave a message from his kidnappers to the President.

C 1 suggested
2 delivered
3 promised
4 presented
5 admitted
6 denounced
7 broken
8 describe
9 demonstrated
10 dictated

Unit 80

A 1 h, 2 c, 3 a, 4 e, 5 f, 6 g, 7 d, 8 b

B 1 Tie the ladder firmly to a branch.
2 Arsenal have reduced Liverpool's lead to six points.
3 He was promoted to Assistant Director in 1968. or In 1968 he was promoted to Assistant Director.
4 I referred her to the hospital for a scan.
5 Details of the bet were transmitted to the central computer.
6 Chase Manhattan and Mellon banks have cut their lending rates to 9 percent.

C 1 accidents
2 job
3 Profits
4 visits
5 applicants
6 fires
7 painting

D 2 Several of the major banks dropped their interest rates from 8 percent to 7.5 percent.
3 Soon after I arrived, I raised our advertising budget from $15 million to $100 million.
4 They have rejected plans to lower the voting age from 20 to 18.
5 The Free Democratic Party was able to increase its vote from 9 percent to 11 percent.

Unit 81

A 2 We have to trace the problem back to its source.
3 His family will have to take measures to prevent him from drinking himself to death.
4 Why should householders be subjected to the same question year after year?
5 Last week thousands were moved to tears at the sombre memorial service in the town.
6 That was the goal to which she had dedicated herself since Franklin's birth.
7 He told me to just ask you to the dance like a normal person.
8 I split up from a long-term girlfriend and started to apply myself to my work in a really concentrated way.

B 1 reduced
2 challenged
3 limited
4 postponed
5 devote
6 condemned
7 prefer
8 bore

C 2 She could be sentenced to death if she is convicted.
3 Your job means a lot to you, doesn't it?
4 Why are we being exposed to all these inconveniences?
5 Callwell also addressed himself/herself to the difficult problem of reprisals.
6 None of his immediate family were invited to his wedding.
7 They still prefer fish and chips to fruit and fibre.

Unit 82

A 2 Marriage was something I believed every girl strove towards.
3 While offering credit, the course would not count toward graduation requirements.
4 We need to pull the British economy out of the recession it now seems to be heading towards.
5 It's a typical political diversion to direct responsibility towards the family.

B 1 He is working towards his Air Transport Pilot's Licence.
2 Firms are edging towards being organised on a regional basis.
3 Inevitably they are pushed towards using bank overdraft facilities. or They are inevitably pushed towards using bank overdraft facilities.
4 The president moved towards decentralizing his country's rigid state-run economy.

C 1 towards   5 to
2 to   6 to
3 towards   7 towards
4 to   8 towards

D 2 We are now rushing towards a terrible war that would be fought with highly destructive bombs.
3 Small businesses had each contributed $3000 towards the event.
4 It is not surprising that they are striving towards separate identities.
5 Some of the president's advisers are leaning towards the use of air attacks.
6 On the surface, the country is gradually moving towards democracy.
7 An increasing number of men are turning towards facial cosmetic surgery.

Unit 83

A 2 I don't know whether I can go through with this.
3 Do you cope well with stress?
4 I found this quite hard to deal with.
5 We are in a country where nature has been interfered with for a very long time.
6 And on the dressing table sits the clutter of make-up that Nikki loved to experiment with.
7 I pleaded with Frances to get a move on as she dawdled to the car.

B 2 He simply carried on with his work.
3 They had planned to go on with their investigation.
4 Meanwhile, the House of Lords select committees have been pressing on with important work.
5 The task of a coalition government would be to push ahead with the creation of a market economy.

C 2 We do not have the resources to cope with a major famine in Mozambique.
3 Volunteers are needed immediately to assist with planning the closing ceremonies for October.
4 Now I don't bother with expensive jewellery.
5 Now is the time to experiment with a softer hair-style.

D 1 integrating   3 interfere
2 reason   4 deal

Unit 84

A 1 laughter   5 relief
2 resentment   6 joy
3 despair   7 terror
4 exhaustion

B 1 g,   2 d,   3 h,   4 b,   5 a,   6 c,   7 e, 8 f

C 1 fell in   6 sympathize
2 compare   7 counter
3 met   8 fits in
4 started   9 check
5 keep up   10 stock up

Unit 85

A 2 Paul and the boys have loaded a wagon with baskets.
3 Sprinkle the fish with chopped chives.
4 The trees should be sprayed with nicotine about a week after the petals have fallen.
5 I was cramming my mouth with sausage when I heard the news.
6 The tickets will be printed with fixed entry times to cut unnecessary queuing.
7 As far as he knew, none of the three had supplied the police with any information prior to the raid.
8 Mr Mandela was to have been presented with the award at the concert in his honour on Monday.
9 The band are so noisy that before taking the stage they stuff their ears with little bits of foam.

B 2 We decorated the dining room with balloons and streamers.
3 Staff will be issued with new grey-and-yellow designer uniforms.
4 Cover your nose and mouth with a clean handkerchief.
5 This provided Frances with a perfect excuse for leaving home.
6 We loaded up carts with all the blankets, bandages, and medication we could spare.

C 1 e, 2 c, 3 f, 4 b, 5 d, 6 a

Unit 86

A 2 We are confronted with the fact that we are aging.

3 Talk all this over with your husband.

4 His victory has been met with enthusiasm from all sides of the party.

5 And what do you suggest we replace it with?

6 It is an episode which few in Hollywood regard with any pride.

7 All the student need concern himself with is reality.

8 There are a lot of players I like to play golf with for a variety of reasons.

9 He views with horror the relentless deterioration in Britain's trade balance over the past four decades.

10 Police have so far given no details of the offences with which those arrested will be charged.

B 1 discuss   5 began
2 confronted   6 conclude
3 replace   7 trust
4 bore   8 met

C 1 He exchanged a quick smile with her.
2 They view each other with hatred.
3 He will be holding talks with the other leaders.
4 The Government has greeted such reports with scepticism.
5 Some start the day with meditation or exercise.
6 I'm sorry to bother you with my troubles.
7 He has nothing to replace them with.
8 Several women offered to help him with his charity work.

Unit 87

A 2 Stephen and I disagree about lots of stuff.
3 Warwickshire and Northamptonshire drew at Edgbaston.
4 My girlfriend and I have just split up.
5 We get on very well.
6 When I broke up with my husband five years ago it was amicable.
7 Why doesn't Johnson team up with Kravis?
8 High-spending countries can coexist with low-spending countries.

9 The interests of the governors should coincide with those of the governed.

10 The Haywards Heath Building Society is to merge with the Yorkshire Building Society.

B 1 to   4 from
2 against   5 against
3 to   6 from

C 1 get married, link up, meet up, pair up, team up
2 break up, fall out, get divorced, part, separate, split up
3 co-operate, get along, get on, go out

Unit 88

A 2 They had clearly been having this conversation for some time.

3 When did you renew contact with your sister?

4 I've been having a chat with that son of yours.

5 And if you have any questions, you can talk them over with Mr. Bacon himself.

6 Why don't we talk it through tomorrow night?

7 Japan and South Korea have reached an agreement on the legal status of Koreans living in Japan.

8 It was reported that contact had been made with nationalist ex-soldiers fighting on the borders.

9 Britain and China have settled their differences over the plan for a new airport in Hong Kong.

10 The two have been trading insults and accusations since well before the start of the campaign.

B 2 Above her head, he and Lloyd exchanged glances.

3 Mr. Bush and Mr. Gorbachev discussed the proposed arms reductions.

4 The only time we really had a conversation was at luncheon in the Elysee.

5 My husband and the children were playing golf on the green outside our house.

6 Nigeria shares a common border with Cameroon.

7 I discussed it with my boyfriend. We just don't think it's necessary.

8 He was supposed to play chess with Grandpa today.

9 I was having a discussion with Patrick about games.
10 Israel has re-established diplomatic relations with Bulgaria after a break of twenty-three years.

Unit 89

A 2 Their militant views matched.
3 The experiences of women and men are beginning to overlap.
4 Despite a declaration of cease-fire in Yugoslavia, Serbians and Croats were fighting this morning in Osijek.
5 Our fingers touched as I gave him the glass.
6 He divorced his first wife in 1939.
7 Richard watched as Henry embraced Joanna.
8 Catherine has been dating John for five months.
9 His ashes will be immersed at the place where the River Ganges meets the River Jamuna.
10 She met her husband ten years ago when he came to Moscow on a business trip.

B 2 We embraced each other, laughing.
3 His guests seemed to agree with each other about everything.
4 Counseling can help two people to learn to get along with each other.
5 Is it true that women are more able to discuss personal things with each other?
6 Lines of longitude all cross each other at the poles.
7 The Association says schools should not compete with each other.
8 Increasingly, people needed better ways to communicate with each other.
9 These orbiting particles collided with each other, and ended up forming a flat disc.

Unit 90

A 2 One of the city's main hotels burned down.
3 The ice on the pond cracked.
4 Her new dress had torn.
5 A warship blew up in the harbour.
6 The gold on the rim of the glass has worn away.
7 The rear window of her patrol car shattered.
8 Apparently, the Titanic's hull had broken twice on or near the surface.

B 2 a) faded   b) fade
3 a) clear up   b) clear up
4 a) melted   b) Melt
5 a) changes   b) change
6 a) improve   b) improve
7 a) cool   b) Cool

Unit 91

A 2 V n   8 V n
3 V n   9 V
4 V n (passive)   10 V n (passive)
5 V n   11 V n
6 V   12 V
7 V

B 2 a) People were beginning to tire in the midday heat.
b) Anyone with this condition should avoid exercise which tires them.
3 a) When one side of the boat began taking in water, people panicked and rushed to the other side, causing the boat to sink.
b) Her screams panicked the men and they fled.
4 a) I was feeling a bit down, and she told me to cheer up.
b) Ethel suggested Paul should cheer up her daughter by visiting her while she recovered from a skiing accident.
5 a) Seeing how free and easy he was, everyone relaxed and started talking freely too.
b) A high-carbohydrate dinner will relax you for sleep during the flight.
6 a) In a few minutes the girls had revived enough to be able to tell their story.
b) Horrified staff tried to revive him but he was dead by the time he reached hospital.
7 a) Don't worry, John, I'm not going to let you down.
b) What worries me is that we might get an increase in inflation.

Unit 92

A 2 We rarely started our meetings on time.
3 His affair broke up his marriage.
4 The two sides are continuing the talks during the afternoon.
5 Both countries have already halted production of chemical weapons.
6 The remaining teams will resume play on Wednesday.
7 He said that decisive action would be taken unless the students ended their protest.

B 1 matches   4 horn
2 bomb   5 heating system
3 bell

C 2 She slammed the door shut.
3 She could be injured if the window blows shut.
4 He snapped open his briefcase.
5 He paused before letting the gate swing shut behind him.

Unit 93

A 2 The house had been converted into a wooden fortress. V n prep (passive)

3 Alan began to tear the portrait in half. V n prep

4 The car reversed out. V adv

5 He backed the car down the driveway. V n prep

6 He restarted the engine, swung the car around and drove back to Hillsden's apartment. V n adv

7 When the plane landed at Stockholm's Arlanda airport, the hijacker gave himself up to police. V prep

8 Teddy galloped around the course at terrific speed. V prep

9 A large number of weapons, explosives and vehicles went missing when British troops were pulled out of Germany. V n prep (passive)

10 Sharpe toyed with the idea of marching his own men into that open space, but he knew he was too late. V n prep

B 2 Coffee spilled onto the carpet.
3 The drum rolled down the hill.
4 His legs swung backwards and forwards.
5 His fist smashed into her cheek.

7 The central hatch cover slid back.
8 The bottle passed from hand to hand around the circle.
9 The drum spins around, creating an unsettling illusion of movement.
10 The film moves through the projector on a series of toothed wheels turned by a motor.

Unit 94

A 2 If more families will now settle in the area, it follows that there will be more children in school.

3 It looked to me as if this gun had been used recently.

4 The break-down of the talks came as it emerged that two protesters died in a demonstration outside the capital.

5 It is simply that owning one's own home is regarded as important to people.

6 In terms of both attainment and behaviour it matters which school a child attends.

7 It doesn't do to grab more than one's fair share.

8 It feels as if spring is in the air.

B 1 came about
2 turned out
3 was

4 hurts
5 matter
6 pays

C 2 It seemed (to me) that I was an important part of their lives.
3 It doesn't matter who won the game.
4 It looks as if you'll have to move house.
5 It helps that I've got a tremendous family.
6 It doesn't sound (to me) as if they're going to pay any attention. or It sounds (to me) as if they're not going to pay any attention.
7 It doesn't matter to them whether or not they sell your product.

Unit 95

A 2 It seems doubtful whether any foreign government would support the plan.

3 It was reported a few minutes ago that oil has come ashore on a headland in South Devon.

4 By the year 2050 it is expected that one out of four persons will be over 65.

5 If it was ever discovered how Beryl had died, they would both be in serious trouble.

6 I mean, it does feel important to have children because it's always been something I've wanted.

7 The 11-plus exam is being brought back, it was announced yesterday.

8 It is understood the airline will begin two weekly services to Cairns in September.

9 It is not known who was responsible for the bomb, which was hidden in a crate in a busy market place in the old city.

10 In ancient Greece, students wore sprays of rosemary in their hair because it was believed that it improved the memory!

B 2 It was revealed that he only had a few weeks until he planned to retire after 41 years.

3 It was proposed that a new town square with surrounding shopping should be developed on the site.

4 It is said that about three million dollars'
worth of property has been destroyed.
5 It is hoped that the vaccine will be
successful.

C 1 b, 3 a, 5 e, 2 f, 4 c, 6 d

Unit 96

A 2 I couldn't face going to the hospital to visit
my brother. It hurt me to see him so sick.
3 It shocked him to think he was capable of
murder.
4 It took us at least two weeks to complete the
assignment.
5 Didn't it strike you that he was awfully
uptight and tense?
6 I could live for a week on what it cost to buy
this shirt.
7 It struck her how self-centred she'd been,
considering only her sorrow, not his.
8 It surprised him that so many had come to
listen to him during lunchtime, but it
saddened him that he did not see his
brother in that audience.
9 It embarrassed her when friends insisted she
was beautiful.
10 It was a pleasure to see my brother and his
family.

B 2 It bothered me that I wasn't as pleased to
see John as I used to be.
3 It worries me that the country is now in a
position to mobilize its forces.
4 It disturbed her that she had not received
either a note or a phone call from him.
5 It amazes me that the Government never
has enough cash for the public's needs but
never fails to provide for MPs' salary
increases.
6 It hadn't occurred to me that he might have
been on the wrong train.

C 1 f, 2 e, 3 a, 4 c, 5 b, 6 d

Unit 97

A 1 g, 2 d, 3 e, 4 b, 5 h, 6 a, 7 f,
8 c

B Here are some possible answers:
I like it when it snows.
I hate it when people play loud music late at
night.

I'd love it if England won the World Cup.
I'd hate it if anything happened to my dog.

C 2 Most analysts see it as almost inevitable
that the alliance will be scrapped.
3 Baron von Malchin wrote that he regarded it
as an honour to have known my father
personally.
4 They saw it as a positive sign that the
university agreed to the contract extension.
5 The Dutch Presidency regarded it as
unhelpful to talk of independence for
Slovenia and Croatia at that stage.
6 The public now expect us to have three
finalists in every championship by right and
view it as abnormal when we don't.

Unit 98

A 2 I think it admirable that she wants to be
independent. Clause: that-clause
3 He believed it unwise to spend large
amounts of money on a few players.
Clause: to-infinitive clause
4 At first I found it difficult to relax.
Clause: to-infinitive clause
5 I consider it my duty to make sure they are
given the proper atmosphere to succeed.
Clause: to-infinitive clause
6 We thought it very strange when she said, 'I
don't have to answer your question.'
Clause: when-clause
7 Mrs Edelman called it a scandal that, in
most states, fewer than 60 percent of
children are immunized. Clause: that-clause
8 The spokesman thought it likely that the tax
officers' visits caught everyone by surprise.
Clause: that-clause
9 The government does not believe it
necessary to hold direct talks with the NLD.
Clause: to-infinitive clause
10 They felt it important that every room had
an individual feel and flavour.
Clause: to-infinitive clause

B Here are some possible answers:
2 I find it sad that there is little that can be
done about this disease.
3 I find it amazing that the press are prepared
to publish unsubstantiated stories.
4 I find it appalling that alcohol is served in
large quantities to young people.
5 I find it extraordinary that people on the
dole receive quite a good deal more money
than students get, for doing nothing.
6 I find it amusing that a 113-year-old Welsh
church is being shipped to Japan to be made
into a golf clubhouse.

Unit 99

A 2 raining, *it* V
3 snowing, *it* V
4 sunny, *it* V adj
5 windy, *it* V adj
6 hot, *it* V adj

C 1 blow, (cannot) hack, have had, lose
2 make
3 be coining, be coining in, live up
4 rough, slum

D 1 I enjoy it at work.
2 I love it there.
3 I prefer it here.
4 I hated it at school. or I couldn't stand it at school.

Unit 100

A 2 At first the authorities denied that there had been a hijack.
3 Remarkably, there have been no weather-related deaths or serious accidents.
4 There hasn't been any decent rain for four years.
5 Do not stop if a passing motorist tells you that there is something wrong with your vehicle.
6 There will inevitably be some friction during this ambitious phase.
7 There followed a series of explosions.
8 There remains one question: who should be tested?

B 2 There are many interesting objects and artifacts in the Museum.
3 There are currently about thirteen thousand people in that camp.
4 In this book, there are over 100 mind-bending puzzles to suit all ages and levels of ability.
5 There are at least 100 names on the waiting list.
6 There are actually no songs on the new Breeders LP.
7 There were more than two hundred thousand people at the rally.

C 2 There were no tables available.
3 There wasn't any other traffic.
4 There is no alternative.
5 There weren't any fresh car tracks in the snow.

Extra Practice

A In the middle of the morning Mrs Pearson *walked* <u>into the Incident Room</u> and *asked* to <u>speak to the officer in charge</u>. Her white hair was uncombed and her cheeks were puffy with crying. '<u>You've got to stop it!</u>' she *said* when she was ushered in to Millson. 'They*'re saying* <u>terrible things</u> in the village <u>about my Lennie</u>. It ain't right. It ain't right at all. And him only dead three days.' Millson put on a sympathetic face. '<u>What</u> *are* they *saying*, Mrs Pearson?' 'They're saying Lennie was meeting the Book Lady on the sly and he *killed* <u>himself</u> 'cos the police *were going to arrest* <u>him</u> <u>for murdering her</u>. He *didn't* even *know* <u>her</u>.'

1	V prep	5	V n
2	V to-inf	6	V pron-refl
3	V with quote	7	V n *for* -ing
4	V n *about* n	8	V n

B *Stepping* <u>from the car</u>, Wade *called*, '<u>Hello, Alma! It's me. I'm just turning around.</u>' She *nodded* somberly, a tall woman in green trousers and plaid flannel shirt, mannish and abrupt, a woman who *kept* <u>herself</u> <u>aloof from the town</u> but *seemed* to love it nevertheless. She *drew* <u>the glass storm door</u> <u>closed</u> and *started* to <u>shut the inner door,</u> when Wade, instead of *getting* <u>back</u> <u>in the car</u>, abruptly strode across the driveway and up the narrow freshly shoveled pathway to the door. Alma *swung* <u>the door</u> <u>open</u> again, and Wade *entered* <u>the house</u>. She *offered* <u>him</u> <u>a cup of tea</u>, and he *accepted* and *followed* <u>her</u> <u>into the kitchen</u>.

1	V prep	8	V adv prep
2	V with quote	9	V n adj
3	V	10	V n
4	V n adj	11	V n n
5	V to-inf	12	V
6	V n adj	13	V n prep
7	V to-inf		

C 1 allow
2 allow
3 let
4 allowed
5 let
6 allow
7 allow/let

Answer Key

D 1 (no preposition needed)
  2 What are you talking about?
  3 It was nice to have someone like that to talk to.
  4 A passer-by talked a gunman into laying down his weapon moments after he shot a policeman in the leg yesterday.
  5 (no preposition needed)
  6 He still talks of Wolverhampton as his home.
  7 Some people tried to talk me out of joining the force, saying it'd be very tough.
  8 Armed with a sheaf of sketches and photographs, he talked his way into the post of chief costume designer.

E a form of the verb *seem*

F a form of the verb *ask*

G a form of the verb *insist*

H 2 looks/looked   11 saw
  3 saw   12 see
  4 looked   13 saw
  5 looked   14 looking
  6 look   15 saw
  7 saw   16 see
  8 looks   17 looked
  9 saw   18 looking
  10 looked

I 1 in   6 about
  2 on   7 as
  3 to   8 to
  4 with   9 with
  5 with   10 by

J 2 bare infinitive, doing something
  3 noun group, becoming something
  4 bare infinitive, doing something
  5 adjective group, becoming something
  6 noun group, becoming something
  7 adjective group, becoming something
  8 noun group, getting something
  9 noun group, becoming something
  10 adjective group, becoming something
  11 noun group, getting something
  12 bare infinitive, becoming something

K 2 speak, V
  3 told, V n to-inf
  4 speak/spoke, V n
  5 told, V that
  6 tell, V n *about* n
  7 speaks, V n as if
  8 tell, V n wh
  9 say, V wh
  10 said, V with quote
  11 speak, V n *about* n
  12 tell, V n
  13 spoken, V *to* n
  14 said, V n *to* n
  15 said, V that
  16 told, V n with quote

246